D0454526

DEMYSTIFYING
THE
AMERICAN
MILITARY

DISCARDED FROM
GARFIELD COUNTY PUBLIC
LIBRARY SYSTEM

Garfield County Libraries
New Castle Branch Library
402 West Main Street
New Castle, CO 81647
(970) 984-2346 • Fax (970) 984-2081
www.GCPLD.org

DEMYSTIFYING THE AMERICAN MILITARY

INSTITUTIONS, EVOLUTION, AND CHALLENGES SINCE 1789

PAULA G. THORNHILL

Naval Institute Press
Annapolis, Maryland

Naval Institute Press
291 Wood Road
Annapolis, MD 21402

© 2019 by Paula G. Thornhill
All rights reserved. No part of this book may be reproduced or
utilized in any form or by any means, electronic or mechanical,
including photocopying and recording, or by any information
storage and retrieval system, without permission in writing from
the publisher.

Library of Congress Cataloging-in-Publication Data
Names: Thornhill, Paula G., author.
Title: Demystifying the American Military : Institutions, Evolution,
    and Challenges since 1789 / Paula G. Thornhill.
Description: Annapolis, Maryland : Naval Institute Press, [2019] |
    Includes bibliographical references and index.
Identifiers: LCCN 2018054259 (print) | LCCN 2018055479
    (ebook) | ISBN 9781682470749 (ePDF) | ISBN 9781682470749
    (epub) | ISBN 9781682470732 (pbk. : alk. paper) | ISBN
    9781682470749 (ebook)
Subjects: LCSH: United States—Armed Forces—History. | United
    States—Military history.
Classification: LCC UA23 (ebook) | LCC UA23 .T475 2019
    (print) | DDC 355.00973—dc23
LC record available at https://lccn.loc.gov/2018054259

♾ Print editions meet the requirements of ANSI/NISO z39.48-1992
(Permanence of Paper).
Printed in the United States of America.

27 26 25 24 23 22 21 20 19   9 8 7 6 5 4 3 2 1
First printing

CONTENTS

Contents

ILLUSTRATIONS

Photographs

Figures

Tables

ACKNOWLEDGMENTS AND DEDICATION

This book has been quite a journey. The structure came from a number of conversations with researchers and students interested in American defense issues but knowing little about the military. When they asked me what they should read to learn more, no single volume came to mind that served as a modest jumping-off point. This book is an attempt to offer one.

Along the way, Dr. Eric Heginbotham, Dr. Mara Karlin, Col. Buzz Phillips, Col. Neal Rappaport (Ret.), Mr. Daniel Strunk, Lt. Col. Kari Thyne (Ret.), and Col. Karen Wilhelm (Ret.) all took time out of demanding schedules to read drafts and give me invaluable feedback. Collectively their expertise covers, among other things, service organizations and culture, military history, civilian-military relations, political philosophy, law, and strategic studies. They improved this work immeasurably. Dr. Liz Allison deserves special mention. She helped to shape this book from the beginning, and without her sage advice it never would have been written. Finally, a heartfelt thanks to Naval Institute Press for trusting me to take on this project. Ms. Laura Davulis, Mr. Glenn Griffith, Ms. Emily Bakely, Ms. Stephanie Attia Evans, and Mr. Pelham Boyer, in particular, have greatly improved this work. Although this material has been reviewed several times to ensure accuracy, some errors may have slipped through. Any mistakes are, of course, my responsibility alone.

Both my parents lived through World War II. My father's division arrived in Europe just in time to fight in the Battle of the Bulge and on into Berlin. My mother watched her three brothers go off to war; they served in the European and Pacific theaters—one on land, one at sea, and one in the air. My parents were civilians at heart, but their wartime experiences convinced them that the military was integral to, rather than apart from, the rest of American society. In this book I hope to capture their spirit and understanding, and it is dedicated to them.

ABBREVIATIONS AND ACRONYMS

A-	attack aircraft
AAC	Army Air Corps
AAF	Army Air Forces
AAV	amphibious assault vehicle
AC	active component
AEF	American Expeditionary Force; Air Expeditionary Force
AFRICOM	Africa Command
ANG	Air National Guard
ASTP	Army Specialized Training Program
ASW	antisubmarine warfare
AUMF	authorization for the use of military force
AVF	all-volunteer force
B-	bomber aircraft
BCT	brigade combat team
BUR	Bottom-Up Review
C-	cargo aircraft
CAF	combat air forces
CCDR	combatant commander (doctrinal)
CENTCOM	Central Command
CinC	commander in chief
CJCS	Chairman of the Joint Chiefs of Staff
CMC	Commandant of the Marine Corps
CNGB	Chief, National Guard Bureau
CNO	Chief of Naval Operations
COCOM	combatant command (informal)
COIN	counterinsurgency

CORM	Commission on Roles and Missions (of the Armed Forces)
CSA	Chief of Staff of the Army; Confederate States of America
CSAF	Chief of Staff of the Air Force
CSG	carrier strike group
CYBERCOM	Cyber Command
DADT	Don't Ask, Don't Tell
DOD	Department of Defense
DPG	defense planning guidance
E-	enlisted
EOD	explosive ordnance disposal
EUCOM	European Command
F-	fighter aircraft
GPS	Global Positioning System
ICBM	intercontinental ballistic missile
IED	improvised explosive device
IFV	infantry fighting vehicle
JCS	Joint Chiefs of Staff
JS	Joint Staff
JSOC	Joint Special Operations Command
LCAC	air-cushioned landing craft
LST	tank landing ship
KC-	tanker aircraft
MACV	Military Assistance Command, Vietnam
MAGTF	Marine air-ground task force
MAF	mobility air forces
MEB	Marine expeditionary brigade
MEF	Marine expeditionary force
MEU	Marine expeditionary unit
NATO	North Atlantic Treaty Organization
NCO	noncommissioned officer
NG	National Guard
NME	National Military Establishment

NSA	National Security Act; National Security Agency
NSC	National Security Council
O-	officer
OEF	Operation Enduring Freedom
OIF	Operation Iraqi Freedom
OSD	Office of the Secretary of Defense
QDR	Quadrennial Defense Review
PACOM	Pacific Command
PPBS	Planning, Programming and Budgeting System
QDR	Quadrennial Defense Review
RC	Reserve component
ROTC	Reserve Officers' Training Corps
SAC	Strategic Air Command
SAM	surface-to-air missile
SEAL	Sea, Air, Land [USN special-warfare component]
SECDEF	Secretary of Defense
SECNAV	Secretary of the Navy [and Marine Corps]
SLBM	sea-launched ballistic missile
SOCOM	Special Operations Command
SOF	special operations forces
SPACECOM	Space Command
SSBN	ballistic-missile nuclear submarine
SSM	surface-to-surface missile
SSN	nuclear-powered attack submarine
STRATCOM	Strategic Command
TRANSCOM	Transportation Command
UAV	unmanned aerial vehicle
UCP	Unified Command Plan
UMT	universal military training
USA	U.S. Army
USAAC	U.S. Army Air Corps
USAAF	U.S. Army Air Forces

USAF	U.S. Air Force
USC	U.S. Code
USG	U.S. government
USMA	U.S. Military Academy
USMC	U.S. Marine Corps
USN	U.S. Navy
WO	warrant officer
VCJCS	Vice Chairman of the Joint Chiefs of Staff

Introduction

The U.S. military has evolved from a tiny and distrusted institution at the margins of government into a central element of the United States of America and its power. Today it is respected and prominent in current events and popular culture, yet it remains mysterious to most Americans. The media, policy establishment, and American people frequently use the expression "the American military" as though it were monolithic and easily understood. Whether in reference to the U.S. military's exploits in World War II, its humanitarian-relief role in the wake of the tsunamis of 2005, the mission to get Osama bin Laden in 2011, or ongoing drone operations in the Middle East, the underlying assumption is that there exists a shared understanding of what it is. Yet, there are myriad ways to approach the U.S. military: organizational and institutional constructs, individual experiences, historical and constitutional debates, concerns about the military-industrial complex or civilian control, expensive acquisition projects, budgetary struggles, technological innovations, or shifting social attitudes about who can, or should, serve in the military. Moreover, the U.S. military itself offers few hints to outsiders on how to think holistically about it. Indeed, it creates its own mysterious, insular world by using a unique language, collecting its members and their families in and around restricted military posts, and fostering an exclusive culture.

The mystery starts with something as small as how people in the military dress. A person in civilian clothes usually goes unnoticed; that same person in a uniform draws attention. The uniform itself is mysterious—what do the insignia, stripes, and ribbons mean? Has that person been in combat, or has she just completed initial training, called boot camp? Moreover, military people seem to act differently than civilians do. They deploy overseas for extended periods, seem to always be working out, and focus strongly on taking care of those under their leadership. Institutionally, the military deepens this mystery. A tank, for instance, is not just a tank; it is either an M1A1 or M1A2. Military services do not simply fight on land, at sea, and in the air; they are "multidomain," providing forces to combatant commanders. Collectively, this argot constitutes an effective way to communicate within the military, but it can easily confuse, even alienate, those who are outside that community.

In short, the U.S. military is a huge, mysterious entity. Even those who are serving or have served see it in a variety of ways. Its fundamental purpose, however, is not in question —the U.S. military provides for the nation's common defense and interests by the threat or use of organized violence. These interests can range from winning a world war to evacuating an embassy to gathering intelligence for the next war; the military can protect such interests only because of its responsibility for acquiring, organizing, using, and sustaining, on behalf of the nation, "violent means"—a term used by theorists to make clear the distinction between individual killing (murder) and nation-state-sanctioned killing (war).[1]

The underlying premise of this work is that understanding the U.S. military is an integral part of understanding the United States and its citizens. Thus, it seeks to demystify this fascinating, complex institution, first, by explaining the basic lexicon and essential organizational structure necessary for mastering and using violent means; second, offering insights into the individuals who serve in these organizations and what they do; and finally, looking in some detail at how these organizations, their structures, and cultures have evolved since the nation's founding. The latter is particularly important, because it reveals how American experiences and society have repeatedly reshaped the military. Furthermore, history offers constant reminders of the extent to which the military is a product of accident and expedience, never perfectly suited to the challenges it faces. Thus, today's military reflects historical adaptation, agglomeration, and contingency; it may only partially reflect the ideal military America would wish to build if working with a blank slate.

There are any number of detailed military histories; exposés of failed reforms; primers on organizational structures, uniforms, and protocol; and analyses of contemporary challenges. Many reflect an implicit assumption that the military is somehow apart from the nation as a whole and will stay that way. This book seeks merely to open a window into this institution in such a way that the reader can, for good or for ill, see the American military for what it fundamentally is—a reflection of the nation, its priorities, and its people.

PART I
THE BASICS

U.S. Military Organizations and Their People

Because the American military is far out of the experience of even some who choose to join it, each service uses an intense, immersive experience known as basic training to convert civilians to service members in a short period of time. This experience typically is structured around six activities:

- Individual memorization and recitation focused on the basics of military organizational structure, rank, history, and culture
- Individual and unit physical fitness accomplished through calisthenics, marching, obstacle courses, timed runs, and similar activities
- Detailed instruction on the proper wear of the uniform, service customs, and service courtesies
- Individual and unit drills—anything from the rifle manual of arms to parades involving thousands—to build discipline and esprit
- Classroom and field instruction on the military justice system, marksmanship, and operation in the field.
- Unit completion of a demanding capstone exercise.

The overriding emphases of basic training are service-specific cultural immersion, discipline, obedience to orders, commitment to excellent performance regardless of the task, and elevation of the success of the unit above the individual. Part I is equivalent to portions of basic training—essential and important, if perhaps not always enjoyable. Chapters 1 and 2 focus on some of the basics needed to understand and discuss the military, such as service organizational structures, equipment, personnel, and uniforms. These essentials open the door to a broader understanding of America's military—past, present, and future.

Military Services, Organizational Integration, and Civilian Oversight

The foundation of the twenty-first-century U.S. military comprises the four military services assigned to the Department of Defense: the U.S. Army, U.S. Navy, U.S. Marine Corps, and U.S. Air Force.[1] No matter what people in uniform do, from special operations to logistics, they must first join one of the four services. All of them share the fundamental responsibility to prepare for, and if necessary wage, war.

The Four Military Services

More specifically, they must master and manage organized violence in order to provide for the common defense of the United States. The focus on organized violence is important. It distinguishes war—the act of political violence against another political unit or nation—and the services' ultimate responsibility for preparing for it, from other violent acts, such as murder, committed by individuals.[2] Each service fulfills this fundamental responsibility by recruiting, organizing, training, and equipping a force specializing in a particular type of organized violence as spelled out in law: Title 10 of the U.S. Code, which governs the military.[3] Someone who enters the military not only joins one of the four services but accepts a share of its responsibility for the mastery, management, and use of organized violence. Paradoxically, though, having accepted the responsibility, a given member might never go near a conflict. This means the military services' vast, latent capabilities for combat are also available for

Table 1-1. U.S. Military Services

	U.S. Army	U.S. Navy	U.S. Marine Corps	U.S. Air Force
Principal Geographic Domain	Land	Sea	Amphibious (ship to shore)	Air and space
Four-Star Leader	Chief of Staff	Chief of Naval Operations	Commandant	Chief of Staff

important peacetime purposes, such as working with allies and providing humanitarian assistance and disaster relief.

The responsibilities assigned to the services are roughly based on their respective physical environments, which, as will be seen in subsequent chapters, create some of the greatest differences among them. Simply speaking, land is the Army's realm; the sea belongs to the Navy; the Marine Corps, originally a body of shipborne foot soldiers, now specializes in ship-to-shore operations; finally, the air and space above the earth are mostly the Air Force's responsibility. All of the services have full-time members, who belong to their active component, and part-time members, who serve in reserve component comprising service-affiliated National Guard units or reserve organizations.[4] The services "recruit, organize, train, and equip" to dominate their respective domains—even as the services recognize that technology has blurred these demarcations considerably. Finally, all the military services are led by senior uniformed executives (four-star general officers or admirals) who are charged with overall direction of their respective services and are responsible to their civilian departmental secretaries. (See chapter 2 for a discussion of ranks.) The four services' specific attributes are laid out in table 1-1.

U.S. Army

Since its founding this nation has had an army, whether to protect the frontier or defeat land forces overseas. The U.S. Constitution, Article 1, Section 8 gives Congress the power "to raise and support Armies." All who serve in the Army

Table 1-2. U.S. Army
Total Size: 988,000 *(as of June 30, 2018)*

Active Component	Reserve Component	
Active Duty	U.S. Army Reserve	National Guard
465,000	189,000	334,000

Source: dmdc.osd.mil

are primarily concerned with land combat and are called soldiers. The Army has always been the nation's largest military service. Arguably, perhaps because of its size, it is also the service Americans know best. Today it numbers approximately 465,000 active-duty soldiers. This total number for the Army (as for the other services), referred to as "end strength," is set by Congress and fluctuates with the perceived threats to the nation. If its reserve component (see below) is included, the Army's total strength today hovers just under one million (table 1-2).[5]

Combat Arms
The Army has organized itself around ground combat: inflicting violence (or preparing to) against an enemy by means of foot soldiers (infantry); self-propelled and towed cannons (artillery); heavily protected tracked vehicles with mounted cannons (armor); aircraft flying in close support of soldiers on the ground (aviation); and unconventional forces (special forces), sometimes in conjunction with the forces of host nations. The Army relies on combat support from engineers, for example, who construct or demolish physical structures (e.g., bridges, airfields) under combat conditions. To employ any of these means successfully also requires considerable expertise in other support areas, such as air defense, intelligence, logistics, cyber, communications, and medical care.

The Brigade Combat Team
The Army, like the other services, uses a hierarchical structure to organize and employ these pieces effectively. Especially in

the years after the 9/11 attacks, the brigade combat team (BCT) has been the Army's core operational unit in places like Afghanistan and Iraq. It is a brigade—approximately four thousand soldiers commanded by a colonel—augmented in a variety of ways to allow it to go, or deploy, anywhere in the world independently and resupply, or sustain, itself there. BCTs can be categorized as any of three types: infantry, Stryker, or armored.[6]

Infantry arriving on foot, by parachute, or by helicopter is at the organizational heart of the infantry BCT. The Stryker BCT puts soldiers riding in, and fighting from, a Stryker—a wheeled, armored vehicle carrying a cannon and troops—at the core of its organization.

For the armored BCT, the Abrams tank (M1A2), the Army's heaviest armored vehicle, is the key piece of equipment. The unit is organized around it.

BCTs have a triangular structure (see figure 1-1). That is, each BCT usually consists of three smaller combat units, known as battalions; each battalion generally has three smaller combat units, called companies; and each company comprises three smaller units, called platoons. The component units of the brigade cannot operate independently

Stryker Combat Vehicle. *U.S. Army*

Abrams Main Battle Tank. *Department of Defense*

without fire (longer-range weapons, such as artillery) and logistics support from specialized units.

Above the BCT Level

Three or more BCTs combine to make a division of ten thousand or more soldiers, three divisions form a corps of 25,000–50,000 soldiers, and corps join to become armies. These organizational structures of division size and larger bring combat and essential support elements together to fight large land conflicts for extended periods of time.[7] This focus on integration of multiple units makes planning and doctrine (formal, standing guidance) critical to the Army's effectiveness; the Army, accordingly, places particular emphasis on development of doctrine.

Land Control

American civilian leaders believe that sending or stationing ground forces overseas is the highest form of national commitment to friends and allies. The Army usually provides the foundation for any major land mission, such as, most recently, Afghanistan and Iraq. As a general rule, wherever the U.S. Army deploys a BCT-sized unit or larger, the nation has made a significant military commitment for sustained operations and displayed an intention to dominate the land with its ground forces. The U.S. Army has an ability unique

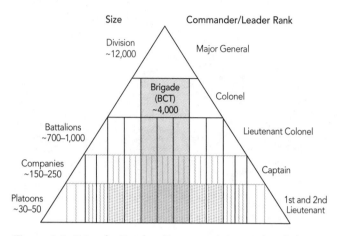

Figure 1-1. Brigade Combat Teams and the "Rule of Three"

among the nation's services to assemble all its combat arms in one place, sustain them with supporting units, and fight lengthy and highly intense land conflicts. In short, the Army is the epicenter of the ability of the United States to control land in military operations.

U.S. Navy

The United States has also had a navy since its founding. The Constitution gives Congress power "to provide and maintain a navy." The Navy focuses on such tasks as defeating adversary fleets and protecting trade, sea lines of communication, coasts, and ports (or attacking those of any enemy). The U.S. Navy (USN) has 270–280 ships.[8] About 324,000 active-duty personnel, sailors, operate the fleet and provide necessary shore support (table 1-3).

The U.S. Navy, like other navies, organizes itself around its most important ship type, traditionally referred to as the capital ship. The capital ship is the key to a navy's success or failure; if a navy's capital ships are destroyed, the fleet fails. The Pacific Fleet's survival despite the loss of several battleships at Pearl Harbor on December 7, 1941, highlighted the emergence of the aircraft carrier as the Navy's capital ship. In the first part of the twenty-first century, the aircraft carrier, with its impressive combat power, remains the capital ship around which the U.S. Navy is organized, despite growing concerns especially about its vulnerabilities to antiship ballistic missiles.

The Aircraft Carrier and Carrier Strike Group

Today's aircraft carriers dwarf those of the World War II era.[9] They are nuclear-powered, floating airports over a thousand feet long and displacing over 100,000 tons. The characteristic flat deck is a runway for catapult launch and arresting-cable recovery of aircraft. Carriers have flight control towers to manage aircraft operations. Each carrier requires a crew of over four thousand sailors to operate and repair the carrier and its aircraft and to defend the ship from attack.

Through the physical presence of the carrier and its aircraft, American power can be projected anywhere around the globe. Carriers are used for a variety of purposes including defending the global commons, humanitarian assistance, and disaster relief. But the core mission of these multibillion-dollar nuclear-powered ships is the employment of organized violence at, and from, the sea.[10] Currently the U.S. Navy has ten *Nimitz*-class carriers and one of the *Gerald Ford* class (about, at this writing, to come into service).[11] Over time all the *Nimitz*-class carriers will be replaced by the newer *Ford*-class ships.

If an aircraft carrier is thought of as a floating airport, it truly comes to life when its seventy to eighty aircraft, organized in squadrons and collectively known as the carrier air wing, arrive on board. These air wings consist of fixed-wing

Table 1-3. U.S. Navy
Total Size: 382,000 *(as of June 30, 2018)*

Active Component	Reserve Component	
Active Duty	U.S. Navy Reserve	National Guard
324,000	58,000	None

Source: dmdc.osd.mil

Carrier Strike Group (includes aircraft carrier, carrier air wing, and other assigned ships). *U.S. Navy*

aircraft and helicopters that, among other things, can strike enemy targets, protect and supply the ship, and recover downed pilots.

Because a carrier's survival is vital to the Navy, it never operates alone. Rather, the carrier is the epicenter of a carrier strike group (CSG), comprising the carrier and smaller ships (e.g., destroyers, attack submarines) that protect and support it. During peacetime, the ships of a CSG often cruise independently and perform a variety of missions. Most notably, nuclear-powered attack submarines (SSNs) operate with considerable autonomy.[12] But in a conflict the strike group assembles, and most ships assigned to it are devoted to protecting the carrier in some way. Some budget skeptics note that this operating concept means that when the nation buys an aircraft carrier it also purchases an air wing and possibly new ships to protect it—potentially increasing an initial investment of well over $13 billion per ship by billions more.

Ballistic-Missile Submarines

An argument can be made that the U.S. Navy has a second class of capital ship—the ballistic-missile nuclear submarine (SSBN), also known as a "boomer." Equipped with twenty-four sea-launched ballistic missiles, each with multiple nuclear warheads, the current *Ohio*-class submarines operate for approximately three months at a time on nuclear deterrence patrols ready to launch their missiles if so directed by the president. These aging, expensive submarines are core to America's nuclear deterrent and slated for replacement by the new, more expensive *Columbia* class starting around 2031.

Culturally, the difference between the missions of ballistic-missile and attack submarines is dramatic. The former stays submerged for weeks at a time, hiding in the ocean's depths and hoping never to launch a missile. In contrast, attack submarines engage in aggressive, risky missions of hide-and-seek against other submarine fleets. Thus, unsurprisingly, most submariners have considerably more enthusiasm for attack submarine assignments than for those associated with the nuclear deterrent mission.

Global Presence

Sailors, wherever they serve, whether they identify with the air, surface, or subsurface aspect of operating at sea, see their service as the embodiment of America's global power, routinely providing presence around the world and protecting the global commons. During peacetime, amidst humanitarian crises, and at war, they are part of a highly visible symbol of the nation's superpower stature.

The U.S. Marine Corps

Although not mentioned in the Constitution, the U.S. Marine Corps (USMC) dates to the nation's founding as well. Originally it provided the Navy with a small contingent of seaborne infantry (as well as shipboard security). Today it remains part of the Department of the Navy and is imbued with a maritime spirit, but it has evolved into a fiercely independent service focused on ship-to-shore crisis response and expeditionary operations. It relies on approximately 185,000 active-duty Marines to execute this expeditionary mission. Even more than for the Army, the infantry shapes the Marine Corps' organizational identity, hence its well-known expression "Every Marine a rifleman" (table 1-4).

Marine Air-Ground Task Force (MAGTF)

To get ashore safely and operate there successfully, the Marine Corps conducts "amphibious assault" via landing craft or arrives by air. Once ashore, the landing force uses its own artillery, armor, and air components to sustain the attack until it can be reinforced. These elements come together in the Marine air-ground task force (MAGTF, pronounced "MAGtaf"). First used in broad concept during World War II—the name was not used formally until 1963— the MAGTF remains central to how the Marine Corps organizes and operates because it can be tailored to perform a variety of missions.

MAGTF Components (Elements)

Closely coordinated ground and air forces are at the heart of the MAGTF. The ground forces are built around infantry riflemen, supported by armor and artillery. Once ashore, whether by air or amphibious assault, these Marine ground forces establish a beachhead, a lodgment, from which to challenge, and ultimately defeat, enemy forces. Marine air elements are essential to the ground force's success. They consist of fighter, attack, and transport aircraft, as well as helicopters to protect and move the ground forces. Command and leadership of the MAGTF vary with its size, as does the composition of its support component—engineers, logisticians, intelligence specialists, and others who keep the MAGTF operational.

Table 1-4. U.S. Marine Corps
Total Size: 223,000 *(as of June 30, 2018)*

Active Component	Reserve Component	
Active Duty	U.S. Marine Corps Reserve*	National Guard
185,000	38,000	None

* To further complicate USMCR nomenclature, it is also known as the Marine Forces Reserve and the U.S. Marine Corps Forces Reserve.

Source: dmdc.osd.mil

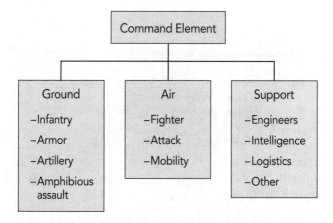

Figure 1-2. Marine Air-Ground Task Force

MAGTF Equipment

Marine ground forces have equipment similar to that of the U.S. Army, with the notable exception of the amphibious assault vehicle (AAV). The AAV is a tracked, armed, and armored fighting vehicle that can disembark from a ship into the water even in rough seas, propel itself ashore, land, and deploy up to twenty-one Marines. The air element is being modernized with the addition of F-35s, which will attack enemy troops, weapons, and equipment engaged with or posing threats to Marine ground forces (a role referred to as "close air support"). The modernized air element also includes the MV-22 Osprey, a tilt-rotor aircraft used to fly Marines directly ashore. It can operate either as a helicopter (especially for takeoff and landing) or a fixed-wing aircraft (for level flight).

MAGTF Types

The Marine Corps emphasizes the "scalability" of the MAGTF —that is, the Marines can assemble smaller or larger ones depending on the mission. There are four types of MAGTFs:

- The special-purpose MAGTF (SP MAGTF), at the smaller end of the scale, can be organized to accomplish a specific mission, such as security cooperation with a partner

Amphibious Assault Vehicle. *U.S. Department of Defense*

nation. For a rough idea of scale, an SP MAGTF consists of approximately five hundred Marines and sailors in air, ground, and support capacities under the command of a lieutenant colonel (see chapter 2).

- The Marine expeditionary unit, or MEU, numbering approximately 2,200 Marines and sailors, is commanded by a colonel. A MEU is typically carried on board amphibious assault ships as a quick-response force for use immediately after a natural or humanitarian disaster, such as the 2004 Indian Ocean tsunami.
- The Marine expeditionary brigade, or MEB, is a larger, combat-focused organization under the command of a one- or two-star general; it ranges from 14,000 to 18,000 in size.
- A Marine expeditionary force, or MEF, is the largest, and principal, combat unit in the Marine Corps. It is commanded by a lieutenant general (three-star) and consists of 20,000 to 90,000 Marines and sailors.

Ship to Shore

Navy sailors are included in the overall composition of the MAGTFs because they are essential for moving Marines from ship to shore and providing personnel (such as combat medics, known as corpsmen) for vital functions ashore. Most notably, the Navy operates a fleet of amphibious ships essential for the Marine Corps' mission. The largest type of such vessels is the amphibious assault ship, frequently mistaken for an aircraft carrier, which can carry an entire MEU, including its aircraft.

Aside from the amphibious assault vehicles and aircraft by which Marines can come ashore, the U.S. Navy operates and maintains a fleet of hovercraft (or LCACs, air-cushion landing craft) to land heavy equipment. In the employment of LCACs, the direct link to the now iconic amphibious operations of World War II is especially apparent.

First to Fight

Regardless of how they get to the fight, Marines believe they belong to the nation's toughest and readiest military service. The Marines' well-honed first to-fight reputation, developed in part to differentiate the Corps from the Army, arguably makes it the preferred service for response to a crisis (recognizing, however, that sustained operations require support from other services). This reputation also puts individual and unit mastery of the means of organized violence at the center of the Marine Corps' organizational identity.

Amphibious Assault Ship with CV-22s on board. *U.S. Navy*

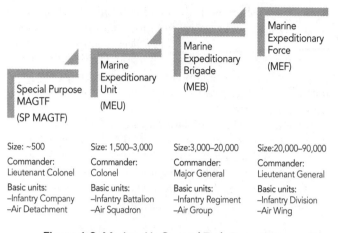

Special Purpose
MAGTF
(SP MAGTF)

Marine
Expeditionary
Unit
(MEU)

Marine
Expeditionary
Brigade
(MEB)

Marine
Expeditionary
Force
(MEF)

Size: ~500

Size: 1,500–3,000

Size:3,000–20,000

Size:20,000–90,000

Commander:
Lieutenant Colonel

Commander:
Colonel

Commander:
Major General

Commander:
Lieutenant General

Basic units:
–Infantry Company
–Air Detachment

Basic units:
–Infantry Battalion
–Air Squadron

Basic units:
–Infantry Regiment
–Air Group

Basic units:
–Infantry Division
–Air Wing

Figure 1-3. Marine Air-Ground Task Force Types

U.S. Air Force

The U.S. Air Force dates its origins to World War I, when the Army explored the potential ability of a revolutionary technology, the airplane, to fly over the trenches to observe and attack the enemy. After the war, during which the promise of aviation was demonstrated, Congress established the U.S. Army Air Corps (USAAC). The USAAC still belonged to the Army, but many airmen passionately argued for organizational independence. They believed that airpower—that is the strategic application of military power from the air (e.g., attacking an enemy nation's economy or the morale of its people)—could win wars alone, but only given an independent air service. World War II provided the opportunity to make this point (although the results have been argued about ever since), and Congress subsequently authorized an independent U.S. Air Force (USAF) in 1947. Today, the Air Force operates a variety of forces: combat, mobility, and unmanned air forces; a nuclear missile force; and a space satellite force. It organizes its forces, smallest to largest, into squadrons, groups, wings, numbered air forces, and major commands. The size and composition of these units vary widely depending on the type of forces involved (table 1-5).

Table 1-5. U.S. Air Force
Total Size: 496,000 *(as of June 30, 2018)*

Active Component	Reserve Component	
Active Duty	U.S. Air Force Reserve	Air National Guard
321,000	68,000	107,000

Source: dmdc.osd.mil

Combat Air Forces

The combat air forces (CAF) within the Air Force consist mostly of bomber and fighter aircraft. Today's bomber aircraft (*B-* designates a bomber) are the B-52, B-1, and B-2. The B-2, a "flying wing," is the most expensive aircraft in the world, costing approximately two billion dollars each to build. Bombers can fly great distances and drop large payloads—primarily conventional but also nuclear weapons—on enemy targets. Fighter and attack aircraft (designated by *F-* and *A-*, respectively) gain and maintain control of the air so other missions can be carried out, suppress enemy air defenses before they can shoot down friendly aircraft, and provide close air support to ground forces. Current aircraft associated with these missions are the new F-22 and F-35 (in Air Force parlance, both fifth-generation fighters), the older (or fourth generation) F-15 and F-16 fighters, and finally the A-10, the Air Force's only single-mission close-air-support aircraft.[13] The combat air forces are considered the epicenter of the Air Force and the embodiment of the pioneering airpower vision. The combined firepower of the bomber and fighter fleets allows the Air Force to project conventional and nuclear global power.

Mobility Air Forces

The Air Force operates a global air cargo network, known collectively and informally as the mobility air forces (MAF). To move the American military anywhere in the world, it flies two large aircraft, the C-5 and C-17 (*C-* designates cargo), capable of carrying large pieces of Army and Navy equipment,

Air Force Fighters: left to right, F-35, F-15 (front), F-22. *U.S Department of Defense*

even the Abrams tank. It also flies a large number of smaller C-130 aircraft to move supplies and people under austere circumstances (minimally developed airfields, for instance). The KC-135 and the KC-46 (soon to enter service) are civilian 707s and 767s, respectively (*KC-* for air refueling), modified to carry large quantities of fuel and transfer it other aircraft in flight. This ability to fly a wide variety of cargo and to refuel aircraft in flight makes the United States capable of sending its military rapidly to any location in the world.

Unmanned Air Forces

Unmanned aerial vehicles (UAV), or drones, have given rise to a new type of Air Force operation. Drone operators fly their aircraft remotely, from hundreds or even thousands of miles away from the actual aircraft, removed from physical risk. Aircrews can fly their drones for hours, even handing them off to new shifts of operators, all the while reconnoitering or ready to strike a target without warning. Some of the commonly known UAVs are the Predator (MQ-1) and the Reaper (MQ-9). More aircraft have been added to this part of the Air Force than to any other in the last decade.

Intercontinental Ballistic Missile Force

Since the early 1960s, the Air Force has operated the land-based nuclear missiles that provide the third component, or leg, of the nation's nuclear deterrent force (the others being bombers and ballistic-missile submarines). After nuclear-arms reductions required by treaty, this force numbers approximately 450 Minuteman III intercontinental ballistic missiles (ICBMs), based mostly in Wyoming, North Dakota, and South Dakota. Like the ballistic-missile submarines, the ICBMs need to be replaced. Collectively, the replacement costs for these two programs, plus a new bomber, approach a trillion dollars, forcing Congress and the nation to consider "how much is enough" for the nation's future nuclear arsenal.

Space Force

Finally, the Air Force operates some of the nation's critical global satellite systems for communication, early-attack warning, and precision navigation and timing. Most notably perhaps, it manages the Global Positioning System, or GPS, a satellite constellation essential to day-to-day operation of such modern necessities as smartphones and vehicle and aircraft navigation systems. Indeed, GPS is so integral to everyday life that most individuals are probably unaware it is a military system, let alone that it was conceived during the Cold War to improve nuclear targeting.

Global Vigilance, Global Reach, Global Power

The Air Force has evolved since its 1947 founding into a diverse force with many missions. The Air Force's "global

Reaper Unmanned Aerial Vehicle. *U.S. Department of Defense*

vigilance, global reach, global power" vision captures the ubiquity of its responsibilities. The variety of forces the Air Force operates gives it the most organizationally diverse culture of the four services. Indeed, some of its missions are quite remote from organized violence, yet integral to the defense of the nation.

The Part-Time Force: The Reserve Component

As the previous tables and chart below show, the military services consist of both active and reserve components. Those serving in the active component (AC) are full-time members of their respective military services, hence the expression "active duty." Historically, the nation also has a proud tradition of part-time military service, today involving the same basic and advanced training as the active component, followed by at least thirty-nine days of military service per year in the reserve component (RC). The reserve component is further divided into the National Guard (Army and Air) and the reserve, composed of the four service reserve organizations.

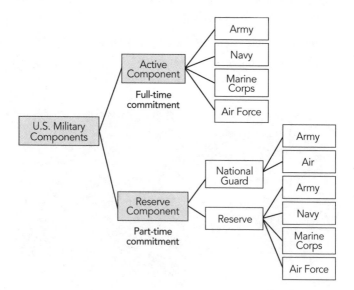

Figure 1-4. Active and Reserve Components

The National Guard

Two services, the Army and the Air Force, have National Guard components. On a day-to-day basis, National Guard units are state, not federal, entities. As such, they are subject to different laws, specifically Title 32 of the U.S. Code rather than Title 10. When they are not in federal service, they are referred to as the Army National Guard of the United States and the Air National Guard of the United States, respectively. Every state, as well as the District of Columbia and three territories, has at least one National Guard unit. Ordinarily these units are activated by, and report to, their respective governors, usually to deal with state-level emergencies, such as civil disturbances and hurricanes. The National Guard promotion process differs considerably from that of the active components. Perhaps the biggest difference is that each state's senior general officer, known as the "state adjutant general," is appointed by the governor or state legislature, making the selection as much a political choice as a military one. The Chief of the National Guard Bureau serves as main adviser to the secretary of defense on nonfederalized National Guard matters.

Once federalized, a National Guard unit is subject to Title 10, its components become known as simply the Army National Guard and the Air National Guard, and civilian control passes from the individual states to the Department of Defense. During early operations in Afghanistan and Iraq, for example, the Army National Guard provided thousands of soldiers to help meet the demand for troops. After the 9/11 attacks, the Air National Guard flew continental air defense patrols in its federalized capacity. As might be expected given these various lines of authorities and responsibilities, the National Guard and its active-duty counterparts have a complicated, and at times contentious, relationship.

The Reserve

All four services have part-time reserve forces that are trained to augment the active-duty forces in times of war or national emergency. These are the U.S. Army Reserve, the U.S. Navy Reserve, the U.S. Marine Corps Reserve, and the U.S. Air

Force Reserve. With some notable exceptions, such as full-time reservists filling active-duty positions, most reservists have civilian jobs. After completing basic and advanced training, they train for one weekend a month and serve a two-week active-duty stint each year. When called to active duty, reservists are integrated into ongoing operations. Whether in their reserve capacities or on active duty, reservists fall under Title 10 of the U.S. Code, the same law that governs active-duty forces, and report directly to the heads of their services.[14]

Organizational Integration

The notion that the military services should try to combine their individual efforts into a single, unified (or joint) fighting force—dates back to World War II. Two specific developments characterized this move to organizational integration, or "jointness": the ad hoc establishment of the Joint Chiefs of Staff and the insistence of Gen. George Marshall, as Army Chief of Staff, on making Gen. Dwight Eisenhower the single, unified commander over all European military operations. In the years after World War II, Congress formally codified both initiatives.

Joint Chiefs of Staff

The Joint Chiefs of Staff (JCS) is a senior military leadership body that consists of the Chairman of the Joint Chiefs of Staff (CJCS), the Vice Chairman (VCJCS), the four service chiefs, and the Chief of the National Guard Bureau (CNGB), who represents the National Guard's interest in its nonfederalized, Title 32 status. Thus, the service chiefs "wear two hats." The first is as the senior military officers in charge of their respective services and responsive to their civilian service secretaries. The second is as members of the Joint Chiefs of Staff. In this latter capacity, they offer strategic insights, operational expertise, and service perspectives to assist the CJCS in giving military advice to the president and secretary of defense. These JCS meetings, informally referred to as "tanks," occur several times a month and ensure that the service chiefs remain immersed in their joint as well as service roles.[15]

Figure 1-5. Joint Chiefs of Staff, 2018

The chairman and the vice chairman are the only two JCS members who are not dual-hatted. The chairman serves as the principal military adviser to the president and the secretary of defense, as well to as the National Security Council and the Homeland Security Council. Civilians may be somewhat surprised to learn that he commands no forces and has no supervisory control over the service chiefs or combatant commanders. The chairman's authority is indirect but significant, lying in his close relationship with the president and secretary and in his power to convene JCS tanks.

The Joint Staff

The chairman and vice chairman are supported by the Joint Staff, an elite, multiservice body of approximately 2,500 personnel that exists exclusively to provide the chairman and the vice chairman with information and expert analysis on issues ranging from personnel, ongoing operations, military strategy, and plans for future requirements. To ensure an integrated, joint perspective, the Joint Staff is explicitly prohibited from supporting other members of the JCS; the service chiefs are expected to draw on their own respective staffs. Organizationally, the Joint Staff mirrors most service and combatant-commander staffs. As the diagram in figure 1-6 shows, all key elements are designated by a *J-* (for joint) followed by a number: J-1, personnel; J-2, intelligence; J-3, operations; J-4, logistics; J-5, strategy and plans; J-6, command, control, communications, computers, and cyber; J-7,

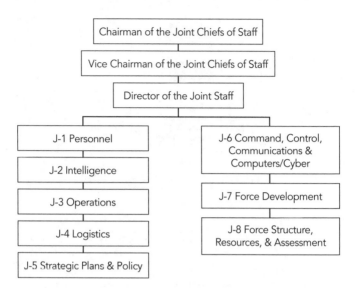

Figure 1-6. The Joint Staff

operational plans and force development; and J-8, force structure, resources, and assessment.[16]

Combatant Commands

The combatant commands, or COCOMs, are the second manifestation of organizational integration.[17] They arc the modern-day descendants of Eisenhower's World War II European Theater of Operation command. COCOMs operate jointly, integrating individual service capabilities. Individual services do *not* conduct operations; the combatant commands do. Because of the evolving roles of combatant commands and their varied organizational histories, they can be arcane, even to civilian leaders. As of this writing, there are ten COCOMs. Six have regional responsibilities, as specified in the Unified Command Plan map (figure 1-7). Four have functional or global responsibilities: Cyber Command (CYBERCOM), Special Operations (SOCOM), Strategic (STRATCOM), and Transportation (TRANSCOM) Commands. In addition, in partial response to President Trump's 2018 call for an independent space service, Secretary

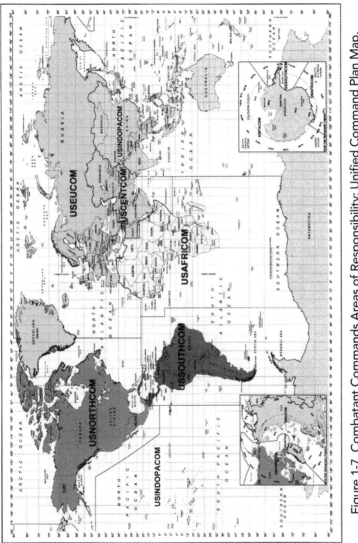
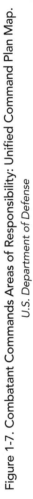

Figure 1-7. Combatant Commands Areas of Responsibility: Unified Command Plan Map.

U.S. Department of Defense

Services chiefs ensure
their services recruit,
organize, train, and
equip their forces...

Army	Their services then turn	Combatant Commands
Air Force	portions of these forces,	- Army Component
Navy	known as components,	- Air Force Component
Marine Corps	over to combatant	- Naval Component
	commands (COCOMs)...	- Marine Component

...COCOMs unite various
service components into
a joint force to perform an
assigned mission. Once
accomplished they return
the forces to the services.

Figure 1-8. Relationship between the Services and Combatant Commands

of Defense James Mattis directed the establishment of a unified Space Command (SPACECOM) in October 2018. Once established, SPACECOM will become the eleventh combatant command and the fifth with functional responsibilities.[18]

Like the chairman, vice chairman, and the service chiefs, the combatant commanders are four-star generals and admirals who come from the four military services. By law, they report directly to the secretary of defense and president, coordinating with the Chairman of the Joint Chiefs of Staff. In contrast, the service chiefs report to their respective service secretaries. Gen. David Petraeus and Gen. James Mattis, both former commanders of Central Command (CENTCOM) are two of the most well-known recent combatant commanders.

Organizationally, perhaps it is easiest to conceive of combatant commands as matrix organizations (figure 1-9). They draw forces from across the services and bring them together under a single leader, the combatant commander or a designated subordinate, to perform a particular mission. Although the combatant commander has an enduring responsibility for a region or a function, specific forces are assigned to that commander for particular missions or operations, the duration of which can range from days to decades. Like project-focused organizations in the business world, when the joint mission is done the forces return to their services.

SERVICES	COMBATANT COMMANDS											
	GEOGRAPHIC						FUNCTIONAL					
	Africa	Central	Europe	North	Indo-Pacific	South	SOCOM	Strategic Command	Transportation Command	Cyber Command	Space Command (To be established)
Army	X	X	X	X	X	X	X	X	X	X	X
Navy	X	X	X	X	X	X	X	X	X	X	X
USMC	X	X	X	X	X	X	X	X	X	X	
Air Force	X	X	X	X	X	X	X	X	X	X	X
SOCOM	X	X	X	X	X	X	X				

CONDUCT OPERATIONS

RECRUIT
ORGANIZE
TRAIN
EQUIP

Figure 1-9. Military Service–Combatant Commands
Matrix Relationship

Special Operations Command is one important exception to this design. SOCOM is a hybrid organization, with some characteristics of a military service. It has forces and their equipment permanently assigned and is responsible for conducting special operations around the globe. Sea, Air, Land (SEAL) team members, for example, might wear Navy uniforms, but they operate as part of SOCOM. This arrangement resulted from the Goldwater-Nichols legislation passed in 1986 (see chapter 10 for more detail). As the matrix shows, all the services, and frequently SOCOM as well, contribute forces to all the combatant commands.

Civilian Control and Oversight

Exercising effective civilian control of the military is one of the toughest challenges for any democratic nation. How does civilian leadership keep a nation's military focused on the nation's needs, rather than more narrowly, and sometimes dangerously, focused on advancing its own interests? The Constitution establishes the basic means of control and places specific responsibilities with Congress and the president. Among other things, Congress controls the military's budget and has the power to declare war, while the president is the commander in chief of the armed forces.[19]

Within the Department of Defense, civilian control is exercised in particular through the president's cabinet-level secretary of defense, supported by the deputy and under secretaries of defense. Subcabinet-level military department secretaries of the Army, Navy, and Air Force also report directly to the secretary of defense. These three department secretaries respectively oversee the four military services (the Secretary of the Navy [SECNAV] oversees both the Navy and Marine Corps) as they fulfill their responsibilities to recruit, organize, train, and equip their particular parts of the military. Organizationally, the service chiefs, in short, do not have direct access to the secretary of defense (military service civilian oversight positions are shaded in gray in table 1-6).

The importance of civilian control extends beyond raising forces to overseeing operations. As mentioned, the secretary of defense, rather than any of the subcabinet secretaries,

Table 1-6. Civilian Control and Oversight

Civilian Cabinet-Level: Position and Department	Secretary of Defense (Cabinet-Level Secretary)			
	Department of Defense			
Civilian Military Department Position (subcabinet)	Secretary of the Army	Secretary of the Navy		Secretary of the Air Force
Civilian-led Military Department	Department of the Army	Department of the Navy		Department of the Air Force
Military Service	Army	Navy	Marine Corps	Air Force
Principal Geographic Domain	Land	Sea	Amphibious (ship to shore)	Air and Space
Senior Service Leader	Chief of Staff	Chief of Naval Operations	Commandant	Chief of Staff

directly controls the combatant commands. Whether or not the nation has struck the right balance of civilian oversight and scrutiny vis-à-vis the military services and the combatant commands is a matter of debate among defense experts and within the military.

At the organizational level, a working familiarity with the military services' structures, their integration, and their oversight is elemental to understanding the American military. Moreover, in the services' evolution rests a deeper story about how the nation has viewed the military and its role over its history. But these sometimes obscure organizations come to life only through the individuals who serve in them. Since the founding, people in uniform have waged the nation's wars, shaped its military's missions, defined the services' organizational cultures, and at times, struggled to secure their services' relevance. The next chapter looks in greater depth at the people who serve today.

Further Reading

Primary sources include: the Constitution of the United States of America; *DoD Personnel, Workforce Reports and Publications*, https://www.dmdc.osd.mil/appj/dwp; Title 10, U.S. Code; the *Unified Command Plan* map at https://www.defense.gov; and White House, "Statement by President Donald J. Trump on the Elevation of Cyber Command," August 18, 2017. Secondary sources include: Hedley Bull, *The Anarchical Society*, 1995; Congressional Budget Office, *U.S. Military Force Structure: A Primer*, 2016; Dave Grossman, *On Killing*, 2009; Karl Marlantes, *What It Is Like to Go to War*, 2011; Richard Myers, *Eyes on the Horizon*, 2009; Harvey Sapolsky et al., *US Defense Politics*, 2009; Barbara Schading, *A Civilian's Guide to the U.S. Military*, 2007; Judith Stiehm, *The U.S. Military: A Basic Introduction*, 2012; and U.S. Marine Corps 101 Briefing (USMC_101 Brief [version 2].pptx).

Those Who Serve and
the Uniforms They Wear

If organizations give structure to the military, the individuals who serve in them bring the military to life. For many nonveteran civilians, typical interactions with the military include seeing recruiters walking the halls in high schools, or watching aircraft perform flyovers before a sporting event, or applauding service members or veterans marching in Memorial or Veterans Day parades, or paying final respects when a veteran has passed away. With the possible exception of the recruiter, who has the specific duty to seek out and chat with qualified high school seniors, these interactions tend to increase, rather than reduce, the mystery surrounding the military, because they lack a context that would connect the event to individual service members.

Transition from Civilian to
Service Member—and Back

Thus it is helpful to remember that all military members enter the service as civilians and, unless they are among the small minority who die while on active duty, return to civilian life after a few years or decades in uniform. When starting on this journey, civilians joining the military who meet the basic medical, moral, and behavioral screening criteria weigh answers to three questions. Which service should I join? Should I join on a full- or a part-time basis? Should I join as an officer or enlisted member? Chapter 1 provided background to consider when answering the first two questions; this chapter will focus mostly on the third.

Officers

An Officer's Purpose, Training, and Commissioning

Commissioned officers occupy the higher positions in the military hierarchy. Traditionally, commissioned officers embody the organizational ethos, leadership, and expertise that characterize their respective services. Individuals who pass the basic screening can seek officers' commissions in any of the services by earning accredited bachelor's degrees and successfully completing initial officer training in one of three ways: enrolling in a Reserve Officers' Training Corps (ROTC) program at a civilian university; attending one of three military academies (at West Point, New York, for the Army; Annapolis, Maryland, for the Navy and Marine Corps; and Colorado Springs, Colorado, for the Air Force); or completing a nine-to-twelve-week basic officer candidate school. If they successfully complete the training, officer candidates—in some settings called cadets or midshipmen—are offered commissions.

Commissions date to the American Revolution, when officers pledged an oath to "diligently discharge" their military duties. The Continental Congress, in turn, presented them formal documents, commissions, acknowledging that "special trust and confidence" had been placed in these officers leading the new republic's revolutionary forces. Today, the ROTC and service academy programs are structured so that academic degrees and officers' commissions are received almost concurrently.

Like their colonial forebears, newly commissioned officers today swear, as their first act, an oath of office to support and defend the U.S. Constitution. The commission carries with it the expectation that new officers will master a skill tied to organized violence, accept a commitment to serve, and develop into leaders of the kind essential to the military's success.[1] This leadership role in particular sets officers apart. It means not only achieving technical mastery but embodying and transmitting the values central to the military ethos, such as duty, honor, service, integrity, and selflessness. For those in command positions, there are also specific roles for leading their units and administering military justice to personnel subject to their command authority.

Officer Pay Designations (Pay Grades)

When someone takes the oath of office, he or she is assigned a pay grade and associated service rank. The pay grade identifies how much basic pay (taxable compensation) the member will receive. Officer pay grades are designated with an O-, for officer, succeeded by a number from 1 to 10. The lower numbers are associated with newer, or junior, members of the officer corps, the lowest pay grade, O-1, being a newly commissioned second lieutenant or Navy ensign, and the highest, O-10, belonging to a full general or admiral with decades of commissioned service. These alphanumerical designations are shared throughout the military.

Officer Progression

Advancement up the levels of traditional white-collar business organizations provides a rough approximation of officer progression. Newer officers (known as company grade, or junior, officers) provide the hands-on, entry-level, small-unit leadership and management essential to the military (table 2-1). These officers are in pay grades between O-1 and O-3 and can be responsible for units ranging in size from a few to a couple of hundred individuals; they may be flying aircraft

Table 2-1. Officer Pay Grades and Progression

Officer Pay Grade (O-)	Categorization	Technical Expertise—Rough Civilian Equivalent	Typical Ages
O-1 to O-3	Company/ junior grades	Entry leadership/ management	Early 20s to early 30s
O-4 to O-6	Field grades	Middle leadership/ management	30s to mid 40s
O-7 to O-10	General/ admiral grades; flag officers	Executive leadership/ management	Late 40s to early 60s

or helping to operate complex and sophisticated systems—perhaps at the same time. If selected for promotion to the intermediate ranks, O-4 to O-6 (known as field- or middle-grade officers), they assume increasingly large responsibilities: leading hundreds or thousands of people and commanding ships, air wings, or military bases. If promoted to general or admiral (in the Navy), pay grades O-7 to O-10, they assume executive responsibilities that roughly equate to the corporate level in the business world.[2] All pay-grade salaries are reviewed annually and are publicly available.

Translating Pay Grades into Ranks

Except in the Navy, the officer ranks to which pay grades correspond have the same names. In the Army, Air Force, and Marine Corps, at the company level O-1 and O-2 equate to second and first lieutenant, respectively, and O-3 to captain. In field grades, O-4 is a major, O-5 a lieutenant colonel, and O-6 a colonel. Finally, at the executive, or general-officer, level, an O-7 is a brigadier general, O-8 a major general, O-9 a lieutenant general, and O-10 a general.

Naval ranks are different. At the company-grade level, O-1 is an ensign, O-2 a lieutenant junior grade, and O-3 a lieutenant. At the mid-grade, O-4 is a lieutenant commander, O-5 a commander, and O-6 a captain. Given the different uses of "lieutenant" and "captain," it is important to know an individual's service so as not to confuse someone quite senior with an officer far more junior, or vice versa. Finally, at the naval executive or flag ranks, O-7 is a rear admiral "lower half" (LH), O-8 is a rear admiral "upper half" (UH), O-9 is vice admiral, and O-10 is admiral.[3]

The Essence of Officership

Officers must master skills and model the military ethos, but arguably the essence of officership rests in using and managing organized violence.[4] Officers are given the unique responsibility of leading groups of people trained and equipped to use violent means on behalf of the nation. Leadership of these individuals is a deep and abiding responsibility, whether they are providing safe passage during an embassy evacuation, destroying a terrorist cell, or attacking a country threatening the United States. Americans should expect the officer corps, at all levels, to manage their responsibilities skillfully, selflessly, honorably, and always in accordance with the direction of civilian leadership.

Warrant Officers

Although they constitute a relatively small portion of the military population, warrant officers exist in all the services except the Air Force; warrant officer (WO) designations are given to individuals with technical skills and tactical expertise that the services need to retain. The Army, for example, uses WOs extensively as helicopter pilots and in logistics specialties, the Marine Corps for specialized infantry positions. The Air Force chose not to use warrant ranks, instead placing such technical expertise in the senior noncommissioned-officer (NCO) ranks. There are successive pay grades to which warrant officers can be promoted within their own ranks, from W-1 to W-5, with names unique to each service. Within the military hierarchy, these individuals rank above enlisted noncommissioned officers and below commissioned officers. They take the same oath as commissioned officers.

Enlisted Personnel

Enlisted Purpose and Training

The majority of individuals who join the military enter the enlisted ranks (in the Navy they are referred to as "rates," a designation that combines pay grade and specialty). In 2017 the enlisted force comprised over one million members of an active-duty force numbering just over 1.3 million. Put another way, there are more than five enlisted personnel for every officer. In general, enlistees are between eighteen and twenty-two years old and about to complete, or are recent graduates of, high school. If they meet all screening criteria, typically they are eligible to enlist, or join, immediately (or right after graduation) at the entry level in one of the military services. Like new officers, new enlistees take an oath, but a different one: to support and defend the Constitution and to obey the orders of the president of the United States and the officers appointed over them.

Whatever service they join, all new enlistees attend some version of basic training. This training teaches new members how to wear their uniforms, inculcates in them the history and traditions of their services, builds physical conditioning, instills the discipline necessary to perform their duties, and plants the seed of an esprit that sets them apart from their former civilian selves. Basic training lasts from eight to twelve weeks, depending on the service. New military members next attend follow-on training programs to begin learning the specific, entry-level skills necessary for their assigned jobs. The young men and women who can be seen walking through airports in new uniforms with only a few decorations are frequently new graduates of basic training on their way to additional schools or perhaps a short vacation, known as "leave."

The enlisted force performs some of the toughest jobs in the military: they fill the bulk of the ranks of BCTs and MAGTFs; serve on the Navy's ships; and protect and maintain aircraft. In general, depending on what organization they join and the amount of training involved, new enlistees serve initially for two to six years. As a rule, the more extensive and expensive an individual's training, the longer the initial commitment of service he or she incurs.

Enlisted Pay-Grade Designations

All enlisted pay grades are designated by an *E-* followed by a number between 1 and 9. The lower the number, the newer a member is to the military and the lower the basic pay. New enlistees, for example, would be E-1s, with entry-level skills and ages from the late teens to early twenties. An E-9, conversely, will have decades of experience and be considered a master in his or her technical field. As in the officer corps, the salary associated with each pay grade is adjusted annually by Congress and is on public record.

Enlisted Progression

Military progression from E-1 to E-9 is roughly equivalent to civilian progression in skilled trades, such as electricians, avionics technicians, pipe fitters, machinists, or paramedics.

Military personnel enter their specialties at the equivalent of the apprentice level—they possess basic skills but need additional training, experience, and supervision. Their pay grades at this level will range from E-1 to E-3, and they are referred to as privates, seamen, lance corporals, or airmen. As they acquire the requisite experience, pass competency exams, and successfully complete increasingly difficult tasks, they progress to the journeyman level. In military parlance, they become NCOs, usually pay grades E-4 through E-6, and are called corporals or sergeants. In the Navy, personnel in these pay grades are called petty officers. In the Air Force, NCO status comes at E-5.

Becoming an NCO is a major accomplishment and is recognized as such throughout the military. NCOs are valued for their technical competence and small-unit leadership (of groups of from three to thirty). Some enlisted members subsequently progress to the master level associated with the pay grades E-7 to E-9. These senior NCOs (called sergeants or chief petty officers in the Navy) are the essential link between the enlisted and officer ranks, providing oversight, mentorship, and leadership, as well as technical expertise. Historically, the high quality of the NCO corps has set the American military apart from others—and is considered the foundation of its effectiveness. But even these long-service

Table 2-2. Enlisted Pay Grades and Progression

Enlisted Pay Grade (E-)	Categorization	Technical Expertise— Rough Civilian Equivalent	Typical Ages
E-1 to E-3	Entry level (privates, seamen, airmen)	Apprentice	18 to early 20s
E-4 to E-6*	Noncommissioned (corporals, sergeants, petty officers)	Journeyman	20s to early 30s
E-7 to E-9	Senior non-commissioned (sergeants, chief petty officers)	Master	30s to early 40s

* The Air Force considers E-5 the first NCO rank.

personnel are young in comparison to the civilian workforce; senior military leaders periodically highlight the overall youth of the nation's enlisted people (table 2-2).

Translating Enlisted Pay Grades into Ranks

While the enlisted pay grades are standard across the military, each service has its own ranks, with corresponding insignia—all involving stripes, chevrons, or some combination thereof. On more formal uniforms (business-suit equivalents), enlisted rank is always worn on one or both sleeves. Ranks suggest what kind of responsibilities individuals have and how long they have served in uniform. Members of the military must learn their respective service's ranks. For those seeking to understand the military, the time it takes to understand ranks is similarly well spent. The effort builds familiarity with the military lexicon, and if one interacts with people in uniform, it demonstrates respect and a level of knowledge about the military that will encourage deeper conversations.[5]

What They Wear: The Uniform as Autobiography

When a new member finishes initial training, whether as an officer or enlistee, he or she earns another identity—soldier, sailor, Marine, or airman. The uniform is the most obvious manifestation of this new identity. To civilians, uniforms seem strange, especially if bedecked with badges, stripes, and other accoutrements. To those with military experience, however, the uniform serves as a visual resume of what someone has and has not done while in the service. Space prevents going into the details of every aspect of every uniform; instead, what follows are some thoughts on how to look at uniforms the way those in the military do—rapidly, and usually unconsciously, "reading" them.

Purpose: Military Equivalents of Civilian Dress

Just as their civilian counterparts might do, the first thing a military member is likely to notice is the type of uniform someone is wearing and assess if it is appropriate to the circumstances. Each service has myriad uniforms, but the vast

Table 2-3. Civilian Dress and Uniform Equivalents

General Type of Civilian Activity	Civilian Dress	Military Uniform Equivalent
Field work/ operations	Work pants, shirts, jackets	Utility (e.g., service-specific camouflage uniforms, flight suits)
Daily office work	Coat and tie; business casual	Service dress without coat (short sleeve shirt, no tie/ long sleeve shirt with tie)
Client meetings	Business suit	Service dress with coat
Formal event	Black or white tie evening wear	Mess dress

majority of them fall into three categories:[6] "utility," "service dress," and "mess dress." A general rule of thumb is that the activity determines the uniform. Table 2-3 summarizes the categories and gives rough civilian equivalents.

Types of Uniforms: Telling the Services Apart

A uniform identifies not only the type of activity of the wearer but the service as well. Service affiliation is revealed in everything from camouflage patterns on utility uniforms to different shades of blue in service dress. Table 2-4 provides some general guidelines for distinguishing the services' uniforms, noting that, as always, there are many exceptions. For quick reference, for service dress only the most distinctive item is highlighted. No attempt is made here to describe the unique camouflage pattern because the services keep changing them (and are again as this book goes to press).[7] However, people dealing with military members should beware: simply referring to everyone in camouflage uniforms as "soldier" is incorrect and could be taken as an insult. "Soldier" is a title specific to Army personnel who go through a great deal to earn it. Individuals of the other services, who work just as hard to be able to call themselves sailors, Marines, or airmen, sometimes take offense at being referred to as "soldiers"—as might actual soldiers overhearing it.

The Story Each Uniform Tells

Each uniform can reveal specific things about the individual wearing it—what she does, how long she has been in, whether she has been overseas or in combat, and so forth. The service-dress uniform, especially when worn with a coat, reveals the most about an individual, but even the utility uniform tells a story. Within moments of meeting, military members assess and make judgments about what is noteworthy or missing on each other's uniform, taking note of rank insignia, patches, badges, and ribbons.

PATCHES

Patches are predominately found on utility uniforms and are most prevalent in the Army. The Army awards them for specific types of training, unit identification, and combat experience. Arguably, in the Army, the Ranger and Special Forces patches are held in the highest esteem. A combat patch on the

Table 2-4. Types of Uniforms by Service

Military Uniform	Army	Navy	Marine Corps	Air Force
Utility (e.g., service-specific camouflage, flight suits)	Specific service is on embroidered tape over left pocket			
Service dress without coat	White shirt over blue pants/skirt	Khaki shirt over khaki or black pants;	Khaki shirt over olive drab pants/skirt	Light blue shirt over blue pants/skirt
Service dress with coat	Above plus blue coat/tie	"Navy blue" (black) suit; open white collar over white pants/skirt	Above plus olive drab coat/tie	Above plus blue coat/tie

Table 2-5. Army Patches

	Criteria	Uniform Location/ Duration
Training	Accomplish specific, rigorous training: airborne, ranger, sapper, special forces	Tab worn on left sleeve; permanent award, e.g.,
Current unit patch	Currently assigned unit	Left sleeve, below any tabs; changes with assignment
Combat unit patch*	Unit patch from time in combat	Right sleeve; permanent award

* Same as combat service identification badge on service-dress uniform

right shoulder is also a keen point of pride and is awarded with ceremony (table 2-5). In units transitioning from conflict to peacetime, tension between those "who've been there" and earned combat patches and those who haven't can become a concern for commanders.

The aviation communities of the Navy, Marine Corps, and Air Force are also known as patch-wearing cultures. For the most part, the patches are tied to specific units and missions. However, one that draws special attention is the weapons-school patch. Especially in the Air Force, to be a weapons-school graduate, and even more so a weapons-school instructor, is tremendously prestigious—the patch marks its wearer as elite and thoroughly professional. The Navy's weapons school, commonly known as "Top Gun," is even more famous than its Air Force counterpart, because of the 1986 movie of the same name.

U.S. Air Force Weapons School Patch. *U.S. Air Force*

BADGES

On the coat of the service-dress uniform especially, a service member wears the personal badges and ribbons he merits. Badges give details about service-specific qualifications individuals have earned and, in some cases, where. Most badges are worn above or below the personal ribbons on the left breast pocket. As more are awarded, they can also appear on the right. The military has scores of specialty occupation badges for all ranks; each with its own criteria. Some badges only officers can earn; some are in different colors (especially in the Navy) for officers and enlisted personnel; some are popular and well known, such as the SEAL and explosive ordnance disposal (EOD) badges.

RIBBONS

If badges identify a service member's job, ribbons are a visual reflection of how well she did it. Ribbons are worn over the left breast pocket. They are small, rectangular, colorful pieces of stiffened cloth that usually, but not always, represent an awarded medal. Medals and ribbons are formally ranked as to precedence; if a uniform has more than one row, the highest is always at the left end (i.e., the wearer's right) of the top row. Most service members receive an award at the end of an assignment, or tour, and the more senior they are the higher this award will be. The ribbons symbolizing these end-of-tour awards are acknowledged, even appreciated, but not necessarily esteemed.

In contrast, one subset of ribbons, associated with personal valor and combat service, garners attention and respect in the military. The most esteemed ribbons signify the award of the Medal of Honor, the nation's highest military award, or the second highest, the Distinguished Service Cross (Army), Navy Cross (Navy and Marine Corps), or Air Force Cross. Because their criteria for award are so strict and involve great personal risk, these ribbons are rarely seen on uniforms. More common are Silver Star medals and Bronze Star Medals with valor devices (small metal Vs).[8] These medals also recognize personal valor in combat and are held in high regard. In addition, each service has a ribbon for valor displayed in peacetime, such as saving a drowning person: the Soldier's, Navy and Marine Corps, or Airman's Medal. Finally, the Marine Corps' rough equivalent of the Army's Combat Unit patch is the Combat Action Ribbon, or CAR. The CAR matters deeply within the Marine Corps, and the cultural divide between Marines who have earned one and those who have not is a challenge for leaders.[9]

"Grading" a Uniform

A deeply ingrained, intuitive habit within the military, inculcated by training, is to look at someone wearing a uniform and ask oneself, "Is that person squared away?" This is a shorthand expression encompassing several other questions: What's her rank? What has he done? Is that person wearing the "prescribed" uniform, the right one for the circumstances? Is it being worn properly? Does it look sharp? Is the head gear correct? (When outside, unless otherwise told, service members always wear a hat, beret, or helmet.) Most important, does the person wearing the uniform reflect the military America expects and deserves? Anyone donning a uniform should wear it proudly and with the understanding that she is a visible symbol of her service and the United States when wearing it.

The expectations and pride that go with wearing a uniform lead some to check into the badges and ribbons others wear. The idea that someone would wear unearned personal ribbons of valor, or elite badges such as the SEAL trident or Combat Infantryman Badge, is especially galling to people who have served. These acts of "stolen valor" have prompted some veterans to become amateur detectives in order to expose such deceptions.

Thus, uniforms are paradoxically intensely personal and yet profoundly unifying. The specifics of each uniform speak to service history, individual qualifications, valor, and accomplishments. But the apparently simple act of donning a uniform tells perhaps the most important fact of all. Military uniforms symbolize a commitment to serve, and they recognize a direct connection, even a debt, to those who have worn them before. Indeed, the uniform ties together servicemen and servicewomen of the past, present, and future in their responsibility to provide for the common defense. Those who wear a uniform might downplay this sentiment, but it is deep and enduring. In that spirit, a military uniform should represent a bridge, not a chasm, between military and civilian cultures.

———

What are the basics about America's military? First, it is organized into four distinct services, the Army, Navy, Marine Corps, and Air Force, each operating primarily in its own physical environment. Second, the services have their own organizational constructs, such as the Army's brigade combat team, the Navy's carrier strike group, the Marine Corps' Marine air-ground task force, and the Air Force's combat, mobility, and unmanned air forces. Third, certain weapons and types of equipment are critical to each service's organizational concepts: the Army's Abrams tanks and Stryker vehicles; the Navy's aircraft carriers, carrier air wings, and ballistic-missile submarines; the Marine Corps' amphibious assault ships and amphibious vehicles; and the Air Force's combat, mobility, and drone aircraft, its ICBMs and satellites. Fourth, the services do not fight in their own right; they provide forces to joint combatant commanders, who are responsible for operations. Fifth, civilian control is enshrined in the U.S. Constitution and is crucial to ensuring that the military stays focused on the nation and not its own institutional interests. Finally, the only reason the twenty-first-century American military works effectively is the dedication and commitment of highly trained active-duty and reserve officers and enlisted personnel, who have volunteered to fill the services' ranks and serve around the world.

Today's American military did not emerge fully formed; nor were its basics predetermined. Rather they reflect the accumulation of experience encountered, decisions made, and actions taken by civilian leaders and the military itself since the nation's founding. To understand how the basics evolved requires an appreciation of the problems the American military has faced over the years and its responses to them. Part II explores this institutional and cultural evolution in some depth.

Further Reading

The most comprehensive reference for this chapter is the official website of the Department of Defense, https://www.defense .gov. From this link users can access the websites of the Joint Chiefs of Staff, Combatant Command, and military services. Other sources include: Samuel Huntington, *The Soldier and the State*, 1981; Barbara Schading, *A Civilian's Guide to the U.S. Military*, 2007; Judith Stiehm, *The U.S. Military*, 2012; and U.S. Department of Defense, *The Armed Forces Officer*, 2007. To study the rank insignia more closely, the Department of Defense has excellent links at https://dod .defense.gov/About/Insignias/Officers/ for officers, and https:// dod.defense.gov/About/Insignias/Enlisted/ for enlisted. One of the best links to learn more about medals and ribbons is https://www.marines.mil/Portals/59/Publications/NAVMC %202897.pdf.

PART II

THE COMMON DEFENSE AND AMERICA'S MILITARY

Debates over the best way to meet the constitutional obligation to provide for the common defense have challenged, fascinated, amazed, and agitated the nation since its founding. The U.S. military's actions over the years reflected, and continue to reflect, how the nation's civilian leaders regarded the military, understood the common defense, and then used the military to provide for it. The twenty-first-century American military described in the first two chapters—its organizations and the individuals who bring it all to life—reflects the outcomes of these debates in its history, as well as its traditions and various organizational cultures. Understanding this long-standing, dynamic relationship is essential to demystifying the American military.

The next part will explore how the U.S. military evolved as a means to provide for the common defense from America's founding to the present. This relationship has been close, enduring, and frequently paradoxical. The focus will be on institutional continuity and change within the military. Each chapter will explore:

- Contemporary understandings of the common defense— During different eras, what American interests, categorized as "the common defense," relied on the military's mastery of organized violence?
- Organizational responses—What did that organizational response look like, service by service?

51

- Personnel—How were the military's personnel needs addressed?
- Organizational integration—To what extent did the services operate in a "joint" manner?
- Civilian control—How did the civilian leadership exercise control over the military?
- Impact on the common defense—How did Americans' understanding of the common defense evolve, if at all, with experience in the use of the military?

As the following chart shows, most chapters are structured so that individual categories can also be read separately across the chapters to reveal how a military institution (e.g., Navy under organizational responses) or practice (e.g., civilian control) evolved over time. The following chapters, however readers approach them, seek to reveal some of the profound tasks, controversies, and decisions that shaped the U.S. military into the uniquely powerful institution it is today.

Chapter (Evolving Common Defense)	Organizational Responses					Personnel	Organizational Integration	Civilian Control
	Army	Air Force	Navy	Marine Corps				
Chap 3 Creation 1787–1860	Small force infantry; frontier-based	None	6 frigates to protect trade & sea lanes	Ship-based infantry		Volunteers	Ad hoc	Found in Constitution, Articles 1 and 2; later established secretaries of War and Navy
Chap 4 Civil War and Aftermath 1861–79	Force of well over 1 million infantry, artillery, cavalry	None	Frigates and riverine craft for blockade & protect trade	Ship-based infantry; guarding navy yards		Volunteers and draft; African Americans serve	Ad hoc	Lincoln hands-on as CinC; expanded War Department
Chap 5 Transition 1880–1917	Small, constabulary force; move to professional focus	Airplane introduced to Army	Move to battleship navy; move to professional focus	Move to amphibious ops; small wars		Volunteers; African Americans serve	Ad hoc; Joint Board (advisory)	President Theodore Roosevelt led naval expansion
Chap 6 WWI and Aftermath 1917–40	Large expeditionary army to Europe; hint of mechanization	Army creates air service	Smaller ships; convoy protection from subs; acft carrier experimentation	Ashore with Army; planning for large amphibious ops		Volunteers and draft; African Americans, women serve; move to standardized training	Joint Board and AEF	President Wilson delegated mostly to military; Congress declared war

Chapter (Evolving Common Defense)	Organizational Responses				Personnel	Organizational Integration	Civilian Control
	Army	Air Force	Navy	Marine Corps			
Chap 7 WWII 1941–45	Over 6 million in uniform; mechanized and integrated, combined arms both theaters	Large USAAF; strategic bombing, case for service independence	Atlantic: convoys, amphibious ops; Pacific: large aircraft carrier, sub fleets; amphibious ops	Amphibious landings in Central Pacific; MAGTF-like concept emerges	Volunteers and draft; African Americans, women serve; standardized initial and advanced training	Ad hoc JCS; combined command, Europe especially	President Franklin Roosevelt hands-on as CinC, created ad hoc JCS; Congress declares and funds war
Chap 8 Atomic Age 1945–49	Dramatic reductions; concern about future relevance	USAF est. 1947; nation's nuclear force in SAC; B-36	Loses fight for nuclear aircraft carrier to USAF B-36	Law codifies amphibious ops	Volunteers and draft; law integrates race and women	UCP and JCS codified; CJCS established, given equal status with rest of JCS	Coordination vs centralization debate; NSA 1947 (SECDEF) and 1949 amendment (DOD) passed; revolt of admirals
Chap 9 Cold War 1950–1973	Unprepared for Korea, fights back; Pentomic division; combined arms Europe, SF takes on COIN in Vietnam	Nuclear USAF includes B-52, ICBMs, space; fighters dominate in Korea and Vietnam	Nuclear aircraft carriers built; project air power from sea; nuclear subs; SEALs and special ops	1952 law codifies division/ wing structure; small wars and COIN; first to fight	Volunteers and draft; RC called up during Korea, not called up during Vietnam	UCP modified, JCS remains consensus org; COCOMs power diffuse	President Truman fires MacArthur; SECDEF McNamara empowers OSD; President Johnson hands-on CinC in Vietnam; AVF legislation, 1973

Chapter (Evolving Common Defense)	Organizational Responses				Personnel	Organizational Integration	Civilian Control
	Army	Air Force	Navy	Marine Corps			
Chap 10 Cold War 1974–91	Focus on major war in Europe until refocused to Middle East	Focus on nuclear mission and major war in Europe	Nuclear aircraft carriers; project airpower from sea; nuclear subs	Expeditionary ops, crisis response; small wars; first to fight	All volunteer force (AVF); women have expanded opportunities	CJCS designated principal adviser; Desert Storm success; COCOMs empowered	Goldwater-Nichols Act, 1986
Chap 11 Expeditionary Military 1991–2001	Reduced force; re-creating expeditionary army	Reduced force; end of SAC, rise of fighter AF; space matures	Reduced force; command of the commons; global presence	Crisis response; first to fight focus	AVF w/ DADT; USG civilians, contractors	Proconsul-era of COCOMs	President Clinton pursues peace dividend; CJCS challenges president on gays in military, leads to DADT
Chap 12 Military Nation Has 2001–2017	COIN dominates; focus on BCTs; need to rebuild ability to wage and win large land operations	Rise of unmanned air force; critical enabler to land forces	Command of the commons; global presence; military power projection from the sea	First to fight; expeditionary ops; long-term land presence Afghanistan and Iraq; COIN	AVF, USG civilians, contractors; DADT repealed, transgender policy in flux; women allowed in all combat arms	CENTCOM dominance; rise of hybrid commands, i.e., SOCOM and CYBERCOM	Congress passes AUMF; President Obama and his SECDEFs direct expanded opportunities for LGBTQ; civilian oversight mechanisms sufficient?

3

America's Military
Creation and Early Challenges

Before creating a national military, the fledgling American republic needed a shared sense of the interests to be protected and of the external threats to them. The new nation struggled to produce such a sense under the Articles of Confederation. Subsequent constitutional debates between the Federalists and the Anti-Federalists to address the weaknesses in the Articles of Confederation revealed a fundamental divide on these core issues. Indeed, these debates highlighted some existential questions for the Framers of the Constitution.

The Common Defense: First Debates

Federalists, led by Alexander Hamilton and James Madison, argued that the common defense of the new nation had to address two problems. First, in order to protect its new land frontier, it needed a national army. Second, the new nation needed at least some protection for its seafaring trade and the Atlantic seaboard. The Federalists discussed these problems and proposed their solutions most famously in the *Federalist Papers*. These papers advocated a national army to address the first issue and a small national navy the second.[1]

Anti-Federalists countered with their own, ultimately less compelling, arguments that the state militias sufficed to meet the new nation's defense needs. They maintained that anything beyond a militia force would encourage expansionist tendencies that the new nation should eschew. Thus, Anti-Federalists believed a national army was unnecessary, even dangerous, especially since powerful memories of the

British army's presence in the colonies lingered. Similarly, a national navy made no sense from the Anti-Federalists' perspective, since, it seemed to them, America's interests stopped at its immediate waters. The creation of an oceangoing navy would unnecessarily raise taxes and centralize power.[2]

After considerable debate, the solutions to these foundational problems that carried the day were codified and ratified in the U.S. Constitution, especially Article 1, Section 8. The language reflected a Federalist victory. In Section 8 the nation established the legal basis for the U.S. military by giving Congress the power to "raise and support Armies" (albeit "no Appropriation of Money to that Use shall be for a longer Term than two Years") and to "provide and maintain a Navy." The stipulation limiting Army funding to two years addressed unease about standing armies by making the Army return often to Congress for funding. The language to provide and maintain a navy differed because of the larger expense associated with building, manning, operating, and maintaining a navy, and the lesser threat a navy inherently posed to the nascent U.S. government. This part of the Constitution also allowed for organizing, training, and equipping the state militias on behalf of the nation if dramatic circumstances, such as repelling an invasion or putting down an insurrection, warranted it.

Organizational Responses

Creating a military and enshrining it in the U.S. Constitution was a critical step, but authorizing a national military proved easier in many ways than structuring, equipping, manning, and paying for it. In the early days those tasks loomed large; in 1789, the nation created the Department of War to assume responsibility for addressing them on land and at sea.

The Army

Because leaders identified perimeter defense, as we might call the defense of the frontier, as a problem that needed solving, the new national military focused on it. Not surprisingly, it created largely a foot-soldier Army, composed of infantry units capable of operating in dense forest. There were also some supporting artillery and engineer units, as well as cavalry trained to fight both dismounted, as infantry, and mounted. By any measure, though, the American army was small, paling in comparison to any of its Western European counterparts.

By 1797 the Army's authorized strength had grown from 1,300 personnel to approximately 3,300 soldiers. The Army grew a bit more during John Adams' presidency, 1797–1801, then dropped during Thomas Jefferson's administration (1801–9) to about 3,200. By the eve of the War of 1812, the force had grown to about 6,700. The Army was still small, and its focus remained in the west, but its composition had changed—the cavalry eliminated, the artillery expanded. The Army abandoned the former due to expense and limited military usefulness and increased the latter for coastal protection against possible British incursions on the eastern seaboard.

One of the Army's most significant achievements during this time was the establishment of the U.S. Military Academy (USMA) at West Point, New York, in 1802. Congress created the military academy to produce officers capable of competent, consistent leadership. West Point's emphasis on engineering gave its graduates technical skills, such as building fortifications and constructing roads, essential to the new nation in peace and war. Although the quality of USMA's early graduates varied, overall their conduct during the War of 1812 as engineers and small-unit leaders ensured their institution's continued existence. Moreover, solidified support for USMA tacitly acknowledged the emergence of the Army itself as a permanent national institution.

The War of 1812 witnessed the first major expansion of the Army since the nation's founding—to over 30,000 regular, or full-time, troops and hundreds of thousands of mobilized state militiamen.[3] The regulars and militia both had mixed success during the War of 1812, but the militia's performance was particularly problematic. From an organizational perspective, the war revealed systemic problems in training, leadership, and logistics. However, it also affirmed the importance of a national standing army. Questions of size, equipment, and garrisoning persisted, but the war clearly answered yes to the existential question: Did the nation need a military? Nonetheless, the Army was a rather suspect institution in the eyes of the population.

The much smaller, postwar Army returned to the frontier. Over the next several decades it largely established and maintained small, isolated garrisons on the periphery. The number of full-time soldiers spiked periodically, as during the Seminole and Mexican Wars, then shrank again to under ten thousand frontier-based soldiers. In the 1840s the War Department introduced a common uniform for the first time, to help create a broader sense of cohesion among its soldiers. Training, however, still lacked standardization, left as it was to individual garrison commanders. In step with the nation's westward expansion, the Army also constructed numerous roads and canals. U.S. Military Academy graduates, in particular, contributed their engineering expertise to the nation's infrastructure. In the process, the academy established itself as one of the few national institutions during a time characterized by regional loyalties and separatist sentiments.

The Navy

The U.S. Navy suffered even more than did the Army after the Revolution. With the sale of its last Revolutionary War frigate in 1785, in fact, it ceased to exist. The action came easily to the new government, which saw a minimal maritime threat and, strapped for cash, faced growing ship maintenance expenses. The ratification of the Constitution opened the possibility of re-creating a navy, but without an immediate threat, Congress had no incentive to do so. When the Barbary States started attacking American shipping in 1793, however, theoretical potential problems became real and present ones. With the Naval Act of 1794, Congress authorized the creation of a six-frigate fleet to address what most thought a temporary problem. The new frigates were smaller and faster than European ships of the line, capable of protecting merchant ships but not of challenging large, established fleets.[4]

As often happens, the Barbary challenge resolved itself before the original naval force was complete. However, even as this maritime issue subsided, another emerged. Relations shifted, and the French, once allies, now posed threats to American commercial shipping, especially in the Caribbean. So the construction of the frigates continued, supplemented with smaller, armed sloops to protect shipping. At the same time, the demands of the Quasi-War with France revealed the difficulty for the Department of War of overseeing both land and sea forces. As a result, Congress created a separate Department of the Navy in 1798.

The future of the Navy, however, was unclear. When Jefferson assumed office in 1801, he had to deal with an escalating, major war between two powerful European powers, France and Britain. Jefferson wanted to stay out of the conflict altogether and focus on protecting American ports. This policy, he believed, required a large fleet of small, cheap gunboats rather than a small number of oceangoing frigates. During Jefferson's second term, well over a hundred of these gunboats were built and deployed to the nation's major harbors.

The War of 1812 made clear that his decision had been ill-advised. The gunboats could not protect American ports: the Royal Navy quickly overwhelmed them. British ships landed forces that marched on and burned much of the new capital, Washington. The U.S. Navy's remaining oceangoing frigates and inland-water brigs (smaller sailing vessels with two square-rigged masts versus the frigates' three), however, engaged the Royal Navy in the Atlantic Ocean and on the Great Lakes. These open-water engagements produced some notable victories, capturing the public's imagination and esteem at the same time.

Shortly after the end of the War of 1812, accordingly, Congress approved funding for aggressive shipbuilding to create a larger, oceangoing navy. This program introduced ships of the line as capital ships and increased the number of frigates. These ships of the line each carried a minimum of seventy-four guns and were expected to protect the republic by opposing other fleets in "blue water," the Atlantic Ocean and Mediterranean Sea. The 1816 legislation appropriated enough money to build nine of these large ships as well as some additional frigates. But these ships were ill-suited to the nation's actual needs; most of them never fought an engagement. Instead, for the next three decades the U.S. Navy played a constabulary role overseas, especially in the Mediterranean and Caribbean, dealing with smuggling, piracy, and slave trading.

The Marine Corps

The U.S. Marine Corps identifies its founding as the issuance of a Continental Congress resolution on November 10, 1775, raising two battalions of Marines. However, when after the Revolution the Navy ceased to exist, so did the Marine Corps, for almost a decade. Only with the launching of the first three new frigates did it return: Congress authorized Marine detachments for the ships. The original Marine force, not surprisingly, was a small one, numbering about 170. Moreover, these Marines belonged to the crews of their respective ships, not to a separate organization. On board, Marines served as sharpshooters, enforced discipline, executed ship-to-shore raids, and sometimes assisted in working the ship.

Soon after creating the Navy Department in 1798, President Adams signed a bill formally establishing a Marine Corps of approximately 350 officers and enlisted Marines, leaving intentionally ambiguous which cabinet department had ultimate authority over it. As initially designed, the Marine Corps belonged to the War Department when ashore, the Navy Department when afloat.[5] Until the War of 1812, the Marine Corps operated largely on board and from warships. During that conflict, however, Marine units served ashore with distinction alongside Army units. The Marine Corps' performance during the war firmly established its reputation as a separate military service.

After the War of 1812, the size of the Marine Corps was tied to the number of ships. Its principal responsibility remained enforcing discipline on board and forming small landing parties to be sent ashore. But Navy and Marine Corps views began to diverge over the number of Marines necessary and their relevance to shipboard discipline. Over the early decades of the nineteenth century, the Navy concluded it could reduce its reliance on the Marines. Moreover, the Marine Corps routinely failed to recruit even its peacetime authorized strength. Individuals who volunteered as Marines received little training, whether officer or enlisted; Marine detachments chronically came into conflict with naval crews, and their members frequently deserted. This mediocrity raised questions about the usefulness of the Marine Corps to the Navy and the nation. A long-serving U.S. Marine Corps commandant, Col. Archibald Henderson, devoted much effort during this period to ensure that it would survive and be assigned solely to the Department of the Navy.[6]

Personnel

The early leaders of the United States had disputed among themselves in the decades after independence whether or not their country, remote as it was from Europe, even needed a national military. Once they took the controversial decision to create one, finding capable volunteers proved even more difficult. The military had no appeal in the nation's early years, even to settlers on the remote frontier, whom the Army protected.

This lack of popular support made it difficult to fill the ranks. Men who enlisted, either on land or at sea, had usually exhausted employment options in the civilian world—foreclosing them by criminal records or excessive drinking—or were new immigrants and simply lacked other opportunities. In any case, the military was their employer of last resort. As might be expected, keeping enlistees from deserting once in uniform proved equally difficult. This disdain for the military prevailed up to the War of 1812, and the services entered that war with less than the congressionally authorized strength.

Producing leaders for this young military was no easier. Congress had established the U.S. Military Academy to inculcate the qualities of officership and establish basic standards of military competence. Any subsequent professional development officers received, however, depended on their individual seniors. For the Navy and the Marine Corps, having then no equivalent to USMA, officer development at all levels occurred solely on the job, perpetuating the considerable unevenness in the quality of officers in both services.

Finally, the War of 1812 was the first test of the state militias since independence. More than half a million answered the call to arms when the nation went to war, signing up for periods ranging from one month to the duration of the war. Militiamen served primarily on land, a few, albeit incompetently, on board ship. These volunteers brought to their respective services, on one hand, their own equipment, but on the other hand, little experience or training—and yet a conviction that they controlled when and for how long they would serve. Collectively these factors gave the militias a reputation for unreliability, and as a result the national government lacked confidence in them.

Organizational Integration

For the most part, service integration did not interest the leaders of the new nation. The complexities discussed above in creating and sustaining even a small military tended toward specialization of the Army, Navy, and Marine Corps. Moreover, given the vast distances, small forces, limited technological means for command and control, and specific geographic responsibilities assigned to the services, few opportunities presented themselves for cooperation.

During the War of 1812, some informal integration did occur, out of necessity. Most notably, Marines fought alongside soldiers, and a few militiamen helped man ships. But all such instances were ad hoc, driven by the immediate demands of war. No integrated planning or training preceded them, no institutional imperative existed to codify the approach, and no senior military or civilian leaders displayed interest in sustaining it. Thus, what little service integration (or "jointness" as the military calls it today) occurred was born of necessity in the War of 1812 and disappeared with its end. The same fate awaited the seeming progress represented by a fairly large Army-Navy amphibious assault at Veracruz in 1847 during the Mexican War. Informal cooperation held the amphibious force together until the city surrendered—at which point it dissipated.

Civilian Control

From the nation's founding, the issue of how the national government would exercise control over the military produced wide-ranging debate. Indignities and intrusions like the Quartering Act imposed by the British army before the American Revolution were to be avoided at all costs. As a result, the Framers of the Constitution believed that civilian, not uniformed, leaders had to control any national military they might establish. The Constitution they produced addressed civilian control most notably in Article 1, Section 8 (which authorized Congress "to make Rules for the Government and Regulation of land and naval Forces") and in Article 2, Section 2 (naming the president as the "Commander in Chief of the Army and Navy of the United States" as well as of state militias when called to federal service). The former gave Congress the authority to pass legislation impacting every aspect of the military. The latter ensured ultimate civilian authority.

However, beyond this language the drafters provided no specifics. In short order it was recognized, as we have seen, that the president needed a department, headed by a cabinet-level secretary, to administer the nation's military. But as so often with the military, changes came only after major setbacks—in this case, defeats on the frontier. Only then did the new department get directly involved in guiding, supporting, and administering the military. President Washington, in contrast, was already comfortable in his role as commander in chief. He had embraced the responsibility for selecting senior officers, such as Gen. "Mad" Anthony Wayne, and for giving them broad direction in their missions on the frontier.

As mentioned, in the mid-1790s the complexity of the construction, commissioning, manning, operations and maintenance of warships led President Washington and, grudgingly, Secretary of War James McHenry to admit the need for specialized naval oversight. It was in 1798, therefore, that Congress created the Department of the Navy and another cabinet-level position, the Secretary of the Navy (table 3-1).

Table 3-1. Civilian Control of the U.S. Military, 1798

	President of United States, Commander in Chief		
Military Service	Army	Navy	Marine Corps* *Becomes a distinct service from Navy, 1834
Legal Authority	Constitution	Constitution	Legislation (1798)
Physical Realm	Land	Sea	Sea, but can operate on land for short periods of time, if needed
Responsible to Civilian Cabinet-Level Secretary	Secretary of War	Secretary of Navy	Secretary of Navy (at sea); Secretary of War (on land)
Executive Branch Department	Department of War	Department of Navy	Department of Navy (at sea); Department of War (on land)

Impact on the Common Defense

In the early decades of the 1800s, the Federalists' views of the military had come to fruition. Even though the force suffered setbacks on land and at sea, when tested by war the country accepted the need for a small standing military to protect the frontier and seaborne trade. But the relationship between the nation and its military was an uncomfortable one.

The small force, on land and at sea, served in remote locations. The people who manned it, lacking better choices, subjected themselves thereby to the tremendous physical hardship, discipline, and numbing routine of isolated outposts. Moreover, the nation had overspent on and over-built its fleet after the War of 1812. The ships of the line that the government assumed would bring protection and prestige were replaced at the heart of the fleet—thanks to declining domestic economy, more peaceful international relations, and shifting overseas demands—by frigates and sloops. Similarly, the exercise of blue-water sea power was displaced by the former purpose of protecting trade abroad. Thus, despite growth during crises and war, safeguarding the nation's expanding periphery on land and its trade at sea remained the core problem for the military to solve through the middle of the nineteenth century, just as the Federalists had envisioned. What they had not anticipated was what would face the military less than a century after the nation's founding—civil war.

Further Reading

Primary sources include: The Constitution of the United States, The Declaration of Independence, and *The Federalist* and *Anti-Federalist Papers*. Secondary sources include: John Chambers, ed., *The Oxford Companion to American Military History*, 1999; Edward Coffman, *The Old Army*, 1988; Raphael Cohen, *Demystifying the Citizen Soldier*, 2015; Richard Kohn, *Eagle and Sword*, 1975; Edward Lengel, *General George Washington*, 2005; Allan Millett, Peter Maslowski, and William Feis, *For the Common Defense*, 2012; Allan Millett, *Semper Fidelis*, 1991; Richard Stewart, ed., *American Military History*, vol. 1, 2009; Craig Symonds, *The U.S. Navy: A Concise History*, 2016; and Ian Toll, *Six Frigates*, 2006.

4

Fighting to Preserve the Union

The Civil War and Its Aftermath

Protecting expanding frontiers and trade in the early decades after American independence proved much easier than addressing the internal tensions among the states. A variety of political, social, and economic problems afflicted the new nation, but the issues of slavery and states' rights threatened to split it into north and south. Abraham Lincoln's election as president in November 1860 proved the final catalyst, leading the southern states to secede and form the Confederate States of America (CSA) in February 1861. Lincoln refused to accept the dissolution of the Union and, within weeks of his March inauguration, the Confederacy fired on Fort Sumter in South Carolina. America now faced an existential challenge to the common defense—it was obliged to fight a civil war to save the nation.

The Common Defense

Prior to the southern secession, the Framers would have recognized the U.S. military. In early 1861, most of the nation's small Army was dispersed at scores of frontier posts west of the Mississippi. The regular Army ostensibly numbered about 13,000 soldiers. Most of these were in the infantry as before, but, due to the distances and demands of the frontier, mounted infantry (dragoons) and cavalry also saw an increase. The Navy had tinkered with steam propulsion, iron-plating its wooden ships, and improving its armament, but a national need to modernize and compete with the great European navies of the day had not materialized. The Marine Corps remained small, its men mostly assigned to ships at sea or naval yards on the East Coast. In all cases the military remained short of volunteers, and because of its continued unpopularity, many who filled the ranks came from the fringes of society, were foreigners, or were new immigrants.

The formation of the CSA had a dramatic impact on the military. When the new Confederate government created its own war department within a few days of secession, it claimed the forces, weapons, and structures that happened to be in its territory. Moreover, some of the best officers, such as Robert E. Lee, left the U.S. Army to assume leadership positions in the Confederate army. Lincoln thus took the nation to war against the Confederacy with a military unprepared for the task of fighting and winning it.

Organizational Responses

The Union needed to solve two major problems: defeat the Confederate army and blockade the Confederacy's supplies in the east and west. In accomplishing these goals, the Army and Navy would face myriad unanticipated challenges. The Army in particular would undergo dramatic changes to fight a war massive in scope and waged on several fronts.

The Army

At the start of the war, the Union army had neither a strategy nor a mobilization plan, or a staff capable of creating either. It also lacked leaders with the experience and expertise necessary to command larger units. As James McPherson comments in *Battle Cry of Freedom*, the country was "less ready for what proved to be its biggest war than for any other war in its history." However, through hard work, trial and error, and the bitter crucible of combat, the nation raised a large, modern military. At its peak, the Union army numbered over one million men, mostly volunteer formations raised by the states. The regular Army itself expanded little, and the state militias remained inconsequential.

In this model, whenever a state raised and equipped a volunteer regiment (each about a thousand men—states received regiment quotas based on their populations), the raw unit was dispatched to one of the newly established federal training centers to be integrated into the larger Union effort. As it received its rudimentary military training, mostly marching in formation and close-order rifle drill, it was grouped with others to make larger tactical units: ideally four regiments to a brigade and three brigades to a division (table 4-1).[1] Above the division level, President Lincoln could direct the combination of divisions into corps (two or three divisions) and even armies (three corps, approximately 80,000 soldiers) as he deemed necessary. Though much remained decentralized, Lincoln and his administration endeavored to create a large federal force from these volunteer regiments rather than rely on a looser amalgamation of state forces. Most of the new volunteers became infantrymen, but advances in technology and the scope of the conflict brought increased need for artillery and cavalry. Indeed, the need for infantrymen, cavalrymen, artillerymen, and engineers was never-ending: the Civil War raged for four years, from the waters off the East Coast to west of the Mississippi River. The cavalry achieved particular prominence because of its ability to cover great distances in long-range patrols and intelligence-gathering missions.

The training and equipping of this vast Union army challenged the military and the nation. Many regiments,

Table 4-1. Union Army Organizational Structure (and Commander Rank), Division-Level and Below

Division (Major General): Total ~ 8,000–10,000					
Brigade (Brigadier General) ~2,600–4,000 soldiers		Brigade		Brigade	
Regiment (Colonel) ~800–1,000	Regiment	Regiment	Regiment	Regiment	Regiment
Regiment	Regiment	Regiment	Regiment	Regiment	Regiment

including their officers, learned how to fight by being thrust into battle. This "on-the-job training" approach to combat, coupled with the effects of disease (for every three soldiers killed on the battlefield, five died of disease owing to poor sanitation, etc.), decimated a regiment's ranks. Combat was particularly deadly for new, inexperienced officers—in battle, officers led from the front, where they were prime targets. Because general officers led large formations, they were especially vulnerable; in combat, they were 50 percent more likely to be killed than the privates under their command.

When it came to supplying the Union army, bureaucratic inefficiency verging on chaos and overreliance on contractors, too many of whom were corrupt, typified the effort. Nonetheless, the Army Quartermaster Corps under the leadership of Maj. Gen. Montgomery Meigs ultimately made great strides to clothe, feed, and equip the Army as it moved south. Meigs' men introduced some interesting innovations along the way. One was the standardization of uniforms across the volunteer regiments—not only designating a single color, as the Army had done in the Mexican War, but introducing graduated measurements for clothing. Establishment of standard sizes allowed manufacturers to mass-produce uniforms, and ultimately civilian clothes too, for the first time.

Three factors decisively shaped a Union soldier's experience during the war—speed, disease, and proximity to violence. Although trains were critical for logistics and troop movements for the first time, the speed with which the Union army engaged Confederate forces still depended on feet—that is, how fast horses could carry their riders, oxen could pull artillery pieces, and most important, soldiers could march. When the Union ranks, sometimes already reduced by disease, reached combat, the fighting was usually directly personal, against enemy combatants at close range—extremely violent, and often lethal. In some battles, such innovations as rifled muskets, Gatling guns (precursors to machine guns), and defensive trenches placed some distance between Union and Confederate forces, but they had yet to reshape the battlefield fundamentally.

The Navy

In the decades before the Civil War, the Navy began its first major modernization since the War of 1812, gradually replacing now-obsolete, wooden sailing ships with steam-powered vessels (still wooden, at this stage, and still equipped with sails). Naval leadership had argued that this modernization required professionalization of the officer corps. In 1845 Congress established the U.S. Naval Academy to provide that core of expertise and leadership. Thus, the Navy entered the war with about half of its forty-two-ship, frigate-centered fleet modernized and a slowly professionalizing officer corps.

Updating, however, was insufficient in itself: the Navy needed to grow quickly to protect U.S. trade and to create, then enforce, the blockade President Lincoln announced at the beginning of the war. It did so largely by minimally modifying commercial steamers, reinforcing the decks to carry naval guns, and installing magazines (secure ammunition storage areas). Although unimpressive even by the standards of the time, these conversion ships allowed the Union fleet to grow quickly and enforce the blockade—which, while imperfect, took a cumulative toll on the Confederate economy and its overall war effort.

The Confederacy lacked the vessels or manufacturing means to match the Union navy in size; it compensated by innovations, notably the famous "ironclads." The Confederacy began covering wooden ships in iron armor and fitting their prows with rams, hoping that a single ironclad would be capable of destroying several wooden ships. The Union navy quickly copied this idea, adopting a more radical design: an entirely new ship type, with a flat deck barely above the waterline and mounting guns in a (first-ever) rotating tower, or turret. The famous battle that ensued between the USS *Monitor* and the CSS *Virginia* (better known as the *Merrimack*, the captured Union ship with whose burned hulk the Confederates had begun) was the first in history between ironclad vessels. It signaled the end of the wooden-ship era of naval warfare. The Confederacy also pursued another important innovation, building an operational submarine, the

Hunley, in an effort to challenge the Union navy's supremacy. The *Hunley* sank one ship but also itself in the process.

The Union blockade needed to interrupt not only the Confederacy's Atlantic shipping but also its trade in the west, which required gaining control of the Mississippi River. This riverine campaign required an updated version of the small vessels Jefferson had advocated decades earlier. Using flat-bottomed gunboats clad in armor, some like the *Monitor* but smaller, the Union navy navigated the shallow waters of the Mississippi, Ohio, and Tennessee Rivers and their tributaries. A series of operations in 1862 and 1863, culminating in the successful, albeit lengthy, siege of Vicksburg, Mississippi, ultimately cut the Confederacy's critical river supply lines in the west.

Thus, after years of simultaneous operations from the eastern seaboard to the Mississippi, the Union navy emerged from the Civil War transformed. It totaled over 670 ships, many of them ironclad steamships. It relied on 100,000 volunteers to man these ships, many of these volunteers having chosen naval service as an alternative to the army. By 1865 the service bore little resemblance to what it had been just ten years earlier.

The Marine Corps

In the history of the Marine Corps, however, the Civil War represented an undistinguished period. Marines did not go ashore to engage meaningfully in the epic land battles. Organizational survival underscored its rationale for staying away. Marine Corps leaders feared that abandoning the Marine Corps' core missions would make it too much like the Army, even effectively a part of the Army. And if that happened, the obvious question for Congress would be, "Why have a Marine Corps?" Operating ashore for extended periods, then, might imperil the Marine Corps' very existence. Congress's 1863 and 1864 explorations of absorbing it into the Army fed these fears.

Thus, aside from some operations on land and at sea, the Marine Corps remained mostly on the periphery. Nevertheless, the Marine Corps grew during the Civil War, largely to keep pace with the growing Navy, doubling from about two thousand officers and enlisted men in 1861 to about four thousand in 1865. Overall, the Marine Corps performed well enough to hold off the minority voices in Congress calling for its abolition. But in 1865, it remained the least remarkable of the three services.

Personnel

At the outbreak of the conflict, expecting a short war, the Union army hoped to rely solely on individual volunteering to fill its ranks. As the war moved into 1862 and casualty lists grew, such enlistments no longer met the need. The War Department first attempted to address personnel shortages through the Militia Act of 1862, a confusing law that levied quotas on the states for both nine-month and three-year volunteers. They were recruited into state militias, forming units that were immediately federalized and integrated into the Union army. Contentious and difficult to implement, the Militia Act nonetheless added over 420,000 three-year volunteers to the Union ranks, as well as the 88,000 "nine-month men" already in the state militias.

By 1863, however, this pool had been nearly exhausted, and Congress passed a conscription act. This controversial legislation assigned quotas by congressional districts, and it sparked riots, most notably in New York City. The act made the obligation to serve less than universal, allowing a potential draftee to hire a substitute or even, initially, pay a fee for an exemption. In the end, the legislation directly drafted about 100,000 men and prompted some 800,000 to enlist or reenlist (and so receive enlistment bonuses). The Navy and Marine Corps benefited from the unpopularity of the draft, as well as from the grim realities of Army life. Both services filled their ranks with volunteers throughout the war.

During the Civil War, the nation and the military wrestled in a new way with questions of who could serve in the military, who should serve, and on what terms. The Militia Act allowed the president to open the ranks to "persons of African descent"—it endorsed, among other things, the enlistment of black soldiers and sailors into the Union forces.

The 1862 Emancipation Proclamation reinforced this policy shift by recognizing the ongoing service of black sailors in the Union navy since the beginning of the war. Thus, the Civil War marked a first step, if a small one (none of these black soldiers or sailors received an officer's commission), in the expansion of the definition of who would be allowed to serve in the military's ranks.

Organizational Integration

During the Civil War, any service integration that occurred was ad hoc, as before. The Navy and Marine Corps continued as they had since the nation's founding. Operationally, that meant small Marine units provided additional shipboard manpower. The most noteworthy examples of service integration occurred in the western theater where the Union army and navy worked together in riverine operations. There the two services cooperated with a closeness for which there was neither precedent nor doctrine. As a result, as it had during the Mexican War, success relied on the willingness of the affected land forces and their naval counterparts, especially their local commanders, to work together.

Union seizures of Forts Henry and Donelson along or near the Tennessee River revealed the effectiveness of such ad hoc Army-Navy operations, but Vicksburg highlighted their utter necessity. After several failed attempts, Gen. Ulysses Grant turned to the local U.S. Navy commander, Rear Adm. David Porter, for assistance in a risky plan to approach and take the city. Under cover of darkness Porter's riverboats skirted Confederate artillery batteries overlooking the Mississippi, picked up Grant's soldiers south of the city, and transported them to the river's eastern bank. Porter's daring move ultimately allowed Grant to surprise the Confederate forces, surround Vicksburg, and on July 4, 1863, capture it.

Such Army-Navy cooperation allowed the Union to control the Mississippi and make the blockade of the Confederacy comprehensive. But it occurred only informally, whether in the east or west. Interservice cooperation reflected the needs and personalities of the local commanders, not a changing, shared perspective on the best way to conduct military operations. Thus, when the Civil War ended in 1865, whatever tendency toward joint military operations had emerged rapidly evaporated.

Civilian Control

President Lincoln used his constitutional authorities brilliantly to exercise civilian control over the Union forces during the Civil War. As commander in chief, he devised the overall Union strategy for defeating the Confederacy, then held the military leaders responsible for its implementation. He questioned and prodded his most senior officers, traveled frequently to the front lines, required timely communications and reports from the battlefield, and sought independent views on the war's progress from junior officers and members of his staff. Famously, Lincoln removed senior leaders he thought lacked understanding of or willingness to execute his war strategy. There was a rapid turnover of commanding generals until Lincoln finally settled on General Grant.

Also, Lincoln effectively delegated administrative responsibilities for raising, training, and equipping the Union forces to his Secretaries of War and the Navy. Both secretaries served

Table 4-2. Civilian Control of the U.S. Military, 1861–1865

	President of United States, Commander in Chief		
Military Service	Army* *Supplemented by states' volunteer armies and militia (if called)	Navy	Marine Corps
Physical Realm	Land	Sea	Sea, but could operate for brief periods on land, if needed
Responsible to	Department of War	Department of Navy	Department of Navy
Civilian Cabinet-Level Secretary	Secretary of War	Secretary of Navy	Secretary of Navy

at the cabinet level with direct and frequent access to the president (table 4-2). Most notably, Secretary of War Edwin Stanton used his position to centralize all activities associated with the Army under the War Department. He delegated important functions to three assistant secretaries and senior staff generals like Meigs. Collectively, they brought some order out of the chaos of the early days and provided sustained leadership and close oversight throughout the war.

In his exercise of civilian control, Lincoln emerged as an exemplar for future presidents. He knew how to hold his civilian and military leaders accountable while at the same time empowering them to exercise the considerable latitude he delegated to them. Even in the twenty-first century, Lincoln remains an exceptional role model for the exercise of civilian control under the most trying circumstances.

Impact on the Common Defense

The United States entered the Civil War in 1861 confronting the ultimate existential problem—Could it survive as a single nation? The answer to this question required a military response, the scope of which the nation's leaders, understandably, had never imagined. As Americans chose sides in the early days of the conflict, all the services suffered, losing men, leaders, forts, and supplies to the new Confederate forces. The Union, however, had the wherewithal to withstand this initial shock, and it eventually built a military, on land and at sea, the likes of which the nation had never seen.

By the time the war ended, the Union forces numbered well over a million men. The Army remained largely an infantry-based organization, moving at the pace its soldiers could walk; nevertheless, the importance of railroads, the speed and mobility of the cavalry, and the battlefield lethality of the artillery grew during this time, and new technologies like the Gatling gun emerged. For the Navy, the change was no less dramatic; the possibilities presented by steam propulsion and iron construction foreshadowed the obsolescence of sail and wood. This technologically advancing Navy required more sophisticated sailors to operate it and fewer Marines to secure it.

Predictably, however, once the Union was reunited, the transformation of the military stalled. For economic and political reasons, in the next decades the military receded to its previous ancillary status. Each service, still tied to its physical geography, started to look anew for a core purpose. The Army was the quickest to find one: although it played a role in Reconstruction, mostly it looked westward to the western territories, where it operated a much-reduced force. In that daunting environment, the cavalry emerged as critical. Despite the sweeping geography of the frontier, the Army's overall size shrank to a fraction of its Civil War size. Within six months of the end of the Civil War, the states' volunteer formations had demobilized over 800,000 soldiers, leaving only the regular Army, which within ten years dropped to a peacetime strength of approximately 25,000 soldiers and 2,100 officers.

The Navy watched its fleet shrink from over 670 ships to 52 in just five years, and its civilian and military leadership imposed what is now known as a "modernization holiday." In part, this dynamic reflected the decommissioning of ships—like those of the river forces—whose unique missions were successfully completed. However, the modernization holiday also reflected "benign neglect" by Congress and a willingness on the part of the Navy to return to its comfortable pre–Civil War mission—protecting the coast and merchant shipping and representing American interests on distant shores. As its warships sailed around the globe, the Navy's leaders saw no urgent reason to add iron plating, let alone build ships of iron, and they declined to convert entirely to steam propulsion because of the lack of coaling stations at which to refuel. Thus, as other navies around the world modernized, the U.S. Navy verged on comprehensive, or block, obsolescence by the early 1880s. Eventually Congress responded, authorizing the construction of four steel ships for the first time. These new ships incorporated the technology that European navies had already adopted.

Finally, the Marine Corps remained small, about two thousand men and eighty officers. A few congressmen advocated its elimination immediately after the war, but the idea gained no traction. The Marine Corps continued in its seagoing-constabulary and landing-party roles in the next decades. Its relationship with the Navy remained close but also fraught with the tensions inevitable between two military cultures confined within the close quarters of a ship. In short, like the other services, the post–Civil War Marine Corps resembled that of 1861.

The American Civil War presented a profound challenge for the U.S. military. In the ultimate, tragic paradox, Americans fought Americans on a previously unimaginable scale in order to preserve the nation. In the course of the war several innovations emerged. From a technology perspective, these included the military use of railroads, the submarine, ironclads, and the forerunner of the machine gun; from an organizational perspective, they included attempts to standardize training and equipment; from an operational perspective, there was informal experimentation with joint operations in response to battlefield demands; and, from a personnel perspective, they included instituting a draft and opening some ranks to free blacks and former slaves. However, almost none of these innovations made a lasting impact on the American military. In the first decades after the Civil War, the military settled back into organizational structures and operational routines recognizable to people who had served in the 1850s. On land, the American military remained focused on North American continental concerns, and at sea it focused on protection of trade. It did not consider itself a world-class military, nor did the nation seek to make it one. A decade after winning an epic civil war, the American military was again a backwater, a peripheral consideration at home and abroad.

Further Reading

Primary sources include: Abraham Lincoln's first and second inaugural speeches and the Emancipation Proclamation. Secondary sources include: Coffman, *Old Army*; Eliot Cohen, *Supreme Command*, 2003; Raphael Cohen, *Demystifying the Citizen Soldier*; Doris Goodwin, *Team of Rivals*, 2006;

James McPherson, *Battle Cry of Freedom*, 2003; Millett, Maslowski, and Feis, *For the Common Defense*; Millett, *Semper Fidelis*; Stewart, *American Military History*, vol. 1; Symonds, *U.S. Navy*; Russell Weigley, *The American Way of War*, 1978.

5

The Military Services in Transition, 1880–1917

Between the 1880s and 1917, the general absence of major challenges to the common defense forced the services to reassess what they did on behalf of the nation and why. This period splits roughly in half, with the Spanish-American War in 1898 the dividing point. The 1880s and 1890s were important to the military, though not because of any particular conflict or struggle—rather the opposite. By this point the frontier had been declared "closed," symbolizing the end of the continental concerns of the Framers. Overseas, the Navy continued to rely on sailing ships (though almost always now with auxiliary steam propulsion as well) to protect seafaring trade routes and to engage in diplomacy in ways the Framers would have recognized. In both cases the nation and the military struggled with the question, What's next? Especially for the Army, which was becoming bogged down by bureaucratization, the question was existential: Did it even have a purpose now that the continent was secured? For the Navy, it was a matter of reaffirming or modifying its national purpose. The Marine Corps, for its part, debated whether its focus should remain serving on board ships, even though new technology called the relevance of that into question.

Organizational Responses: The Military at the End of the Nineteenth Century

The Army

The Army had achieved the objectives for which the Framers created it. An eye needed to be kept on the borders to the north and south, but the frontier dangers no longer existed.

Gen. W. T. Sherman, Civil War hero turned commanding general, led the Army through this institutionally turbulent period.

Under his leadership, the Army took some important steps. First, having defeated Native Americans in the struggle for control of western lands, it consolidated its outposts. Most of the Army would remain dispersed throughout the west, but between 1889 and 1891 alone it abandoned 25 percent of its frontier posts. Second, it modernized its infantry and artillery arms, prodded especially by junior officers who feared falling hopelessly behind their European counterparts. Third, the Army worked to professionalize its officer corps. Sherman emphasized the importance of military education, arguing that the military was a demanding profession requiring life-long learning, study, and practice. To that end he directed the establishment of the School of Application for Infantry and Cavalry in 1881 at Fort Leavenworth, Kansas. The mere fact that a figure like Sherman could publicly advocate professionalizing the officer corps indicated that any lingering concerns among national leaders about a standing army had eased considerably.

Sherman also supported reforms previously proposed by a protégé, Col. Emory Upton (who had been a brevet brigadier general during the Civil War). In the late 1870s, Upton studied European militaries and found the German military an especially suitable institution to emulate. Among other things, Upton suggested reducing political influence in the promotion process, routinely assessing performance through an evaluation system, and rotating officers between field and Army staff positions so they would develop a fuller appreciation for the demands on their service. Finally, Upton recommended a reorganization and centralization of the Army's field and staff structures, the latter specifically based on what he had seen in the German general staff.

Sherman urged the adoption of these reforms, but many in Congress—not to mention powerful entities within the Army itself—did not agree. Eventually the proposals stalled, largely owing to strong parochial interests and the lack of consensus regarding the need for change. After all, as defenders of the status quo hastened to point out, the old ways had won the nation's wars. In this context, any proposed change needed to answer persuasively the question, Change to what end? Through the middle 1890s, the Army lacked a convincing answer to that question.

For a while after the frontier closed, the Army looked more like a constabulary, a gendarmerie, than an army. Thus, on the eve of the Spanish-American War, of the Army's total of about 26,000 men almost 50 percent were foreign by birth. It lacked a unifying national mission; it remained fragmented, its units no larger than companies or battalions; it lacked a coherent staff or command structure; it did not train in large formations; and it barely entertained the notion of mobilization, whether for the Army itself or the national guard.[1] In short, it approached the twentieth century unprepared for the challenges that awaited.

The Navy

While the Navy did not face an existential crisis, its prospects were discouraging. By the 1880s, Civil War–era ships patrolling the sea-lanes desperately needed to be replaced if the Navy was to continue to fulfill this foundational mission. Congress agreed to fund four new ships to continue these patrols. The ships possessed some updated technology but had much in common with their predecessors. This modernization gap perturbed some of the more junior, technologically savvy officers who saw their senior leaders as unwilling to embrace the new. These younger officers emerged as some of the strongest advocates for more aggressive fleet modernization.

Even more so than in the Army, however, during the 1880s the Navy's senior leadership embraced professionalization of its officer corps. Commodore Stephen Luce spearheaded a movement away from traditional "on-the-job" officer development, calling for a naval war college; the new institution was established in Newport, Rhode Island, with Luce its first president. This school would create theorists and scholars of its naval-officer students conversant in naval strategy and the science of war. Graduates would both command ships and articulate why and how best to use them on the nation's behalf. Establishment of the Naval War College and the beginnings of a professional class of naval officers further manifested the nation's acceptance of a standing professional military.

Luce made an inspired decision when he appointed Capt. Alfred Thayer Mahan to the Naval War College's faculty. While at Newport (he would later become its second president) Mahan collected his lectures into his famous work, *The Influence of Sea Power upon History, 1660–1783*. In it he argued for a strong U.S. Navy and the need to acquire overseas bases to support it. Mahan, looking at Great Britain's rise to global power, argued that Britain's wealth came from global trade enabled by its command of the seas. The United States, he implicitly argued, could follow a similar path to greatness, if it so chose.

Not only the Navy, but the nation's leaders more broadly, mused about the possibilities of attaining such greatness. In Mahan they found a potential new national purpose—Could the United States use its navy to duplicate Great Britain's global rise? To achieve this, the United States obviously would need a fleet able to command the seas. Congress took the lead this time, authorizing an aggressive shipbuilding program of a new class of large, state-of-the-art, heavily armed ocean-going battleships. Unlike their predecessors, built to protect merchant vessels and sea-lanes, the primary mission of these ships was to fight and defeat battleships in other fleets. In sum, America had decided to create a world-class navy.

The Marine Corps

For the Marine Corps, this shift in the Navy's emphasis raised the vital question of where it would fit. Should Marine Corps leaders argue that Marines remained integral to the ships' companies of this new, modern fleet, even though the Navy itself saw little use for them? Or should the Marine Corps focus more on missions ashore, thereby risking assimilation into the Army? This dilemma consumed Marine Corps leaders in the last decade of the nineteenth century. They feared, with some reason, for their service's continued existence.

Whether the dilemma's solution rested at sea or ashore, they knew they had to remake the Corps into a unique, elite force within the Department of the Navy if it was to survive. For them, the Spanish-American War came none too soon.

The Spanish-American War and Its Aftermath: Harbinger of Things to Come

When America decided to challenge Spain's colonial dominance in the Caribbean and in the Philippines at the end of the nineteenth century, it extended the common defense overseas for the first time. In 1898 the U.S. military, despite some significant missteps, especially in mobilization and joint operations, quickly defeated Spain in the Spanish-American War. With this victory, the United States acquired Cuba, the Philippines, Puerto Rico, Guam, and Wake Island—becoming both a Caribbean Sea and a Pacific Ocean power.

The war with Spain both highlighted the need for organizational reform and elevated the public stature of the services. The Army recognized its profound mobilization problems yet reveled in the highly publicized success of Lt. Col. Theodore Roosevelt's volunteer cavalry, the "Rough Riders," at the battle of San Juan Hill. The Navy likewise acknowledged that interservice cooperation had failed while basking in Adm. George Dewey's victory at Manila Bay. The Marine Corps alone skirted major organizational issues while garnering its own iconic moment when it landed at Guantanamo Bay. The Marine Corps seized its objective in the face of great odds—fortunately, with several national reporters (including Stephen Crane, journalist and author of the popular *The Red Badge of Courage*) in tow. The American public learned of the victory in the reporters' glowing columns, and the Marine Corps captured its imagination. Indeed, the Spanish-American War proved a decisive moment for the Marine Corps, more than for any other service. The once floundering organization emerged with the esteem of the American people for its bravery and discipline under fire, its daring spirit, its tenacity, and its competence.

Organizational Responses: 1898–1917

The Army

The Army's response to the Spanish-American War was marked by chaos. Many national guardsmen refused to respond to the federal call-up, forcing the creation of a federally controlled volunteer force to fill out the ranks. The Army's training and equipping proved equally problematic, largely validating the need for the reforms advocated by Sherman and Upton. Although ultimately successful in the war, many in the Army felt their institution had displayed systemic problems mobilizing, deploying, and operating. The collective experience of the Spanish-American War finally convinced most Army leaders of the need to reform.

Secretary of War Elihu Root led the effort this time, and he started it within months of the war's end. Root undertook a weapons modernization program; pushed changes along the lines Sherman and Upton had proposed, centralizing command, administration, and planning by means of an Army Chief of Staff supported by a general staff; planned for three larger, division-sized units; revolutionized education by revamping West Point's curriculum and creating an Army War College akin to its naval counterpart; and persuaded Congress to pass the Dick Act in 1903. This legislation overhauled the hopelessly obsolete 1792 Militia Act, creating the modern National Guard and Reserve and making them eligible for federal funding in return for greater federal authority over them. The Army concentrated on reform throughout the decade after the war, even while operating in the new overseas territories acquired during the war and along the Mexican border.

The Navy

The Spanish-American War dramatically increased the Navy's size and national prestige. In particular, the need for a consistent diplomatic and military presence in America's new territories elevated the fleet's importance, public profile, and size. Within a decade after the war, at least thirteen additional battleships entered service. To test the effectiveness of this new battleship fleet, the president—now Theodore

Roosevelt, who was an admirer of Mahan—dispatched sixteen battleships—dubbed the Great White Fleet because the ships were painted "peacetime white"—on a round-the-world cruise. The stated purposes of this circumnavigation of the globe were to build diplomatic relations and to test the fleet's ability to execute a long voyage. With this fourteen-month-long, successful mission, Roosevelt sent a signal: the United States intended to wield its power in the international arena. The battleship and its global mission symbolized the elevated purpose and prestige of the Navy.

The Marine Corps

The Marine Corps emerged from the Spanish-American War with high public esteem and new missions as well. Most notably, it now provided forces to protect American interests overseas, in places ranging from the Caribbean Basin to China. It also started to specialize in seizing and defending advanced naval bases at which the fleet would be able to repair and resupply its ships in wartime. Paradoxically, the Marine Corps also waged a successful political fight to retain one of its foundational missions—providing shipboard guards. Roosevelt had signed an executive order eliminating them in order to free up Marines for duties ashore, and the Corps' leaders feared duplicity. They believed President Roosevelt intensely disliked the Marine Corps and sought its elimination; they interpreted the loss of the afloat mission as the first step toward amalgamation into the Army. The result was an ironic battle on Capitol Hill to preserve a mission even many inside the Corps considered anachronistic. That the Marine Corps won that battle, and was able to mobilize Congress to preserve an outdated mission, symbolized its emergence not only as an autonomous military institution but, arguably, as the most politically astute of the three services.

Organizational Integration

After the public embarrassment of their service-centric, uncoordinated performances during the Spanish-American War, the Army and Navy both developed broader staff planning.[2] In 1903 they agreed to create a Joint Army and Navy Board, or Joint Board, of two admirals and two generals to devise joint plans. This Joint Board lacked authority to direct changes to service plans, it convened on an ad hoc basis, and it divided quickly on substantive issues that threatened service interests. Nonetheless it represented the first, specific interservice attempt to plan together, or jointly, to address military problems. War Plan Orange, the plan for a possible conflict with Japan for primacy in the Western Pacific, was the most famous of its plans. First submitted to the Joint Board prior to America's entry into World War I, it went through a number of iterations over the next several years. Worried about the perils of "entangling alliances," the Army and Navy believed that working with allies (in what is known as combined cooperation) was inappropriate and, as a result, did no such planning.

Impact on the Common Defense

America and its military were on the cusp of a new, larger global role in the first decade of the twentieth century. The Army, Navy, and Marine Corps now operated the bulk of their respective forces overseas and they started to compare themselves to other militaries around the globe. This overseas role took America beyond its borders and caused its leaders to rethink fundamentally the locus of, and provision for, the common defense. Moreover, the services' modern organizational cultures came into sharper relief. As their missions began to overlap, they cooperated loosely but also competed more for the nation's attention and resources. In particular, despite its small size, the Marine Corps' expanding, overlapping missions on land and at sea presaged the competition for public esteem and funding in the decades ahead. The decade after the Spanish-American War foreshadowed the forces that would shape the twentieth-century American military; they would reveal themselves more clearly in 1917, when the United States entered World War I.

Further Reading

Secondary sources include: Edward Coffman, *The Regulars*, 2004, and *Old Army*; Cohen, *Demystifying the Citizen Soldier*; James Hewes, *From Root to McNamara: Army Organization and Administration, 1900–1963*, 2005; Peter Karsten, *The Naval Aristocracy*, 2008; Millett, Maslowski, William Feis, *For the Common Defense*; Millett, *Semper Fidelis*; Capt. William Parker, *A Concise History of the Marine Corps, 1775–1969*, 1970; Stewart, *American Military History*, vol. 1; Symonds, *U.S. Navy*; Weigley, *American Way of War*.

The Common Defense
Moves "Over There"
World War I and Its Aftermath

The Spanish-American War shifted America's military focus overseas, away from the continental United States and toward the Caribbean and the Pacific. Less than two decades later the military changed its focus again: the nation sent it to fight in the war engulfing Europe. The military had not anticipated involvement in an overseas conflict. Indeed, when war broke out in Europe in 1914, the United States had immediately declared its neutrality. Public sympathies favored the British and the French, especially after the sinking of the *Lusitania* by Germany in 1915. The consensus among President Woodrow Wilson, Congress, and the American people, however, was for supplying Britain and France with war materiel but staying out of the fighting.

The Common Defense

Ultimately, it was Germany's revolutionary employment of unrestricted submarine warfare, announced in February 1917, against merchant vessels supplying Britain and France that triggered America's entry. Germany's decision was a calculated gamble: on one hand, attacking American merchant vessels would prompt the United States to declare war; on the other hand, Germany believed that even if so, by breaking the allies' overseas supply lines it could win the war before America's military mobilized. In March, German submarines, or U-boats, sank three U.S. ships, inflicting heavy casualties. In response to these attacks on American vessels and citizens, President Wilson asked Congress for a declaration of war against Germany on April 2. As the United States pulled together its approach to the war, it found that providing for the common defense in this instance involved waging war predominately "over there" (in the words of a popular wartime song), on the European continent.

Organizational Responses

By any measure, the U.S. military faced a daunting challenge. For the first time in its history, the nation was asking it to undertake a huge campaign overseas. This mission required raising, organizing, and training a large force at home; making it "expeditionary," transportable overseas to where it could actually confront the enemy; and once in Europe, somehow integrating the force into the allied war effort without giving direct authority over it to the British or French. This multi-level problem would require an astonishing effort; indeed, many thought it impossible, especially given the small size of the prewar military (see table 6-1). In the problem's solution, other large problems and important innovations emerged.

The Army

Less than a year before America's entry into World War I, Congress passed the National Defense Act of 1916. Congress had been spurred to action by the Mexican revolutionary general Pancho Villa's raids on the southern border, as well as by growing concern about the nation's overall unpreparedness against the backdrop of the European war. The law reflected a more tolerant attitude toward military service on the part of the American public. Among other things, it allowed for a

Table 6-1. Active-Duty Military, 1916
Total: 179,400

Department of War	Department of Navy
Army: 108,400	Navy: 60,400
	Marine Corps: 10,600

Source: dmdc.osd.mil

peacetime expansion of the Army to 175,000 (still extraordinarily small by European standards); established the ROTC at colleges and universities; and expanded the president's authority to call up the National Guard for federal purposes. Nonetheless, America's declaration of war revealed an army singularly unready for the task at hand.

The emergency required the Army to rethink its fundamentals. To acquire sufficient manpower, the Army would have to rely on a draft (discussed below). Identifying people to serve was complex but just the beginning: a new type of industrialized warfare required the Army to think anew about organizing, training, and equipping these raw troops. The Army would number well over three million soldiers by war's end; senior leaders needed to change the service's organizational structure fundamentally to control it. It had been operating in small units in the Philippines and Caribbean; now its leaders would have to command and move large numbers of soldiers. To accomplish this, they quickly designed the "square" division, a new concept that comprised four regiments and placed almost 18,000 soldiers (eventually more) under a single division commander (table 6-2). This distinctive structure solved two problems. First, it allowed the Army to run a division with fewer officers, an important objective since its rapid expansion meant experienced officers were in short supply. Second, it created a unit large enough to operate as an independent command, autonomous from allies desperate for additional manpower to fill their ranks, depleted by years of war.

Table 6-2. The "Square" Division
Total: ~17,700

Brigade 1 (~8,850)	Brigade 2 (~8,850)
Regiment 1 (~4,425)	Regiment 3 (~4,425)
Regiment 2 (~4,425)	Regiment 4 (~4,425)

From a training perspective, the urgency of getting American troops to Europe led to the creation of a two-tier training system. Initial, or basic, training would be conducted eventually at thirty-two camps established throughout the United States. Basic training was standardized: it covered how to use violent means (e.g., rifles, artillery) from the individual up to the battalion level. Basic training created a shared experience across the Army for the first time, but it did not integrate individual specialties into an effective, combined-arms force ready to fight on the battlefield.

That responsibility rested with Gen. John J. Pershing, the newly appointed, overall commander of the American Expeditionary Force (AEF) in Europe. Only after smaller units arrived in Europe were they assembled into divisions and trained for the actual demands of the battlefield. For this training General Pershing relied heavily on regular Army officers who had graduated from the Army's former School of Application at Fort Leavenworth.[1] Leavenworth graduates impressed Pershing with their ability to take on big problems and handle large units. The actual amount of training new troops received in the theater varied considerably, based on the allied pressures to move them to the front lines.

But first, the new American troops had to be moved as quickly as possible three thousand miles across the Atlantic, a daunting and novel task. By the latter part of 1917, four divisions had been assembled overseas—an impressive number, perhaps, by U.S. standards, but one that did not begin to meet the reinforcement needs of the allies, struggling to replace millions of casualties. Shipping proved the critical bottleneck. Only when the British offered up a large number of transports, about a year after the declaration of war, did the American military achieve a considerable presence in Europe.

The industrialized trench warfare of World War I called on American industry to mobilize for war to an unprecedented degree. Only a war economy could produce uniforms, rifles, machine guns, artillery pieces, and munitions sufficient for the multimillion-man force, let alone the three innovations—the automobile, tank, and airplane—introduced to the battlefield. A national commitment was made, but while American industry mobilized, the United States had to rely on allies to supply certain kinds of equipment.

Machine guns and heavy artillery had shaped the defensive, stalemated characteristics of the western front years before, but the automobile, tank, and airplane foreshadowed a future revolutionary reshaping of the battlefield. Automobiles (including trucks), used as ambulances, personnel transports, and supply vehicles, eventually gave troops on the battlefield previously unknown mobility and sustainability. By replacing automobile tires with tracks and adding armor protection and a gun, military innovators produced the tank, which could potentially drive over trenches and into no-man's-land. The tank, in turn, ultimately suggested an offensive means to break the western-front stalemate.

The airplane, however, surpassed both of these in its revolutionary impact on the western front. In 1909, six years after the Ohio-born Wright brothers' first flight at Kitty Hawk, North Carolina, the Army ordered the first American military airplanes. Unsure what their mission should be, the Army initially assigned the airplanes to the Signal Corps, to enhance communications among Army units, collect operational intelligence, and reconnoiter enemy positions. Fragile, temperamental machines, airplanes not only captured imaginations but claimed the lives of quite a few men who flew them in the early days of aviation. Because of the high number of fatalities, the Army offered hazardous-duty pay as an incentive.

By the time the United States entered the war, European battlefield adaptations to the airplane had demonstrated it could serve as a bomber—that is, an aircraft capable of dropping weapons from the air to earth—and also as a pursuit, or fighter, plane, armed with weapons capable of shooting at other aircraft or enemy forces on the ground. By the end of the war, the nascent Army Air Service, still ostensibly under the Signal Corps, numbered almost 200,000 men (including over 1,500 pilots) and about 740 aircraft (almost five hundred of them from Britain or France). Early air pioneers like Brig. Gen. William L. "Billy" Mitchell declared passionately that the airplane was the new, decisive instrument in war—one best operated beyond the front lines, independently of the more conservative ground forces. This line of argument became the opening salvo in a deep institutional debate between land-focused soldiers and air-focused soldiers, a debate that in many ways remains unsettled today.

Meanwhile, whatever equipment the AEF used and wherever it came from, General Pershing was determined that the AEF would fight as an independent entity. After three years of catastrophic stalemate on the western front, he did not trust the allies to employ American troops effectively. As a result, he demanded, over strong objections of his British and French counterparts, that AEF units would fight under American command in a separate sector of the front, albeit one integrated into the allied effort.

General Pershing had initially estimated that the AEF would not be ready for such action until 1919. However, three catastrophic developments in 1917—France's failed Nivelle Offensive and the subsequent French army mutinies, Britain's failed Passchendaele campaign, and Russia's withdrawal from the war—changed this calculation. Determined to keep the allied effort alive despite these major setbacks, the AEF accelerated every aspect of its formation and deployment overseas. As a result, it found itself in action by April 1918, about a year after the declaration of war. From May until Germany's surrender in November 1918, the AEF fought in important battles, now iconic in the American military tradition: Chateau-Thierry, Belleau Wood, the Marne, St. Mihiel, and Meuse-Argonne.

At the war's end, the Army stood transformed. A force that less than two years earlier had numbered approximately 200,000 had grown to over fifteen times that size. In November 1918, 2 million of the Army's over 3 million soldiers had shipped overseas; 1.3 million AEF soldiers saw frontline duty; and approximately 117,000 died there. America's army, for all of its problems getting "over there," had accomplished what many previously thought unnecessary and, in any case, impossible—organizing, training, equipping, and employing a large land force overseas.

The Navy

The Navy's experience during World War I differed dramatically from the Army's. The year before the American entry, the U.S. Navy believed it saw its future modeled in the great clash of the British and German fleets at Jutland (May 31–June 1, 1916). This massive, albeit strategically indecisive, battleship confrontation prompted Congress to pass the Naval Act of 1916 (also known as the "Big Navy Act") a couple of months later. The act outlined another massive naval expansion program, this one projecting a large number of battleships and battle cruisers. However, America entered the war before the completion of any of these vessels, and, Germany's unrestricted submarine warfare, which had brought the United States into the conflict, suggested that a different navy was needed anyway.

That is, winning surface-fleet actions was not the big problem facing the Navy; rather, it was defeating the threat below the surface. Germany's revolutionary U-boats sank allied shipping at a terrific pace, and American and British shipyards could not replace these vessels fast enough. Given the vital importance of the Atlantic supply lines, over which personnel and equipment were to be shipped to the western front, the U.S. Navy's key mission shifted to protecting merchant vessels. Accordingly, it began to learn how to conduct a new kind of campaign, antisubmarine warfare (ASW), rather than preparing for a decisive surface engagement with Germany. It would not need a Mahanian main fleet of huge battleships but a large number of smaller ships, such as destroyers, to escort merchant vessels across the Atlantic, into the coastal waters off Britain and France, and throughout the Mediterranean Sea. The Navy's 1916 construction plan dramatically changed; resources were shifted to build a fleet of destroyers for escort duty.

The escort mission meant adopting the British technique of having merchant vessels travel together in convoys, where they could be protected. Unlike the AEF, the Navy frequently integrated itself within Royal Navy operations bringing those supply and troop ships safely to port. As essential as the convoy mission was, the Navy loathed it. It replaced the glamour, excitement, and decisiveness of confronting an enemy battle fleet with the day-to-day tedium of protecting slow, lumbering merchant ships in all types of weather. It also meant that the number of troops and tonnage of supplies moved were the measures of victory, not the number of enemy warships destroyed. The sailors responsible for keeping the supply lines open found this support mission, however indispensable, uninspiring. Nevertheless, the Navy responded to the new ASW mission with innovations to roll back the U-boat campaign. First, it placed thousands of submerged mines in the waters between Norway and Scotland. Second, it employed airplanes to scout for U-boat submarines, to protect convoys, and even to bomb continental targets. By the end of the war, naval aviation had over 37,000 men and two thousand aircraft.

In November 1918 the Navy totaled 774 active ships, the vast majority destroyers and smaller. To man all of these escort ships and perform other missions, the Navy needed a significant increase in manpower. By the end of the war, the Navy had grown from approximately 60,000 sailors in 1916 to over 500,000. Like the Army, it started to standardize basic training for the first time before sending new sailors to the fleet. A few years earlier, in 1911, the Navy had opened its Great Lakes basic training facility, near Chicago. The idea was to inculcate new enlistees with a shared sense of naval traditions, values, and discipline before sending them to advanced training in their specialties. Even the Navy, despite its long-standing commitment to learning on the job, especially on board ship, now recognized the importance of institutionalizing a common, early training experience for all who joined its ranks.

At the end of the war, the Navy could look back on some impressive accomplishments. It had successfully adapted to a new type of warfare, fighting naval vessels operating below the surface; changed its shipbuilding program dramatically; trained a force ten times larger than its peacetime one had been; and learned how to operate closely with its British counterpart. It had also experimented with new types of weapons, undersea mines and naval aircraft to complement the surface

ASW campaign. Its efforts might have been unglamorous, but they had significantly contributed to winning the war.

The Marine Corps

World War I started to solidify the Marine Corps' worldwide reputation as an aggressive, effective fighting force, building on what it had gained during the Spanish-American War and then sustained through its involvements in Latin America, the Philippines, and China. From a training and personnel perspective, this latest wartime performance represented the culmination of two prewar initiatives. First, as part of the 1916 Naval Act, the Marine Corps' authorized strength increased by 5,250 personnel over its existing 11,000. Second, like the other services, the Marine Corps had embarked on a formalized training program for all of officer candidates and recruits. Shortly before America's entry into the war, the Marine Corps activated three bases, in Quantico (Virginia), Parris Island (South Carolina), and San Diego (California) to conduct rigorous initial training.

By the time the war ended two years later, the Marine Corps numbered about 73,000. A Marine Corps regiment was part of the first Army division to arrive in France in July 1917. In February 1918, the Marine 4th Brigade became a stand-alone element of the Army's 2nd Infantry Division of the AEF. Moreover, when the 2nd Division's commander was suddenly transferred to deal with a crisis elsewhere, a Marine brigadier general, John A. Lejeune, was given the division and commanded it for much of the war. Lejeune's Marines of the 4th Brigade went on to fight with distinction most famously in 1918 at Belleau Wood, where Marine Corps lore claims the Germans called them "Devil Dogs" in grudging tribute to their fierce fighting.

Marines also experimented with air operations during the war, ably threading the organizational needle between the Navy (which wanted to use any maritime air assets available to hunt and attack submarines) and the Army (which believed it was solely responsible for air missions ashore). Although the contribution of Marine aviation to this conflict was modest at best, the experience convinced the Corps' leadership that it had a distinct role to play in the advanced-base mission articulated after the Spanish-American War.

The Marine Corps received considerable publicity in the domestic press as a tough, competent fighting force, frequently at the Army's expense, further endearing itself to the American people but exacerbating tensions with its sister land service. Paradoxically, however, its focus on land combat far from the sea resurrected a fundamental question—What did the Marine Corps uniquely provide the nation that justified its existence as a separate service? Although the Corps' continued existence was not now really in doubt, the old, almost irrational, worry about being absorbed by the Army, combined with this new interservice tension, again made some Marines fearful for their service's future.

Personnel

To accomplish the required rapid expansion of the military, the nation looked to three new sources of personnel: the first-ever universal draft, African Americans, and women. President Wilson proposed a universal draft—called "selective service," to blunt accusations that it amounted to involuntary conscription—shortly after America declared war. Selective service would be comprehensive, involving all qualified males between ages twenty-one and thirty, but executed at the state and local levels. Despite implementation difficulties and concern in some quarters that Wilson's request would cause rioting reminiscent of that during the Civil War, it received widespread support. By July 1, 1917, almost 10 million men had registered for the draft, and by the end of the war about 2.8 million of them had been called to active duty. Ultimately draftees, not enlistees into the regular forces or the National Guard, accounted for more than half of the over 4 million personnel in uniform during the war (table 6-3).[2] Clearly, the nation had accepted that the scope of the problem facing it demanded a national call to arms.

Moreover, the draft brought a large number of African Americans into the military. By the end of the war, about 200,000 were in Europe as part of the AEF. Because of the racism and racist laws of that day, they served in segregated

Table 6-3. World War I Approximate Personnel by Service
Total: ~4,200,000

Department of War	Department of Navy
Army 3,600,000	Navy 500,000
Army Air Service: 200,000 (included in Army total above)	Marine Corps 73,000

Note: Reported numbers vary due to the rapid growth and contraction of the services from April 1917 until November 1918. The Army Air Service was controlled by U.S. Army but operated with considerable latitude.

Source: dmdc.osd.mil

units. For the first time, they had black officers, but only at the lower levels; white officers retained the more senior positions. Most of these soldiers were in manual-labor units, but some served in combat arms. General Pershing seized an opportunity, in fact, to assign four black infantry regiments to serve with the French army, where they fought with distinction throughout the war. Under pressure from domestic constituencies, the War Department also created the segregated 92nd Division. Unfortunately, afflicted by poor training and racial clashes between the white and African American officers, the division performed poorly in combat, feeding postwar prejudice within the military about the effectiveness of African American troops.

Also for the first time, the nation allowed women to join the military in World War I. Approximately 23,000 women served as Army and Navy nurses overseas and in the United States. In addition, the Navy and Marine Corps opened up reserve enlisted ranks to women. Women assumed administrative responsibilities in order to free up men to go overseas. The vast majority of these women, about 13,000, served in the Navy, 300 or so in the Marine Corps. Immediately after the war, with the exception of a few nurses, the services demobilized all the women in their ranks. With the emergency over, their need for most minorities and women passed.

Organizational Integration

World War I's complexity, scope, and technological advances spurred joint and, for the first time, combined cooperation. From a joint perspective, the Marine Corps continued to work closely with the Navy; the Corps moved ashore to fight alongside the Army in the AEF; and soldiers, sailors, and Marines took to the air for the first time in history to experiment with employing weapons in and from the air. From a combined perspective, the United States recognized that it needed to work with allies. U.S. Navy and Royal Navy ships protected convoys together, and the AEF itself, though in its own part of the land front, was an integral part of a much larger allied effort to defeat Germany and its partners.

However, the fact that the services' physical environments began to overlap did not make systematic interservice or even intraservice cooperation inevitable—far from it. Indeed, in the case of airpower the opposite occurred. Most notably, the Army Air Service approached cooperation and integration from a completely different perspective: rather than work more closely with land forces, it sought to distance itself from its parent service, the U.S. Army. Amidst the fighting on the western front, the Army's own air pioneers argued that creating a unique, air-focused organization would better serve the Army and the nation. Thus, another controversy started over the nature of a military service. Should the nation create a new military service devoted to air warfare? Early airpower pioneers emphatically believed it should, arguing vociferously that the airplane represented a new, decisively violent technology that the Army was unsuited to exploit.

Civilian Control

Once Congress declared war, it largely handed off civilian control to the executive branch. President Wilson, in turn, exercised civilian control during the war almost exclusively through cabinet secretaries. He met with General Pershing once before sending the AEF overseas. During that meeting, he directed the general to ensure that American forces operated separately from the allies but otherwise offered only strong (if vague) confidence that Pershing would succeed. The president conducted his few subsequent interactions with Pershing through Secretary of War Newton Baker, bypassing the newly appointed Army Chief of Staff, Gen. Peyton March, although March was keen to assert his own authority over Pershing. In short, Wilson gave Pershing his intent as commander in chief and remarkable latitude to execute it.

A similar relationship played out for maritime operations. Wilson worked through Secretary of the Navy Josephus Daniels, who in turn empowered Adm. William Sims, the commander of U.S. naval forces in European waters, to work out all aspects of convoy operations. Sims, like Pershing, had a more decisive voice with the civilian chain of command than his Washington, D.C.–based service chief.

Impact on the Common Defense

America's success in World War I signaled a profound movement with regard to the nation's common defense. In its twenty months of war, the nation addressed the major, at times seemingly impossible, problem of creating, equipping, moving, and using a large fighting force overseas. The wartime experience suggested that the front line of the common defense now rested "over there," not in the continental United States. The issues associated with this shift proved the military's overriding challenge after World War I. They were all the more difficult in that the military addressed them in the context of a national rush to "return to normalcy" (as the new president termed it).

Despite rapid demobilization, arms limitations, much smaller defense budgets, and national indifference, military leaders needed to understand how to organize, train, and equip large numbers of citizens in the event the nation fought overseas again. Congress directed the Army to look first to the politically powerful National Guard as a federal source of manpower in the event of another large mobilization. The military also needed a clearer understanding of America's industrial base and how to mobilize it to equip a rapidly expanding force. These latter two problems led to the creation of the Army Industrial College and absorbed the attention of future national leaders like George Marshall in the years after World War I.[3]

For the Army, the question of what might require a large mobilization effort in the first place sparked an internal debate. Even if the common defense had shifted overseas, what now was the dominant problem for the Army? Was it a Japanese attack on the Philippines or the Panama Canal Zone, a new European threat, or resurgent trouble on the Mexican border? The vagueness of the Army's sense of purpose allowed it to justify a wide variety of forces, not necessarily of types that would prove most critical. For example, the Army should have embraced the tank in hindsight, yet it did not, because of the organizational and cultural threats that innovation posed for the infantry and cavalry. Many senior Army leaders viewed the tank as simply a supporting weapon for the infantry, and some continued to argue that horse cavalry still had a role to play. As a result, in the 1920s junior officers like George S. Patton Jr. and Dwight D. Eisenhower who advocated independent tank, or armored, forces found themselves out of step with their leadership.

The greatest source of contention within the Army, however, was still the airplane. Should air forces be tied to ground operations, or should they be allowed to operate independently? In the two decades after World War I, early Army aviators like Billy Mitchell, James H. "Jimmy" Doolittle, and Henry H. "Hap" Arnold continued to insist on the decisiveness of airpower in future wars. They believed that airpower rendered land warfare obsolete, that if applied strategically it could destroy the industrial heart and national will of any enemy. But victory through airpower required independence —air forces needed to be untethered from their outdated land counterparts. Ironically, however, like the Army spokesmen on their service's future purpose, air advocates lacked clarity on how airpower contributed to the common defense. Eventually, they settled on defending the nation's coasts and overseas territories from enemy fleets. That choice led to an emphasis on larger, longer-range aircraft rather than the shorter-range aircraft needed to support ground troops.

The Navy traversed an equally delicate course after World War I. Eager to shed its World War I legacy as a convoy-support force, the Navy focused on winning a future conflict with Japan. To that end, its planners devoted considerable time and energy to refinement of War Plan Orange, experimenting with new concepts for Pacific operations, fleet size, and fleet composition. In the latter connection, the Navy needed to wrestle with the implications of new technology: How should it address undersea and naval air operations? Aircraft flown from a new type of ship, the aircraft carrier, seemed especially likely to revolutionize naval warfare. Battleship officers resisted the idea, and even in those years of naval arms limitation, they engaged in the intense internal controversy over the Navy's next capital ship: the battleship or the nascent aircraft carrier?

For its part, the Marine Corps embraced the Navy's concentration on Japan. It still needed to distinguish itself from the Army: longtime critics were asking, "Why do we need a second land force? Shouldn't the Marine Corps just be integrated into the Army?" In part, the Marines answered those questions by staying overseas, sending small, independent forces into "contingencies" in Nicaragua and China. But it was their interest in the Navy's Pacific basing problem identified in War Plan Orange that was to generate their unique post–World War I mission. The Marine Corps began to look at how to conduct ship-to-shore, or amphibious, operations to establish advanced naval bases in wartime—hoping to solve both the Navy's problem and its own. In 1927 the Joint Board recognized the Marine Corps as responsible for developing amphibious techniques to seize advanced bases in support of naval campaigns. This acknowledgment reassured Marine Corps leadership and represented a crucial development in the identification of a unique mission and of the doctrine it would make necessary.

In the years after World War I, America's military services found themselves in an unsettled state. Drastically reduced in numbers and budget, they struggled to understand and then integrate new technologies for organized violence, means that operated in three dimensions—not only on the earth's surface but underwater and in the air. At the same time, they contemplated the complexities of large-scale mobilization of personnel and industry that might be made necessary by threats to American interests in the Western Hemisphere, eastward in Europe, or westward in the Asia-Pacific. Absent direction from civilian leadership, the individual services emphasized threats with which they were respectively best suited to deal. World War I, in short, was a profoundly disruptive experience for America's military. Its aftermath revealed myriad potential overseas threats. Yet, none of them remotely suggested the scope of what the military would face when it entered World War II in 1941.

Further Reading

Primary sources and memoirs include: William Sims, *The Victory at Sea*, 1920; U.S. Department of Defense, *Selected Manpower Statistics, Fiscal Year 1997*. Secondary sources include: John Chambers, *To Raise an Army*, 1987; Chambers, ed., *Oxford Companion to American Military History*; Coffman, *Old Army*; Coffman, *Regulars*; Cohen, *Demystifying the Citizen Soldier*; Edward Miller, *War Plan Orange*, 2007; Millett, *Semper Fidelis*; Millett, Maslowski, and Feis, *For the Common Defense*; Parker, *Concise History of the Marine Corps*; Symonds, *U.S. Navy*; Stewart, *American Military History*, vols. 1 and 2; Frank E. Vandiver, "Commander-in-Chief—Commander Relationships: Wilson and Pershing," *Rice University Studies*, 1971; Weigley, *American Way of War*.

7

Global Expeditionary Conflict, 1941–1945

After World War I, a "return to normalcy" and domestic issues dominated the nation's attention. Political isolationism and the Great Depression turned America's attention inward for most of the 1920s and into the 1930s. By the mid-1930s, the U.S. Army was a shadow of the force of World War I. Tight budgets had reduced its active-duty ranks to below 200,000 soldiers and limited the most basic supplies, like rifles and bullets, as well as the newest equipment, like airplanes and tanks. Major armies around the world dismissed the U.S. Army as inconsequential. The U.S. Navy, although it fared better through the 1920s and 1930s, fell short of its long-articulated goal to build a Navy "second to none." The Marine Corps too, at the start of the Great Depression, saw its numbers dwindle to just over 16,000 men. These reductions went so deep that by 1931 the Corps could barely fulfill commitments to protect American citizens and interests in China and Nicaragua.

The Common Defense

By the late 1930s, hostile acts by Germany, Japan, and Italy had started to alarm President Franklin Roosevelt and his key civilian and military leaders. The increasingly violent international environment suggested the emergence of new threats to the common defense that could require America to fight overseas simultaneously in two separate theaters. By the time Germany invaded Poland on September 1, 1939, the American military's newly conceived Rainbow Plans postulated that the United States would indeed have to fight in a coalition against Japan or Germany, or perhaps both at the same time.

The December 7, 1941, Japanese attack on Pearl Harbor and Germany's declaration of war a few days later, on December 11, tragically confirmed that the U.S. military would need to cross the Pacific to defeat Japan and the Atlantic to defeat Germany. To do so, the United States would have to create and sustain a military large enough not only to go "over there" but to do so twice, at the same time, and then fight in partnership with allies where possible or, at a minimum, to provide materiel assistance to them. On every level, the nation and its military faced herculean tasks. In short, achieving this objective demanded virtually the complete mobilization of America.[1]

Organizational Responses

To begin with, to defeat the Axis powers led by Germany, Japan, and Italy, the U.S. military needed to expand dramatically. America's active-duty, peacetime military was to go from about 334,000 in 1939 (table 7-1) to over 12,000,000 just six years later, in 1945. To create, train, equip, move, and sustain a force over thirty-five times larger than it had less than a decade before, the formerly neutral United States would have to become a nation in arms.

The Army

In the last few years before the nation went to war for the second time in the twentieth century, the Army pursued a variety of initiatives. Organizationally, one of the most important was to reassess the square division. That structure

Table 7-1. Active-Duty U.S. Military, 1939
Total: ~334,400

Department of War	Department of Navy
Army: 189,800	Navy: 125,200
Army Air Corps: ~20,000 (included in Army total)	Marine Corps: 19,400

Source: dmdc.osd.mil

had provided the mass necessary to fight autonomously in World War I, but having grown to about 25,000 men, it required considerable support and lacked battlefield flexibility. After vigorous debate, the Army adopted a new triangular division of 10,000 to 15,000 men. The triangular concept (figure 7-1) diminished the role of the brigade structure; three regiments rather than four now constituted the heart of the division. This change required fewer supporting units, was better suited to rapid expansion of the Army, made the division more maneuverable on the battlefield, and, perhaps most important, much easier to ship around the globe. With this seemingly unremarkable organizational change the Army confronted the need to create large expeditionary forces that could ship out quickly to fight overseas.

The expeditionary U.S. Army of World War II had much greater battlefield mobility than had the AEF. Confined to the trenches during World War I, the AEF, when it moved at all, did so at the marching pace of the foot soldier. In World War II, the mechanization of the battlefield foreshadowed by the introduction of the automobile, tank, and airplane two decades earlier came to fruition. Mechanization produced a

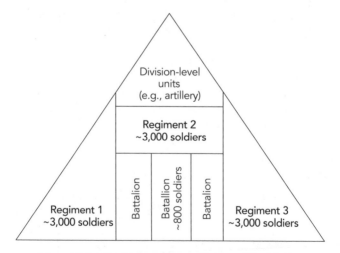

Figure 7-1. Triangular Infantry Division, World War II
Regimental Focus: 10,000–15,000 Soldiers

mobility revolution that reshaped the infantry and cavalry and gave them new speed and maneuverability. The most famous of these vehicles was the four-wheel-drive Jeep; with it and other motorized vehicles like transport trucks and half-tracks (an early armored personnel carrier with wheels in the front, tracks in the rear), the infantry could cover distances over land faster than ever before. The tank's firepower, speed, and lethality ended any lingering hope of relevance for the horse cavalry; hereafter the cavalry rode not horses but tanks (and later their derivatives). Indeed, by the end of war the United States had produced enough tanks to equip twenty new divisions devoted to armored warfare.

Army organizational innovations also explored the use of the airplane to move infantry. Most notably, after some experimentation, the Army concluded that infantrymen could be dropped or landed from the sky in large numbers onto the battlefield ("vertical envelopment," in modern Army parlance) to disrupt or confound the enemy. During World War II, the Army reconstituted two infantry divisions, the 82nd and the 101st, as airborne for this purpose. Hardened by intensive physical and technical training, these soldiers hoped to surprise the enemy by approaching the battlefield via parachutes or gliders. Ultimately they were to distinguish themselves in some of the most iconic actions of the war, including the Normandy invasion of June 6, 1944.

Finally, inspired by the daring feats of British commandos earlier in World War II, the Army created the Rangers, a highly trained elite force for very specialized and dangerous missions. Infantrymen in these units scouted and raided behind enemy lines. In Europe, these Rangers would win acclaim as the "boys of Pointe du Hoc" on Normandy's Omaha Beach;[2] in the Pacific they won the nation's esteem as Merrill's Marauders (named after their commander, Brig. Gen. Frank Merrill). These Rangers, supplied by airdrop, operated for extended periods behind Japanese lines in Burma.

Excluding the Air Corps, the Army now had to find and then train over six million men in ninety divisions. The nation activated the reserves, federalized the National Guard, and drafted millions to fill the Army's ranks (see table 7.4). To turn this raw material into soldiers, the Army mixed prewar and ad hoc wartime approaches to training. Existing units trained mostly at the Army's main training bases. The bulk of the World War II Army, however, comprised scores of new divisions. To train them the Army developed cadres of trainers at the main training bases then sent the cadres to train the new divisions as they were "stood up." This approach placed much of the training at the division level and yet standardized training across the force. To prepare a division to go overseas took roughly a year of training, both basic and advanced. Training frequently culminated with complex maneuvers in places like Tennessee and Louisiana, exercises that prepared soldiers for the demands of the battlefield.

Creating the officer corps to lead these new units required additional measures. The U.S. Military Academy enlarged its classes and accelerated graduations but could still provide only a small portion of the officers needed. Activated reserve and Guard officers provided some more. The highly selective, accelerated Army Specialized Training Program (ASTP) was another source of officers; ASTP replaced the ROTC program, compressing four years of undergraduate education and officer training into eighteen months. Another active-duty program put qualified candidates through Officer Candidate Schools (OCSs) lasting seventeen weeks. Finally, enlisted personnel who proved outstanding combat soldiers often received battlefield commissions, in almost every case to second lieutenant. Audie Murphy, the most decorated soldier of World War II, earned his commission this way.

Thousands of volumes, not least the Army's own, invaluable official histories (the "green books"), address virtually every aspect of the Army's performance: grand strategy, Washington politics, senior and field leadership, combat-arms integration, training, and of course the conduct of battles and campaigns. The Army experienced tragic failures and terrific successes, ultimately becoming the largest American contributor to the greatest military victory of the twentieth century. (The Soviet Union was the single largest land-forces contributor to Allied victory, fielding over 20 million men to fight on the eastern front.) Whether fighting on some of the famous battlefields of Europe, losing the Philippines to the Japanese and then returning to liberate them, operating in the neglected China-Burma-India theater, or garrisoning the frozen Aleutian Islands, this citizen-soldier force of World War II shaped the modern psyche of the U.S. Army. Despite the intervening years and conflicts, understanding how the twenty-first-century Army thinks about its role in America's defense requires a deep appreciation for its epic World War II experience.

The Army Air Forces

During World War II, an additional 2 million individuals wearing Army uniforms served in a specialized component of that service, the U.S. Army Air Forces (USAAF). By the late 1930s, air pioneers and theorists had argued persuasively that an enemy could be defeated decisively from the air by destroying its war economy and demoralizing its citizens. Large planes capable of flying into enemy airspace would drop enormous numbers of bombs on strategic economic targets (e.g., war production plants and oil refineries). Airmen referred to these planes as bombers and this revolutionary approach to war as strategic bombing.

However, as they had since World War I, senior airmen argued that if strategic bombing was to succeed, they needed to be in charge of it—airplanes were simply too revolutionary for traditional Army officers to use decisively. Early assessments of Britain's Royal Air Force and the German Luftwaffe's wartime performance pointed to the importance of having an independent air force and of centralizing control over it. Thus, just months before the United States entered the war and over the protests of many Army officers, President Roosevelt and Army Chief of Staff General Marshall agreed to Gen. "Hap" Arnold's appointment as the chief of the Army Air Forces (AAF). This arrangement gave Arnold an autonomous staff and direct access to the president on air matters. A subsequent change (in March 1942) designated him as Commanding General, AAF. Despite some limitations, these changes and the authority embedded in them gave the AAF de facto independence to design and wage a strategic bombing campaign throughout the war.

To do that, the Army Air Forces needed several thousand bombers; trained aircrews and maintenance specialists to fly and keep them operational; and thousands of overseas and U.S. air bases from which to operate them. In 1939 all this was virtually unimaginable. That year the AAF's predecessor, the Army Air Corps, had approximately 2,400 planes total, of which only eight hundred were combat capable and even fewer were bombers. Somehow American industry needed to produce tens of thousands of bombers to destroy the Axis powers' economies. When the bombers' ability to protect themselves from enemy attack proved limited, American industry also needed to produce tens of thousands of pursuit (designated in a *P-* series), or fighter, aircraft to defend them on the way to and from targets, as well as for a wide range of other missions. By 1945 industry produced close to 300,000 planes; some of the largest categories are listed in table 7-2.

Some of the bombers and fighters of the era are among the most legendary planes in aviation history: the B-17 Flying Fortress, B-24 Liberator, B-29 Superfortress, P-47 Thunderbolt, and P-51 Mustang.

Creating and maintaining such a technology-intensive force presented the Army and the AAF yet another challenge. The AAF's leaders argued that about 75 percent of the Army's inductees lacked the intelligence necessary to master the AAF's technical tasks. The AAF was ultimately given preferential treatment in personnel: it picked the most

Table 7-2. Aircraft Production in World War II

Aircraft Type	Total
Bomber	97,810
Pursuit/Fighter	99,950
Reconnaissance	3,918
Transport	23,929
Trainer	57,623

talented servicemen in the Army's ranks to fill its own. To train them the AAF created new flight- and ground-training programs. It was to be the aviation cadet program that produced the vast number of flight-crew officers (i.e., pilots, navigators, and bombardiers) needed. This program combined the military discipline of the Army's officer candidate school with basic flight training to determine a trainee's aptitude for aviation. Enlisted crew members and maintenance specialists underwent technical preparation for specific tasks after completing basic training. Only then did air and ground elements come together organizationally as an air group.

The group was the fundamental air combat unit. Comprising two or more squadrons (what the Army considered roughly battalion equivalents), the group had both combat and support elements so that it could operate independently, much as an Army regiment did. A heavy bomber group built around B-17s or B-24s, for example, would consist of over seventy aircraft and 2,200 personnel. The AAF created over 300 combat groups over the course of World War II, of which approximately 250 remained operational when the war ended in 1945. To manage this large force, the AAF combined two or more groups into wings, two or more wings into air divisions, and two or more air divisions into numbered air forces, such as the Eighth Air Force of European theater fame (table 7-3).

Overall, then, the AAF differed greatly from its parent service, the Army. AAF training took longer and was more technical. The AAF organized itself differently and focused

Table 7-3. USAAF Organizational Structure, Numbered Air Force (e.g., 8 AF, 20 AF)

Air Division				Air Division			
Wing		Wing		Wing		Wing	
Group	Group	Group	Group	Group	Group	Group	Group

Note: The U.S. Air Force continues to use the numbered air force, wing, and group nomenclature.

on the particular attributes of aircraft and air operations rather than on supporting ground combat forces. Moreover, the AAF's single-minded concentration on strategic bombing and its perceived entitlement when it came to personnel and equipment caused tension with the Army, a strain that some would argue persists today. Army/AAF friction was especially evident over the issue of battlefield missions: close air support for frontline forces and interdiction of enemy supply lines. Some Army leaders believed that the AAF refused to embrace these vital roles because it perceived them as not strategically important. The AAF countered that it more than met the Army's battlefield needs, albeit not according to Army doctrine. The AAF held firm to the proposition that to be decisive, airpower had to focus on strategic missions. The Army recognized the need for service independence for the AAF, but the nature of air operations that the latter insisted on produced distance, even distrust, between the two.

Much has been written about U.S. air operations during World War II. From the storied, and sometimes controversial, bombing missions over Berlin and Schweinfurt in Germany and over Tokyo in Japan, to the resupply missions in the China-Burma-India theater, to the battlefield missions flown in every theater, the AAF impacted the Axis powers' economies and national will, if not as dramatically as airmen hoped. In the process, the AAF made a strong case for full service independence after the war. Airmen would then argue that the dropping of the two atomic bombs ultimately demonstrated the effectiveness and importance of strategic bombing. To their minds, only an independent Air Force could be entrusted with this revolutionary new weapon.

The Navy

The U.S. Navy went to war in a stronger position than did either the Army or the Army Air Forces, despite the lingering constraints of the 1922 Washington Naval Conference agreement. The signatories of this pact, including the United States, Great Britain, and Japan, had agreed to, among other things, post–World War I battleship and aircraft-carrier limitations. The treaty framework, however, started to break down when Japan withdrew in 1936 and failed completely when Europe went to war in September 1939.

President Franklin Roosevelt, as a former Assistant Secretary of the Navy, unabashedly favored the Navy over the other services; and he heartily supported the Two-Ocean Navy Act of July 1940. The law more than doubled the number of authorized ships for the Navy to 257 warships, including 18 aircraft carriers and 43 submarines. Warships, however, took longer than military aircraft to build. Thus, when the Japanese attacked Pearl Harbor, the fleet was not appreciably larger than in 1940 and certainly was not ready for offensive operations in both oceans.

Waging a two-ocean war required a vast and varied navy and sailors to man it. The Navy greatly increased the number of officers and enlisted members it put through basic training. For officers this involved accelerated graduation of midshipmen from Annapolis, the creation of the U.S. Navy Reserve Midshipmen's School (the Navy's equivalent of OCS), and the establishment of the V-12 Navy College Training Program (roughly equivalent to ASTP). For the enlisted ranks, the Navy ultimately opened seven "boot" (basic training) camps. Standardized training emphasized discipline, physical fitness, and basic familiarization with shipboard life.

In the Atlantic Ocean, some of the naval requirements resembled those of World War I. The hard-fought Battle of the Atlantic—in which the Allies fought to protect transatlantic cargo shipping from a sustained German attempt to destroy it—proved one of the most unglamorous, dangerous, nerve-wrecking, and crucial campaigns of the war. The scope of the effort to supply Britain and the Soviet Union and the effectiveness of the German U-boats, frequently operating in "wolf packs," made this a harrowing operational theater. Destroyers and other small surface ships once again provided most of the crucial convoy escort force, supplemented over the course of the war by land- and sea-based aircraft.

The Navy's responsibilities in the European theater, however, extended beyond the Battle of the Atlantic. Here, as in the Pacific theater, the Navy had to prepare for and execute amphibious operations. These massive yet intricate evolutions involved the shelling of land targets, then the moving of soldiers (and Marines in the Pacific) from American ships to enemy-held shores. Such operations required thousands of new amphibious vessels, large and small, to move men and materiel to the theater and then ashore in North Africa, Italy, and France. The June 6, 1944, landing at the Normandy beaches in France remains the largest amphibious operation in history.

Despite the Navy's importance to the Atlantic theater, its institutional heart resided firmly in the Pacific. Not only had the Navy experienced catastrophic losses in its battleship fleet at Pearl Harbor, but the Pacific's vast expanse lent itself to Mahanian, fleet-on-fleet, naval warfare. To retake captured islands and invade Japan, the Navy needed first to challenge Japan's naval dominance in the Pacific. The attack on Pearl Harbor had dramatically signaled, it seemed, the end of the battleship era. For months after this tragic attack, only the aircraft carrier remained to the Pacific Fleet, and so it—not the battleship—would be at the heart of any Pacific Fleet action.

Since the early days of flight, naval aviation pioneers had experimented with launching and recovering airplanes at sea. Shortly after World War I, the U.S. Navy modified some ships with flat landing surfaces for aircraft. It created its first operational aircraft carriers (or as journalists liked to call them, "flattops") in the 1920s, and by 1941 four large carriers operated in the Pacific Fleet. During the war the carrier, with its scores of aircraft, extended the fleet's reach well beyond visual range. For the first time in history, major fleet encounters occurred without the ships ever sighting each other. From the launching of Jimmy Doolittle's Army bombers off the USS *Hornet* to bomb Tokyo to the great carrier battles of the Coral Sea and Midway, the aircraft carrier had by the end of 1942 clearly emerged as the most important warship for control of the seas and other key missions.

In the Pacific theater, U.S. Navy submarines also played important roles. Submarines went on secretive long-range patrols, cruising as far as Tokyo Bay to sink Japanese shipping and disrupt Japan's war economy. In this way, the Navy's submarines functioned in the Pacific much as the German U-boats did in the Atlantic. These same American submarines also played an important covert role, landing and extracting forces onto and off enemy-held islands.

Finally, the island-hopping campaign of capturing key islands while bypassing and isolating others required the Navy to execute amphibious operations throughout the Pacific. These campaigns meant preinvasion bombardment by aircraft, battleships, cruisers, and specialized craft followed by the landing of Marines and soldiers along with their materiel from, sometimes, hundreds of amphibious ships and craft. As in the Atlantic theater, tank landing ships (LSTs), capable of carrying twenty-five tanks thousands of miles and landing them directly onto unimproved beaches, and small landing craft called "Higgins boats" proved vital. A bloody assault on the Tarawa Atoll in November 1943, one of the earliest of these amphibious operations, taught the Navy and Marine Corps tough lessons about the deadliness of such operations when tides were miscalculated and Marines and soldiers were forced to disembark too far from shore. Subsequent landings on islands such as Saipan, Iwo Jima, and Okinawa applied these hard-learned lessons, but the Japanese had learned as well. The ferocity of an already horrific campaign increased as U.S. forces moved toward Japan.

To fight and win in the Atlantic and Pacific theaters, the Navy underwent a profound expansion. Shipyards built a staggering number of vessels during the war, including approximately a hundred aircraft carriers (including smaller escort carriers), 120 battleships and cruisers, 260 submarines, 1,000 LSTs, and tens of thousands of Higgins boats and other specialized landing ships and craft. To man this vast force, the Navy grew to over three million personnel. This number included U.S. Coast Guardsmen brought into the Navy under a legal proviso that subsumed the Coast Guard into the Navy during wartime.

Notwithstanding the Navy's inauspicious start in World War II, its multifaceted approach to global war had been validated by the end of the conflict. The service had devised innovative options for major fleet actions, for protection of supply lines, and for amphibious operations. As it was for the other services, World War II was the Navy's institutional pinnacle in terms of protecting the nation.

The Marine Corps

By the time the United States declared war, the Marine Corps numbered approximately 50,000 strong. It had established itself as the most experienced military service in amphibious operations, having used exercises during the interwar period to refine operational doctrine, to improve movement of a military force from sea to shore, and then to conduct an offensive operation there. But the demands for amphibious operations in the Atlantic and Pacific were so numerous that the Marine Corps was unable to execute all of them. Interservice rivalry also had much to do with the extent to which the Marine Corps would control amphibious operations in either theater. The Army believed landing forces needed much more in the way of artillery and vehicles than did the Marine Corps. Moreover, senior leaders in both services were loath to serve under officers of the other, as old institutional hostilities reemerged. A compromise emerged in early 1942, after acrimonious debate: the Army proposed, and the Marine Corps and Navy happily accepted, that the Marine Corps devote all its attention and units to the Pacific.

Meanwhile, at the entry level, the Marine Corps was experiencing the same problems of rapid expansion as the other services were. The Corps continued to train at two recruit depots, Parris Island on the East Coast and the new Camp Pendleton, California, on the West Coast. Both put Marine recruits through a seven-week training cycle (shortened from the interwar period of twelve weeks) with a focus on building discipline, physical fitness, and esprit. The last three weeks, longer than in the other services, were devoted to rifle marksmanship, to reinforce the Marine Corps ethos, "Every Marine a rifleman." The Marine Corps drew its future officers from the Navy's commissioning sources and then put them through its own OCS course before sending them out to units. It also expanded other bases, mostly on the East and West Coasts, to train for the particular demands of amphibious operations.

The Marine Corps organized its expansion on a framework of building new regiments. Once a full regiment was trained, it immediately forfeited one of its three battalions to become the core for the next new regiment. Regiments, then, were triangular, and three of them largely made a Marine division.[3] By the end of the war, the Marine Corps had six divisions. It also had created five Marine air wings, roughly associated with these divisions, to provide them close air support. The air wings belonged entirely to the Marines: aircraft, pilots, and maintenance support. Marine aviation's performance during the 1942 Guadalcanal campaign confirmed for the Marine Corps the importance of having its own ("dedicated" or "organic") aviation. Throughout the war, the Marine Corps stressed the integration of its air-ground fighting forces, even when geographic circumstances did not allow for much air support. From this single-minded focus, what would become the modern MAGTF was born.

Despite the Marine Corps' expansion, the scale of Pacific theater operations required substantial Army ground forces as well. But it was the Marine Corps story that captured the public's imagination. It did so, in part, because of the Marines' courageous fighting in the Solomons and the Central Pacific, on islands like Guadalcanal, Tarawa, Iwo Jima, and Okinawa, but also because of its proactive attitude toward the media. By 1943, in addition to encouraging coverage by civilian journalists, the Marine Corps had trained almost three hundred journalists as Marines, who in turn covered every aspect of any amphibious operation, producing over three thousand articles a month, along with photographs or newsreels. Thus, the Marine Corps' version of Pacific campaign received more press than the Army's large force in the Pacific, and ultimately the Corps' mystique as America's premier fighting service grew.

Personnel

The personnel numbers from the U.S. participation in World War II are staggering. During the war over 16 million Americans served in the military, more than 73 percent of them overseas; when the war ended in 1945, over 12 million were still in uniform (table 7-4). Some of these, as noted, were in reserve and National Guard units activated for the duration of the war. More were volunteers who flooded into the recruiting offices in the months after Pearl Harbor. Nonetheless, filling the ranks required an energetic national draft. By the end of the war, local draft boards had registered for selective service 36 million men, of whom over 10 million were inducted. Even the Marine Corps resorted to creative methods to increase intake while retaining its identity as a volunteer, fighting elite. It did so by urging draftees at induction centers to "volunteer" for the Marine Corps rather than be drafted into other services and by recruiting seventeen-year-olds before they registered for the draft. Thus, even though almost half of the Marines during World War II were, in essence, draftees, only 70,000 appeared on its rosters as such.

Vast personnel requirements also brought African Americans, Japanese Americans, and women into the military in large numbers. Official racial and gender integration of military ranks remained in the future, but enough people from minority groups served during the war to stimulate a broad conversation about integration. Most notable were the over 1.2 million African Americans. The majority performed support duties in the Army, including loading and driving the trucks of the famous "Red Ball Express,"

Table 7-4. U.S. Military, Approximate Size, 1945
Total: ~12,000,000

Department of War	Department of Navy
Army: 6,200,000	Navy: 3,300,000
Army Air Forces: 2,000,000	Marine Corps: 500,000

which delivered supplies throughout France. But they also distinguished themselves in the infantry, in the Navy and Marine Corps, and in the Army Air Forces. For example, the AAF's Tuskegee Airmen (so known for the Alabama base where they trained) formed the 332nd Fighter Group (which became one of the most heralded fighter units of the war) and the 477th Bombardment Group.

In a similar vein, Japanese American men, initially considered security risks and excluded from military service, were eventually allowed to join the Army and serve in Europe. Most were assigned to the now-legendary 442nd Infantry Regiment, the most highly decorated combat unit of the war. Also, the Army and Marine Corps put hundreds of Native Americans through specialized training to provide secure communications in both the Atlantic and Pacific theaters. These Americans, who became known as the "code talkers," fought in some of the toughest battles of the war, including Normandy and Iwo Jima. Finally, approximately 266,000 women, including African Americans, volunteered to serve in women-only units of each of the services during the war.[4] They were nurses, administrative support personnel, and even pilots, ferrying aircraft from the factories to their initial bases, some of them overseas.

Wartime demands, in short, saw millions of citizens previously excluded from the military services invited into their ranks to address a profound national need. However, as had been the case in World War I, how the nation would treat these individuals once the crisis passed remained an open question.

Organizational Integration

The Atlantic and Pacific theaters differed dramatically when it came to organizational integration at the strategic and operational levels. Allied organizational integration in Europe surpassed anything imagined in World War I. General Eisenhower, as Commander, Supreme Headquarters Allied Expeditionary Force, commanded the largest joint (i.e., more than one U.S. service) and also combined (allied) force the world had ever seen. He answered to President Roosevelt and General Marshall but had considerable latitude in his command. His key subordinates were British and American, and they came from the two nations' armies, navies, and air services. These component commanders (in modern parlance) could be exceptionally difficult to work with at times, but they never doubted Eisenhower's authority as the overall theater commander. Centralized command of combined operations and land, sea, and air integration, especially for critical undertakings like the Normandy invasion, dominated the operational approach in Europe.

In the Pacific theater, the approach was different. Since the non-U.S. contribution of forces was much smaller, combined operations were less important. Much more important might have been joint organizational integration of the U.S. military forces, but that largely failed. Adm. Ernest J. King, the Chief of Naval Operations, considered the Pacific a naval theater and insisted the Navy should be responsible for strategy and execution there. King's logic made theater strategy the preserve of Adm. Chester A. Nimitz, the commander in chief of the U.S. Pacific Fleet and Pacific Ocean Areas. From a naval perspective, that strategy envisioned first the establishment of control of the seas (especially those of the Solomons Archipelago in the South Pacific, already being contested), then an island-hopping campaign through the Central Pacific until American forces were close enough to invade Japan itself. The Navy argued that this approach, strongly influenced by Mahan's writing, was the fastest way to victory.

In Washington, King passionately argued for this strategic preference, but it directly clashed with that of Gen. Douglas MacArthur, who had been the commander of all forces in East Asia in December 1941. In early 1942, as the Philippines, where MacArthur had his headquarters, were about to fall, President Roosevelt ordered him to Australia to establish and command the Southwest Pacific theater. From this vantage point, MacArthur directly challenged King's concept, vigorously arguing that the best strategy was to fight northward from Australia to recapture New Guinea, return to and liberate the Philippines, and then, finally, take the war directly to Japan.

Strong service parochialism, Roosevelt's enduring affinity for the Navy, and the outsized personalities of King and MacArthur all contributed to disinclination on the part of the president to choose one strategy over the other. Instead, the U.S. military waged two independent theater operations in the Pacific. The Central Pacific became known as the Navy and Marine Corps theater, the Southwest Pacific as the Army and Army Air Forces theater. Many argue that in retrospect this two-pronged strategy was probably optimal and that, informally at least, forces from all the services operated successfully together in both Pacific theaters. However that may be, from an organizational-integration perspective, the two Pacific command structures remained separate, and any thought of single integrated joint strategy for the theater was flatly dismissed.

Thus, World War II simultaneously gave rise to one of America's most joint military campaigns ever, in Europe, and a theater split between two independent, service-focused campaigns, in the Pacific. Moreover, except for the president and his informal JCS, as discussed below, no committee or organization attempted to integrate all of these into a single, global military campaign at the highest level of government. Harry S. Truman became acutely aware of this lack of integration when Roosevelt's sudden death abruptly thrust him into the presidency in April 1945.

Civilian Control

Even before America's entry into the war, President Franklin Roosevelt made it clear that he was commander in chief and would direct the war effort. As one author notes, Roosevelt believed the Framers made it clear in the Constitution and *Federalist* 74 that the president was the commander in chief, and so, unlike Woodrow Wilson, he refused to delegate conduct of the war to the military.[5] How President Roosevelt would exercise that control over such a vast enterprise, however, was unclear. When the war started, his formal control still passed through his secretaries of war and the Navy. The secretaries provided essential administrative control and handled much of the mobilization effort, but when it came to directing the course of so vast a war, the arrangement proved inadequate.

To address this shortcoming, the executive branch established under Roosevelt's direction a myriad of agencies and boards to oversee almost every dimension of the war effort. However, one of Roosevelt's most important innovations—the Joint Chiefs of Staff—first met as an unofficial group, in December 1941, and remained such throughout the war. Initially, the JCS consisted of the Army Chief of Staff, General Marshall; the Chief of Naval Operations (CNO), Admiral King; and the Chief of the Army Air Forces, General Arnold. Notably, the JCS excluded the Commandant of the Marine Corps (CMC). The Chief of Naval Operations was to represent Marine Corps as well as the Navy.

Roosevelt first pulled together the Joint Chiefs to prepare for a planning conference with the British shortly after Pearl Harbor; he needed a counterpart to the Chiefs of Staff Committee that would accompany Churchill. At the conference, it quickly became apparent that British military leaders surpassed their American counterparts in their capacities for both strategic and operational planning. If Roosevelt wanted to drive overall Allied war strategy, he would need a standing, and capable, advisory group to do it. Thus, the ad hoc JCS soon had a vital role in Roosevelt's war planning.[6]

One additional innovation of the JCS structure was Roosevelt's appointment of Adm. William Leahy as the chief of staff to the commander in chief in July 1942. In this capacity, Leahy served as a direct link between the president and the JCS. He briefed the president every morning on military issues and communicated White House decisions to the Joint Chiefs. His function, like that of the JCS itself, was completely informal, but because of Leahy's close relationship with the president, some see his position as the precursor to the modern chairmanship of the Joint Chiefs of Staff.

President Roosevelt used the JCS to communicate his intent to the military and to shape the war effort, but that did not mean he deferred to it. He frequently disagreed with the JCS, even on critical matters such as the timing and location of the "second front" in Europe (i.e., to supplement the Soviet front). The disagreements were, at times, so profound that the JCS feared that Churchill, in particular, had undue influence over Roosevelt. This informal system suffered from such imperfections throughout the war, but it offered the president an effective means to direct the war's overall strategy, seek military advice, and exercise civilian control.

Impact on the Common Defense

The war ended abruptly in August 1945 with the use of a revolutionary new weapon—the atomic bomb—against Japan. Less than four years after Pearl Harbor, America and its military stood transformed. The inconsequential force of 1939 had emerged from the global conflict as one of the largest, most effective in history. Almost every aspect of American society had willingly mobilized to produce it. Through enlistments and the draft, citizens had accepted the call for the duration of the conflict. American industry activated its latent production capacity to produce ships, planes, tanks, and other weapons to arm this force, move it overseas, and then keep it supplied. The small, barely mechanized military of the late 1930s was now, less than a decade later, fully mechanized and in possession of the world's only atomic weapons. By any measure—number of theaters and personnel, war production figures, cost, shipping, and so forth—the American military's accomplishment in World War II was vast and awe inspiring.

Yet, ironically, the nature and scale of the services' wartime achievements provoked major identity crises when the war ended. Army, Navy, Marine Corps, and Army Air Forces leaders feared for their respective services' futures; none of them wanted to return to the backwater status of the 1930s, yet the postwar demobilization was so rapid that it seemed that might happen. After all, the nation had won a global war and received the unconditional surrenders of its enemies. Why should it retain and maintain a large military?

Predictably, new and fierce interservice competition erupted almost immediately. In particular, the anticipated creation of an independent Air Force meant that resources would now be allocated among four services rather than three. Thus, as the nation celebrated a great victory, it also struggled to envision the post–World War II military that would be necessary for the common defense. It proved a mighty struggle—one that created many of the organizations, structures, and insecurities evident today.

Further Reading

Primary sources include: U.S. Department of Defense, *Selected Manpower Statistics, Fiscal Year 1997*. Secondary sources include: *U.S. Army in World War II* (the "Green Books"); Chambers, *Oxford Companion to American Military History*; Coffman, *Regulars*; Cohen, *Demystifying the Citizen Soldier*; W. F Craven and J. L. Cate, eds., *The Army Air Forces in World War II*, 1948–58; Nigel Hamilton, *The Mantle of Command: FDR at War, 1941–1942*, 2014; David Jablonsky, *War by Land, Sea and Air*, 2010; Miller, *War Plan Orange*; Millett, *Semper Fidelis*; Millett, Maslowski, and Feis, *For the Common Defense*; Samuel Morison, *The Two-Ocean War*, 1963; Parker, *Concise History of the Marine Corps*; Steven Rearden, *The Council of War*, 2012; Symonds, *U.S. Navy*; Stewart, *American Military History*, vol. 2; Ian Toll, *The Conquering Tide*, 2015; Weigley, *American Way of War*.

8

The Services' Struggles for Relevance in the Atomic Age, 1945–1949

The sudden end of the war caught American military and civilian leaders off guard. After the German surrender, they had begun to plan for a postwar world, but, because of the need to invade and subdue Japan, they had anticipated the war continuing well into 1946. This gave them, in theory, time to address major questions about the size, composition, and purpose of the military afterward. With the official Japanese surrender on September 2, 1945, this timeline accelerated dramatically and, with it, interservice rivalry for postwar relevance. One of the great paradoxes of the war's end was that even as the services celebrated an unparalleled military victory, they started worrying about their postwar futures. What did the nation need this large, victorious military to do? Without a meaningful postwar mission, military leaders feared that loss of skilled personnel and severe reductions of budgets would once again place their services' effectiveness at risk. As a result, an unseemly chapter in American military history followed in the immediate aftermath of the war, as the services struggled to reinvent themselves and ensure their continued relevance.

Amidst the rapid demobilization that dominated the military's attention immediately after Japan's surrender, President Truman supplied impetus for the public postwar rivalry by asking two questions as commander in chief. First, what did the nation need to do militarily to prevent another Pearl Harbor? Second, how should the military internalize the hard-learned lessons of the war, especially with the advent of atomic weapons? These searching questions prompted major interservice debates, one over unification, the other over service roles and missions.

Unification Debate, 1945–1947

The unification debate had both cabinet- and service-level components. In the former, Truman sought more centralized presidential control over the independent military departments. In the latter, he looked for service-headquarters and theater-command structures that served the same end. At both levels, the main issue was centralization, rather than continued coordination.

Centralization: The Preferred Approach of the Army and Army Air Forces

President Truman found kindred spirits in the Army Chief of Staff, General Marshall, and the AAF chief, General Arnold. At the cabinet level, centralization meant a single, unified Department of the Armed Forces under a single, civilian, cabinet-level secretary of the armed forces. From a uniformed perspective, this meant a single chief of staff of the armed forces to unify functionally the service branches for land, sea, and air warfare, much as Eisenhower had in Europe during the war. The services chiefs of the Army, Navy, and Air Force would report to the chief of staff of the armed forces.

Organizationally, this option meant a separate air force to handle the responsibilities for air warfare and potentially a Marine Corps with a reduced role in land warfare, no amphibious assault mission, and more subordinate to the Navy. Supporters of this approach argued that it offered a clear command structure, would be more efficient, and would allow better civilian control. Those who disagreed, including the Chief of Naval Operations, the Commandant of the Marine Corps, and some powerful members of Congress, insisted that centralization strengthened the Army at a time when the new atomic age was raising questions about the continued relevance of sustained land operations. They saw the centralization approach as an indirect way of protecting Army force structure and increasing its budget share even as its importance to the nation diminished.

Coordination: The Preferred Approach of the Navy and Marine Corps

The Navy and Marine Corps argued publicly and passionately that centralization posed a threat to civilian control and to military effectiveness. Internally, both services saw it as a direct challenge to their futures. The Navy feared losing its air arm to the new air force, and the Marine Corps sensed it would lose its identity if it lost the amphibious mission. To protect themselves, the Navy and Marine Corps sidestepped the military centralization issue by advocating a much broader, national approach based on interagency, national-security coordination.

They argued that enhanced national coordination would best serve the president and address the larger issues that had been raised: unity of command and unity of effort. The separate military departments and the JCS should, in this view, continue to function as they had during the war; even if Congress created a separate air force and associated military department, there would be no need to change what the services did. Instead, the president simply needed a mechanism to ease civilian-military coordination. This line of argumentation gave rise to a Navy–Marine Corps proposal to create a National Security Council (NSC) to take an all-of-government view of foreign policy; to institutionalize the JCS, but without a chairman; and to keep the military departments largely autonomous.

Unification Debate Resolution: The National Security Act of 1947

The unification debate raged in Washington for almost two years. Congress held a number of contentious hearings involving the service chiefs and the Commandant. President Truman repeatedly made clear that he preferred the Army's centralization approach; the Navy and the Marine Corps took their case to the Congress and the press and won public support. The Marine Corps in particular waged an all-out, public-relations battle to secure its post–World War II future. Ultimately, the sea services' approach largely shaped the legislation that emerged from this debate.

Despite his disappointment over the outcome of the debate, on July 26, 1947, Truman signed into law the National Security Act (figure 8-1). At the presidential level this legislation established structures, including the NSC, to coordinate and integrate national security policies.[1] Specifically to help the president oversee the military, the legislation brought the services together under a new rubric, the National Military Establishment (NME). The act stated that a secretary of defense (SECDEF) would be the head of the NME and serve as the "principal assistant to the President" on national security matters. However, the act defined the NME only vaguely, authorized the SECDEF virtually no staff, and left to the service secretaries, although now formally denied cabinet status, their privileged access to the president, as long as they informed the SECDEF first.

At the joint level, the legislation established formally the Joint Chiefs of Staff consisting of the Chief of Staff of the

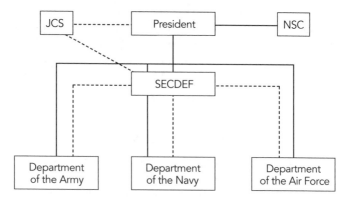

Figure 8-1. National Security Act, 1947:
National Military Establishment Relationships

Army, the new Chief of Staff of the Air Force (CSAF), and the Chief of Naval Operations. The Commandant of the Marine Corps was still excluded. Even more strikingly, the legislation failed to create a single head of the JCS, Admiral Leahy's de facto role. Instead, it designated *all* of the service chiefs as "principal military advisers to the President and Secretary of Defense."

At the service level, it renamed the Department of War the Department of the Army and created a separate Department of the Air Force, with its own service secretary, to oversee the newly independent U.S. Air Force. On one hand this legislation marked the culmination of the airpower advocates' dream of a separate air force. It gave the new service broad responsibility to conduct "prompt and sustained offensive and defensive air operations." However, it also allowed the Army, Navy, and Marine Corps to retain any service-specific, or organic, aviation necessary to perform their missions. This language set up an inevitable and enduring tension between the new Air Force and the three other services over which aviation forces should be operated by which service. Finally, the legislation rewarded the Marine Corps' campaign to protect its mission. It put into law the Marine Corps' primary responsibility for amphibious assault and seizure of advanced naval bases, thereby ensuring further friction with the Army.

The impact of National Security Act of 1947 continues to be debated. It created many of the national-security coordinating activities that remain in place today, including the NSC, the Air Force, the secretary of defense position, and the JCS. Concomitantly, it left control of the military decentralized, resting as before with the military departments and their associated services. Decentralization heightened the postwar competition among the services for mission and influence as resources became scarcer. Creating an independent air force, a fourth service, exacerbated this organizational competition. Thus, arguably, and ironically, rather than reducing interservice rivalry, the National Security Act of 1947 worsened it.

Service Roles and Missions Debate, 1947–1949

The next round in the interservice rivalry started immediately after passage of the 1947 National Security Act. As soon as he had signed the new legislation, President Truman issued Executive Order (EO) 9877, which assigned the four services their primary duties. These duties, known as "roles and missions," carried implied budgetary and administrative authority to execute them.

As a general rule, EO9877, like the National Security Act, assigned each service its roles and missions based on its principal physical environment: the Army was responsible for "prompt and sustained combat incident to operations on the land," the Navy for "prompt and sustained combat operations at sea" (to include sea control, although it had to coordinate with the Air Force on some air operations), the Air Force for "prompt and sustained air offensive and defensive operations," and the Marine Corps for the "seizure or defense of advanced naval bases and for the conduct of limited land operations in connection therewith." Navy and Marine Corps leaders vehemently objected that the executive order required the Navy to work more closely with the Air Force, left unclear the Navy's role in strategic air operations, and placed some limitations on Marine Corps responsibilities.

The Key West and Newport Conferences

In January 1948 the new secretary of defense, James Forrestal, directed the service leaders to solve the dispute among themselves and propose revised roles-and-missions language more consistent with the 1947 legislation. Unsurprisingly, the effort failed, so Forrestal convened a small conference in Key West, Florida, March 11–14, at which he and the Joint Chiefs would draft new language. The subsequent Key West Agreement allowed for the assignment of secondary roles and missions that would allay organizational fears and reassure all the services of their relevance. A month later President Truman rescinded EO9877, and on April 21, 1948, Forrestal issued in its place a new directive, "Functions of the Armed Forces and the Joint Chiefs of Staff," based on the Key West Agreement.

Any hope that the functions paper resolved key differences, however, was short-lived. Fierce interservice competition and distrust remained, especially between the Navy and the Air Force over responsibility for atomic weapons. Airmen insisted that "offensive air operations" meant sole authority to carry, and if necessary use, the atomic bomb. The Navy argued that it too needed the wherewithal to deliver atomic weapons if it was to fulfill its assigned role. A second conference convened at Newport, Rhode Island, August 20–22, 1948, to take on this and related issues. Participants again were limited to the secretary and the JCS. Among other things, the Newport conference supposedly clarified the definition of the Air Force's primary mission in a way that allowed the Navy to air-deliver atomic weapons against land targets from its aircraft carriers. To the Air Force, however, this provision proved unacceptable, calling into question its core airpower responsibility.

The B-36-versus-Supercarrier Controversy

This acrimonious debate between the Navy and the Air Force spilled into the public domain as the services fought over budgetary resources for modernization. The Chief of Naval Operations insisted that the Navy needed a "supercarrier" (informally, an aircraft carrier displacing 70,000 or more tons) capable of launching aircraft armed with atomic bombs to perform its primary sea missions. The Air Force's Chief of Staff responded that here was a clear duplication of the Air Force's primary air mission and that, in a time of limited defense funding, dollars should be spent on the B-36 intercontinental bombers instead. When Louis Johnson abruptly took over as secretary of defense on March 28, 1949, the controversy erupted publicly. Johnson had assumed office because Forrestal had suffered a nervous breakdown caused, at least in part, by the pressures of the secretaryship.[2] Truman directed Johnson to curb interservice rivalry and implement a much smaller defense budget. Less than three weeks after coming into office, Johnson questioned the JCS about the supercarrier's viability. The CNO and CSAF positions remained unchanged. The Army chief of staff sided largely with the Air Force, challenging the need for more aircraft carriers; that made two services to one. Johnson, after consulting with Truman but not the SECNAV, canceled the supercarrier on April 15, 1949.

The SECNAV promptly resigned, and the Navy's uniformed leadership, in what became known as the "revolt of the admirals," refused to accept Johnson's decision. Instead the admirals took their case public, seeking to convince the American people and Congress of the importance of the supercarrier. They also launched a bitter campaign against the B-36, criticizing the fundamental soundness of the aircraft and the Air Force's plan for operating it. The Navy's campaign prompted a series of high-stakes congressional hearings, which would grip the public's attention between August and October 1949. These hearings culminated in Congress' eventual endorsement of the B-36 as the primary delivery means for atomic bombs and the dismissal by Secretary Johnson of the Chief of Naval Operations.

Reform amidst Debate: The 1949 Amendment to the National Security Act

By this time, the roles-and-missions debates had highlighted the need to amend the original National Security Act. Early that year, Secretary Forrestal, an original supporter of coordination over centralization, had observed that his office's lack of authority not only fostered service rivalries but perpetuated budgetary inefficiencies at a time when the nation wanted to cut defense spending dramatically. Truman had readily agreed and backed Forrestal's call for new legislative action. Johnson, when he succeeded Forrestal, felt the challenges of his new position even more acutely and pursued legislative reform as well. Thus, even as the B-36-versus-supercarrier controversy approached its climax, Congress passed a modification to the original act; on August 10, 1949, Truman signed it into law.

The amendment addressed some of the most glaring shortcomings of the 1947 legislation: it abolished the NME and established a single cabinet-level Department of Defense (DOD) in its place; it downgraded all the military

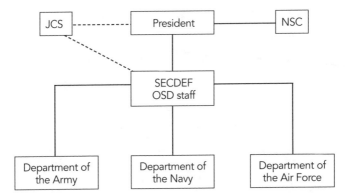

Figure 8-2. National Security Act, 1949 Amendment:
Department of Defense Relationships

departments to subcabinet level and subordinated them to the DOD; it gave the secretary of defense "direction, authority, and control" over the entire department and authorized a sizeable staff, with a deputy and assistants, to help the secretary exercise that responsibility; and it authorized the appointment of a chairman of the Joint Chiefs of Staff, albeit with limited authority over the rest of the JCS (table 8-1). In the aggregate, the amended legislation put in place some of the vital organizations and relationships that exist today.

By the time the B-36-versus-supercarrier controversy ended in October 1949, America's military and the nation it served were in a very different place than four years earlier. In those years, the nation had established its first new, independent military service since the founding of the republic. The Air Force brought with it not only new national capabilities but new sources of interservice competition, its existence upsetting a long-standing status quo with regard to basic service responsibilities. Dramatic decreases in defense spending aggravated these tensions. In the absence of an overarching national problem that demanded the attention of all the services, competition between them boiled over into acrimonious exchanges. Ostensibly the arguments concerned major programs (now generically referred to as "platforms") like

Table 8-1. Department of Defense, 1949 Amendment to National Security Act of 1947

	President			
Cabinet-Level Department/ *Secretary*	Department of Defense (1949) *Secretary of Defense* Chairman and JCS (advisory)‡			
Subcabinet-Level Military Departments/ *Civilian Secretary** *demoted from cabinet level (1949)	Department of Army/ *Secretary of Army*** **until 1947 called Department of War and Secretary of War	Department of Navy/ *Secretary of Navy*		Department of Air Force/ *Secretary of Air Force**** ***new military department and secretary (1947)
Military Services/ *Military Leaders*	U.S. Army/ *Chief of Staff, Army*	U.S. Navy/ *Chief of Naval Operations*	U.S. Marine Corps/ *Commandant Marine Corps*	U.S. Air Force/ *Chief of Staff, Air Force*

‡ JCS includes CJCS, CSA, CNO, and CSAF but not CMC.

bombers or aircraft carriers, but the debates actually went much deeper. They were fundamentally about how the services envisioned the evolving nature of the common defense and their specific roles in providing for it. At the most basic level, these debates reflected service organizational cultures and values—and associated insecurities as to how the nation viewed the services and assessed the continued relevance of each. Because of the scarcity of defense dollars, the budgets became the metric of the value to the nation of each service.

———

Service tensions and insecurities could well have erupted again, but by 1950 the Soviet Union had emerged as a significant threat to the ever-evolving common defense. A series of important activities and events led up to U.S. acknowledgment of this state of affairs. The now-famous Long Telegram sent to the State Department in 1946 by George Kennan, the American chargé d'affaires in Moscow, had warned of the difficulties posed by the Soviet Union and argued for the need to contain it. The 1947 Truman Doctrine outlined a foreign policy to stem the global spread of Soviet communism. By late June 1948, the Soviet Union had directly challenged the United States by blockading access to West Berlin; the U.S. military, especially the Air Force, had responded with an around-the-clock airlift to keep West Berlin supplied. The Berlin Airlift persisted until the Soviets reopened the main roads in May 1949. National Security Council Report 68, better known as NSC-68, presented to Truman in April 1950, concluded that Kennan's containment policy needed to be militarized and called for a tripling of defense spending. Finally, just two months after the issuing of NSC-68, North Korea invaded South Korea with the approval and help of the Soviet Union and China. Collectively, these events created a wholly new defense picture. Suddenly America found itself in a burgeoning Cold War with the Soviet Union and, in June 1950, at war on the Korean Peninsula. The four military services had struggled for mission, purpose, and money just a few years earlier; now they had all these in abundance.

Further Reading

Primary sources include: the National Security Act of 1947 and the National Security Act of 1947 as amended in 1949; NSC-68; and Executive Order 9877. Secondary sources include: Thomas Boettcher, *First Call: The Making of the Modern U.S. Military, 1945–1953*, 1992; Chambers, *Oxford Companion to American Military History*; Cohen, *Demystifying the Citizen Soldier*; Miller, *War Plan Orange*; Millet, *Semper Fidelis*; Millett, Maslowski, and Feis, *For the Common Defense*; Aaron O'Connell, *Underdogs: The Making of the Modern Marine Corps*, 2012; Parker, *Concise History of the Marine Corps*; Steven Rearden, *The Formative*

Years, 1984; Stewart, *American Military History*, vol. 2; Douglas Stuart, *Creating the National Security State*, 2008; Symonds, *U.S. Navy*; Weigley, *American Way of War*; Amy Zegart, *Flawed by Design*, 2000.

Containment and the
Emergence of Two Militaries

The Cold War, 1950–1973

NSC-68, Korea, and later Vietnam set the institutional boundaries for how the services would provide military options during the first decades of the Cold War. The containment doctrine ensured that America's common defense would remain overseas, pursued in ways firmly intertwined with friends and allies in Europe and Asia. But nuclear technology as well as the diverse nature of overseas commitments meant that containment placed some demands on the military that were different from those experienced during World War II. The Cold War was global, focused on stopping the spread of communism, but unlike in the world wars, the actual conflicts during the Cold War occurred in relatively small nations.

The Common Defense

Throughout these early decades of the Cold War, the services wrestled with one of the major questions raised at the end of World War II: How fundamental were nuclear weapons —the most revolutionary military weapons introduced since the founding of the republic—to America's postwar vision of the common defense and to the individual services? Competition occurred both among and within the services, its nature depending on how important their respective chiefs perceived the nuclear mission to be and the extent to which civilian leaders agreed with those assessments. In the end, America created a Janus-faced military to execute the containment strategy. There were, on one hand, nuclear forces;

these were concentrated in the Air Force and Navy and were meant to deter a major nuclear war with the Soviet Union. There were, on the other hand, also nonnuclear forces; these were intended to fight conflicts that emerged under the global nuclear umbrella.

The services offered different solutions to the multifaceted containment problem, based on a variety of factors: presidential direction, each service's understanding of its larger purpose and the role of nuclear weapons in fulfilling that purpose, each service's culture, and, more selfishly, the potential each saw for expanded missions and resources. The services' success in fulfilling their responsibilities varied over the decades. But by the time the United States withdrew from Vietnam in 1973, it was clear that the services had failed on some fundamental level. The military's reputation plummeted from its post–World War II glory to a nadir during Vietnam.

Organizational Responses

The Army

The Army's national prominence peaked during the nonnuclear, or conventional, conflicts in Korea and Vietnam. At the start of the Korean War, the drastically reduced U.S. Army numbered only 590,000 active-duty personnel—almost 5.5 million fewer soldiers than five years earlier. More importantly, rapid demobilization and the shift to nuclear weapons left the remaining Army units understrength and unprepared. Even the occupation forces in post–World War II Japan were unready; but when North Korea invaded the South in June 1950, these were some of the first units called into action, in a hastily assembled coalition under a United Nations mandate.

The early weeks of the Korean War revealed the depths of the Army's unpreparedness. By August U.S., South Korean, and other UN ground forces had fallen back to a perimeter around the southeastern port city of Pusan. There the Army units regrouped, received reinforcements, and reequipped. Army and Marine Corps forces in the perimeter, decisively aided by an aggressive amphibious operation in which the Navy put ashore an Army–Marine Corps landing force at Inchon, to the north just west of Seoul, eventually broke out in September 1950. They went on an offensive that subsequently took American and UN forces deep into North Korea. At that point, in October 1950, China entered the war; by January 1951 the Chinese had pushed the UN back south of the 38th parallel where the war had started. A stalemate ensued in this general area and continued until an armistice was signed in July 1953.

By that time, the Army had grown to twenty divisions and numbered about 1.5 million personnel, the increased numbers achieved by reinvigorating the draft and calling up reserves. Interestingly, with the exception of the use of helicopters in reconnaissance and medical evacuations ("medevacs," later made familiar to Americans by the movie and TV show *M*A*S*H*), the U.S. Army of the Korean War was remarkably similar to its World War II antecedent.

The absence of a decisive outcome in Korea did not bode well for the Army. Newly elected President Eisenhower and his key advisers concluded that proxy wars like Korea weakened the United States by undermining its economic strength. The administration decided to pursue instead what it called the New Look, a policy that heavily emphasized air-power and nuclear retaliation. Eisenhower's support of the New Look raised fundamental questions about the Army's continued relevance and precipitated an identity crisis for that service—an irony, Eisenhower having served a distinguished career as an Army officer. The fact that the Air Force represented the main challenge to the Army's relevance only deepened the irony: a decade ago the Air Force had been subordinate to, even a part of, the Army, but now it supplanted the Army in the eyes of many Americans.

Army leaders believed their service needed to find a place in the New Look. With respect to weapon systems, they chose to compete directly with the Air Force over the emerging guided-missile technology. The Army argued it needed guided surface-to-air missiles (SAMs) to fulfill its air-defense responsibilities, including protection of the United States itself. Its Chief of Staff, Gen. Maxwell Taylor, pointedly noted that the Air Force had "left the battlefield" in its pursuit of long-range bombers and supersonic fighters and could no longer be trusted to support soldiers on the ground; as a result, the Army, he argued, had to provide that support and protection itself. Moreover, it needed guided, shorter-range surface-to-surface missiles (SSMs) to prevail on expansive future battlefields, especially those on which the new North Atlantic Treaty Organization (NATO) might fight in Europe. With this logic, the Army won authority to pursue both SAM and SSM programs despite the Air Force's vehement protests that they violated the Key West Agreement.

For a short period in the late 1950s, the Army also looked to increase its own reliance on nuclear weapons, actually redesigning its organizational structure to accommodate tactical nuclear weapons. The resulting concept proved one of the oddest in the Army's history—the pentomic division. Smaller overall than its predecessors, the pentomic division consisted of five battle groups (basically expanded battalions) and was specifically structured for "dispersion, flexibility, and mobility" on a nuclear battlefield. The Army even staged exercises using actual nuclear weapons to demonstrate that pentomic ground forces could both employ them and fight through enemy nuclear detonations.

This radical change carried with it profound implications for the soldiers and how they understood what the Army and nation expected from them. However, before the Army could address, let alone fully understand, these implications, the Eisenhower administration gave way to the John F. Kennedy administration and the New Look gave way to Flexible Response. Amidst these leadership and policy changes, the pentomic division quickly disappeared.

Flexible Response allowed the Army to return to some of the basics of land warfare. Kennedy wanted a way to challenge the spread of communism that was cheaper, non-nuclear, and more nuanced than sole reliance on nuclear weapons. In this Kennedy had been inspired by General Taylor's 1960 book *The Uncertain Trumpet*, a critique of recent U.S. strategic policy; he had taken note especially of the threat of communist guerrilla insurgencies.[1] Kennedy had concluded that the best way to oppose communism was to provide military assistance to national governments friendly to the United States and under attack by communist guerrillas. Military assistance would be in the form of small, elite Army units that would train and equip a host nation's forces to wage a counterinsurgency (COIN) campaign. Thus, Kennedy's Flexible Response replaced primary reliance on nuclear weapons with reinvigoration of conventional land warfare capabilities like infantry and armor and the creation of special military forces devoted to military assistance.

President Kennedy's interest in COIN operations marked the moment when the Army's modern special forces came into their own. The Army had retained its various special forces, albeit in much smaller numbers, after World War II and even established the Special Warfare Center at Fort Bragg, North Carolina, in the early 1950s. Special Forces, as they were known officially after 1952, managed to avoid the most debilitating effects of the Army's post-Korea focus on nuclear warfare, continuing to hone their expertise in counterinsurgency and the training of foreign militaries. Although they believed themselves elite in training and mission, the Army's leadership refused to recognize them as such, for fear of undermining esprit in the rest of the Army. Kennedy, however, disagreed. During his October 12, 1961, visit to the Special Warfare Center, Kennedy authorized Special Forces soldiers to wear distinctive green berets. With that gesture, he turned the Army's Special Forces into the legendary Green Berets.

The Green Berets soon found themselves at the vanguard of Kennedy's COIN effort. In the early 1960s, constant demand for their expertise led to their expansion to allow them to provide military assistance around the globe, most notably in Vietnam. As this Vietnamese assistance effort morphed into a combat mission, the Green Berets were complemented by another elite force, the Rangers, who, as they had since World War II, routinely made long-range patrols into enemy territory. Green Berets and Rangers ultimately made up only a small part of America's army in Vietnam numerically, but their performance ensured continued support for such elite units after the war ended.

Beyond special operations forces, the vastly increased role of helicopters emerged as one of the Army's most remarkable conventional innovations. In Korea helicopters had revolutionized medical evacuations from the battlefield; in the next decade the Army experimented with using them to support its soldiers and increase their mobility and firepower. The Army's expansion of its air arm to deliver troops to the battlefield and then protect them implied a further criticism of the Air Force's willingness to provide mobility and close air support for ground troops. The reconstitution, over the Air Force's protestations, of the Army's 1st Cavalry Division as an air-mobile formation during Vietnam suggested the Army had won its case to develop its own aviation. The 1st Cavalry had about 15,000 soldiers, and it was armed and equipped much more lightly than an infantry division. Its well over four hundred helicopters moved its soldiers and their equipment, provided direct fire support, and performed medevacs in combat.[2]

By 1971 the Army's helicopters numbered over 9,500. The Army's reliance on helicopters revolutionized its approach to warfare in Vietnam as much as the jeep and tank had revolutionized the battlefields of World War II. Nevertheless, the helicopter's centrality to combat operations heightened tension between the Army and the Air Force over roles and responsibilities. Army organizational integration of guided missiles over the previous two decades had also strained the now aging Key West Agreement. However, a national loss of confidence in the military, especially the Army, during Vietnam dwarfed these internecine conflicts. After a decade of fighting, billions of dollars in defense spending, and over 58,000 killed in action, the U.S. military left Vietnam in 1973 defeated and in disarray.

The Air Force

Almost from the moment of its independence, the Air Force emerged as the Army's biggest challenger for roles and budget. In the first half of the Cold War, the Air Force committed itself to becoming the nation's predominant nuclear service. Its organizational logic went like this: first, nuclear weapons revolutionized warfare; second, the Air Force's bombers carried these weapons; third, long-range strategic bombing was the Air Force's foundational mission; fourth, therefore, long-range strategic nuclear bombing was central to the Air Force's purpose. If the nation's civilian leadership accepted this logic, the newest military service would not only surpass the Army but become the nation's preeminent military service. However, given this focus on the nuclear mission, conventional capabilities mattered only to the extent they supported the nuclear ones. Paradoxically then, the Air Force found itself well prepared for the Cold War with the Soviet Union but poorly prepared for the limited conventional wars in Korea and Vietnam.

By the start of the Korean War, and consistent with Truman's endorsement of NSC-68, the expansion of the Air Force's strategic bomber force was well under way. The Strategic Air Command (SAC), created in December 1946, predated the formal establishment of the U.S. Air Force. When Gen. Curtis LeMay took over as SAC's commander in 1948, he began an aggressive campaign to turn it into an elite combat-ready, strategic nuclear bombing force. With the establishment of NATO in April 1949, the Soviet Union was clearly the presumed adversary of this nuclear force, and the United States for the first time explicitly linked its security interests to those of Western Europe. Under LeMay, SAC quickly became known for its hair-trigger alert status and its frontline role as the nation's dominant strategic deterrent against the Soviet Union. The Air Force prioritized deterrence of Soviet attacks against the United States and NATO above all other missions. Thus, even at the height of the Korean War, a significant number of Air Force aircraft remained in the United States or Europe solely for the nuclear mission.

Truman had made it clear that no nuclear weapons would be used on the Korean Peninsula and that no strikes beyond Korea's borders would be approved. Airmen in Korea accordingly found themselves waging a limited war, not preparing for the unrestricted nuclear conflagration SAC envisioned. As a result, as a group they did much less strategic bombing and more air superiority (controlling the air), interdiction of supply lines, and close air support to the ground forces. For these tasks, they frequently had the wrong aircraft. With the notable exception of the new F-86 jet fighter, they flew either obsolete World War II aircraft or new jets designed to escort long-range nuclear bombers. In short, the airmen who fought in this conventional, limited air war in Korea experienced a much different Air Force than did their SAC counterparts.

For some years after the Korean War ended, Eisenhower's New Look ensured that the Air Force received the bulk of the budget for nuclear deterrence. Where the Army floundered in this environment, the Air Force flourished. SAC's requirements, in particular, received priority throughout the 1950s, leading to the rapid modernization of the Air Force's nuclear bomber force, culminating in the purchase of hundreds of B-52s starting in the mid-1950s. In addition, the Air Force procured hundreds of KC-135 (modified civilian Boeing 707s) air-fueling aircraft, or tankers, capable of refueling these B-52s in flight so they could attack anywhere in the world. As nuclear weapons became smaller, SAC even added nuclear-capable fighter aircraft to its force. The Air Force also expanded its basing structure, especially at home and in Europe, to accommodate this expanded force and mission.

As the Soviet Union developed significant nuclear capabilities of its own, American policy makers began to question the nation's reliance on the bomber as the sole deterrent. Civilian Air Force leaders urged the development of nuclear-tipped missiles for the deterrent force. Over the objections of General LeMay, the Air Force began to develop such a weapon, an intercontinental ballistic missile (ICBM), to compete with those of the Soviet Union. By 1960 the Air Force had twelve Atlas ICBMs stationed in the United States and the Minuteman ICBM under development. On the one hand, both represented major technological accomplishments. On the other hand, less than fifteen years after the Air Force's institutional independence, civilian leaders had directed the creation of an unmanned system to perform a deterrent mission that, if executed properly, would mean the ICBMs would never be used. Through this lens, LeMay's reluctance to add missiles to the Air Force's inventory of weapons made sense: they diverted resources and diluted the strategic bombing mission.

The Air Force was forging close, enduring ties with key intelligence agencies in these years, especially the Central Intelligence Agency and the National Security Agency. Most notably, in conjunction with the CIA, it experimented with a variety of means to collect intelligence on the Soviet Union. This effort led to the development of such new reconnaissance planes as the U-2 and SR-71 and the modification of existing booster rockets to launch surveillance satellites into space. The Air Force pursued the space mission so aggressively that the Department of Defense had designated it as its "executive agent" for space by the early 1960s. Indeed, adaptation to changing nuclear, missile, and space technologies, as well as those of aeronautics, appeared a promising way for the Air Force to secure its own niche among the services. However, as the war in Vietnam expanded, it reminded Air Force leaders what Korea had first taught them—the requirements for confrontation with the Soviet Union were fundamentally different from those of limited war.

In Vietnam, once again the Air Force entered the skies with aircraft largely unsuited to the conflict. Although fighters improved over the course of the war, at its start, the main ones had been designed for war with the Soviet Union. The F-105, for example, had been created to deliver a single nuclear bomb at low altitude. The F-4, one of the more successful Air Force fighter aircraft in Vietnam, had been initially designed for the Navy; the Air Force had adopted it only when directed to do so by Secretary of Defense Robert McNamara. As in Korea, these fighters were used for establishing air superiority, interdicting supply lines, and providing close air support. But these demanding missions proved even more difficult than they should have been because of unsuitable equipment and lack of training. Collectively, these factors added credibility to the Army's accusations of inadequate Air Force support. The issue was especially acute when it came to interdicting the flow of personnel along North Vietnam's principal supply route, the Ho Chi Minh Trail.

The Air Force used B-52s to bomb targets in North Vietnam but, again as in Korea, the conventional strategic bombing campaign produced inconclusive results. Finally, Vietnam highlighted the need for effective cargo transport capability, or airlift. To meet this need, the Air Force developed an impressive global capability to move American ground personnel and their supplies to Vietnam, and then within Vietnam (where jungles made road travel difficult) with its C-130 turboprop transports, capable of operating from unprepared runways. The Air Force's Military Airlift Command (MAC) came into its own during this conflict.

Overall, air operations in Vietnam left Air Force leaders dissatisfied with their service's performance. But these same leaders frequently placed the responsibility elsewhere. They believed that much of the Air Force's ineffectiveness in Vietnam (and Korea) had stemmed from the failure of civilian leaders to grasp the importance of unleashing airpower if they wanted to win wars. Arguably, the Air Force left Vietnam the most bifurcated of all the services: airmen who operated in the conventional, fighter-oriented force largely concerned themselves with the demands of limited war, those on the nuclear and fledgling space side focused on strategic deterrence. Only infrequently did these two realms intermix. Not surprisingly, these factions started to compete for influence and resources as Vietnam faded in memory.

The Navy

The Korean War quickly brought the Navy out of its "post–revolt of the admirals" doldrums. Like the other services it benefited from a rapid influx of resources, even restoration of the supercarrier to its shipbuilding budget. Operationally, North Korea's limited naval capabilities allowed the U.S. Navy to cruise in the seas off Korea with impunity. This meant it could use its carrier-based aircraft for interdiction and close air support ashore, as the Air Force did. Its control of the sea also allowed the Navy to execute the landing at Inchon. Nevertheless, the Navy, like the Air Force, saw itself as playing a supporting role to the ground forces during the Korean War, the Navy's primary mission of winning and retaining command of the seas being moot.

As the Cold War tensions grew in the 1950s, American lawmakers increased the Navy's budget and expanded its global presence. The Navy used its additional resources, in part, to support the recently established Sixth Fleet, in the Mediterranean. This new fleet's emphasis was on readiness to project its sea-based airpower ashore to deter Soviet aggression. By the mid-1950s it would also be capable of air-delivering nuclear weapons from its carriers at sea. Remarkably, just a few years after the revolt of the admirals one of the service's most important organizational developments in the 1950s was the rise of the nuclear Navy, spearheaded by Adm. Hyman Rickover.

Admiral Rickover devoted himself single-mindedly to bringing nuclear-powered propulsion to the Navy, especially to the submarine fleet. Nuclear power would exponentially improve the survivability of submarines by allowing them to operate submerged for weeks, even months, at a time rather than the few days possible with diesel-electric power. Through a mix of engineering and bureaucratic brilliance, Rickover obtained permission to build the USS *Nautilus*, the world's first nuclear-powered submarine, in 1951. Launched in 1954, she went on to set several records for endurance and survivability. In Rickover's view, the *Nautilus* demonstrated the immense potential of nuclear-powered submarines: they would quickly become integral to the U.S. Navy's strategy to control the seas, since they could attack any Soviet ship at will.

However, the new CNO, Adm. Arleigh Burke, saw another important application for these nuclear-powered submarines—as nuclear-missile carriers. Burke's vision reflected the convergence of a number of factors. First, the Soviet Union had just launched the world's first sea-launched ballistic missile (SLBM), from a converted, diesel-powered submarine. This development fed fears in policy circles that the U.S. Navy was falling behind its Soviet counterpart. Second, SLBMs offered senior American civilian policy makers another alternative to ensure the survival of the U.S.

nuclear arsenal and thus deter a Soviet nuclear attack. Third, SLBMs represented an opportunity for the Navy to reclaim a significant portion of the nuclear mission from the Air Force. Just five years later, in 1960, the Navy launched the USS *George Washington*, its first fleet ballistic-missile submarine, armed with sixteen Polaris SLBMs. The *George Washington* represented the "third leg" of a nuclear triad: nuclear-armed bombers, land-based ICBMs, and SSBNs. Thus, the now-canonical nuclear triad emerged from a series of incremental policy debates and bureaucratic competitions, not a sweeping strategic concept of nuclear deterrence.

The conventional surface Navy returned to the public's attention with the Kennedy administration's shift to Flexible Response in the 1960s. The partial naval blockade of Cuba during the 1962 missile crisis was one of its most famous moments on the national stage. As the 1960s progressed and the Vietnam War expanded, the Navy returned to traditional roles like power projection ashore and added emphasis to others, including coastal patrol, riverine warfare, and special operations.

As it had in the Korean War, naval power projection ashore consisted of launching carrier-based aircraft to strike strategic targets (this time, in North Vietnam), interdict supply lines (especially along the Ho Chi Minh Trail), and provide close-air and naval-gunfire support to ground forces. Collectively, these constituted the largest and most visible of the Navy's contributions to the war. In addition, other smaller surface vessels tried to prevent supplies from flowing to enemy forces along the South Vietnamese coast and to interdict enemy communications and supply in the vast Mekong Delta. Riverine operations involved small gunboats that more closely resembled pleasure craft than warships. As so often in Vietnam, the enemy remained elusive, and consequently, so was a useful assessment of the overall impact of these "brown-water," or inshore, operations.

Finally, the Vietnam War witnessed the resurgence of special operations in the Navy. Responding to President Kennedy's call for an increased emphasis on unconventional warfare, the Navy reinvigorated its special-warfare capabilities, which dated back to the frogmen of World War II, by formally establishing SEAL teams on January 1, 1962. SEAL members underwent specialized, demanding training before entering operational units. Fully qualified SEALs, organized in two teams at that time, went on to distinguish themselves in counterguerrilla, advisory, scouting, direct action (e.g., damaging, capturing, or destroying a specific target), and rescue missions in Vietnam and neighboring Laos and Cambodia. Once the war ended, however, the nation eagerly left COIN warfare behind, and the SEALs struggled for resources and relevance.

The Navy, in some ways even more than the Air Force, was a divided organization during this era. For example, from a nonnuclear perspective, it found the Vietnam War frustrating and disheartening. Decisive engagements proved elusive, the sustained operations simultaneously demanding and broadly debilitating. The latter is perhaps best exemplified by a race riot on board the USS *Kitty Hawk* off the coast of Vietnam in 1972. Restoration to health of the surface Navy clearly needed leadership, time, and resources. The nuclear-submarine Navy, on the other hand, emerged from the Vietnam War in decent shape because, paradoxically, it had been deterring the Soviet Union all that time, not fighting a counterinsurgency. Rebalancing the Navy's submarine, surface, and air forces would be a priority in the years after Vietnam.

The Marine Corps

Only the Marine Corps shunned the idea of making nuclear weapons central to its purpose and doctrine during the Cold War. What experimentation it did with tactical nuclear weapons focused on amphibious assault in a nuclear environment. Other than that, nuclear weapons remained ancillary to providing the nation a force-in-readiness expert in amphibious warfare. As a result, and unlike the other services, the Korean War and its aftermath fit easily into the Marine Corps' long-standing narrative of battlefield prowess and success. To Marines, Korea would be anything but "the forgotten war."

Marine Corps lore about its role in the Korean War began with MacArthur's request early in the war that the Corps rush a brigade from the United States to Pusan to shore up the perimeter. This brigade was instrumental in stopping the enemy's advance and then spearheading the breakout. Shortly thereafter, the 1st Marine Division played a conspicuous part in the daring amphibious landing at Inchon that pushed the North Korean army back almost to the Chinese border. This division ultimately conducted one of the most epic withdrawals in modern military history, from the Chosin Reservoir area, when Chinese forces flooded into North Korea to stop the UN advance. The doggedness and courage Marines displayed during this withdrawal encapsulated the Marine experience in Korea. It seemed, at least to the American public, that the Marine Corps was fighting at a higher level than the other services.

The Marine Corps worked hard to capitalize on this reputation. It celebrated its prowess, calling attention to its battlefield performance on Capitol Hill, to the press, and in Hollywood. Indeed, at the height of the Korean War, Marine leaders heavily lobbied congressional supporters to draft legislation to protect the Marine Corps institutionally and elevate its status within the Department of the Navy. President Truman's signing of Public Law 416 on June 28, 1952, further amending the National Security Act of 1947, rewarded their efforts. It laid down that the Fleet Marine Force (as its operating elements were collectively known) would consist of a minimum of three divisions and three air wings; that the Marine Corps' assigned roles and missions were distinct from the Navy's; that the Commandant of the Marine Corps was on a coequal footing with the CNO within the Department of the Navy; and that the Commandant could sit on, and vote as a member of, the JCS on all matters related to the Marine Corps. As the war ended and the Army experienced another existential crisis and the Navy and Air Force embraced nuclear weapons, this legislation gave the Marine Corps equal standing among the services.

In the decade after the Korean War, Marine Corps leaders expected that the Corps, as an effective amphibious force-in-readiness, would be protected institutionally from dismemberment to support the other services. Culturally, the role was well suited to the Marine Corps, which eschewed not only nuclear weapons but what it categorized as the technological, managerial approach to war that the other services had adopted.

Part of its program was permanently stationing Marines overseas, especially on Okinawa, where those in Korea were moved after the war. Even more essential to this shift was a critical decision taken in 1954 to adopt officially the Marine air-ground task force for use whenever Marines deployed outside the United States. Under this structure, in any crisis around the globe to which Marines responded, a single MAGTF commander would be responsible for all the Marine air, ground, and support elements involved. The air element would fly close air support, and the support element would supply the ground element until other services could bring reinforcements. The MAGTF proved tailor-made for the low-level, shorter-duration contingencies that were to come and that the other services believed belonged to the past. Once the capability existed, presidents found it highly valuable because of the flexibility it offered. Thus, Marines found themselves in great demand throughout the 1950s for contingencies in places like Lebanon, Taiwan, Ceylon, and Venezuela.

The innovative integration of helicopters into the MAGTF's air element was one of the reasons the MAGTF was so versatile. Originally the Marine Corps experimented with the helicopter for amphibious operations during a nuclear attack. But it was the helicopter's potential to move Marines from specially configured ships to shore that captivated the imaginations of their leaders. Amphibious landing craft remained essential to moving forces ashore, but helicopters offered an option to move them quickly.

By the end of the 1950s, the MAGTF was an integral part of Marine Corps operations. In 1962, doctrine was issued that specified different types of MAGTFs. They would range from the smallest, the Marine expeditionary unit, built around a battalion and a helicopter squadron; to the Marine expeditionary brigade, composed of a regiment and a Marine air group with helicopters and close-air-support aircraft; to the largest, the Marine expeditionary force, organized around a minimum of a division and a Marine air wing.

In the early days of Vietnam, the versatility and importance of the MAGTF were again on display. When in March 1965, President Lyndon B. Johnson authorized the first substantial commitment of ground forces to protect the Da Nang air base, a MEB landed to meet this requirement. As the military presence in Vietnam grew, the Marine Corps easily scaled up the MEB to a MEF, which would grow to almost 86,000 Marines at the height of the conflict. The Marine Corps, however, had a tougher time accepting the overall strategy for conducting the war. Gen. William Westmoreland, U.S. Army, commander of the Military Assistance Command, Vietnam (MACV), believed a conventional, large-unit strategy would win the war. Marine Corps leaders disagreed, seeing the conflict as a counterinsurgency problem that required intensive pacification efforts. This disagreement never fully resolved itself during the war; the Marine Corps supported Westmoreland's strategy when necessary but pursued its own strategic approach when it could.

As befitted the first force into Vietnam, the Marine Corps was also the first service out. Once President Richard M. Nixon announced the national withdrawal in 1969, the Marine Corps argued that it should redeploy soonest so it could return to its amphibious mission and rebuild its readiness to respond to other crises. It carried this argument, and by July 1971, only five hundred Marines remained in Vietnam. For the first time since the Civil War, however, a war had failed to burnish the Marine Corps' reputation. The same racial tensions and drug problems that were tearing apart the other services afflicted the Marine Corps as well. Restoring its luster in the eyes of policy makers and of the American public as *the* tough combat-ready, first-to-fight force emerged as a key objective in the post-Vietnam era.

Personnel and Training

By pre–World War II standards, even after the dramatic drawdowns at the end of that war, the armed forces remained huge. The late 1940s peacetime military was approximately five times larger than its 1938 peacetime antecedent. The active-duty ranks in the late 1940s and through the end of the Vietnam War were filled from three sources: volunteers; coerced volunteers who joined to avoid being drafted, usually into the Army; and conscripts (table 9-1).

Volunteers

Recruiting of volunteers continued in local recruiting stations around the country. For the most part, the Navy, Air Force, and Marine Corps met their personnel needs by enlisting volunteers seeking either to serve or simply to avoid the Army. The first two services tended to stress to potential recruits the building of technical skills, travel, and advanced education. The Marine Corps focused on building tough, first-to-fight warriors out of a soft civilian culture. The Army also sought volunteers but given its size and competition from other services, it ultimately relied on the draft.

Conscription

Congress allowed the draft to lapse for a short time during the rapid drawdown after World War II, but escalation of the Cold War brought it back in 1948. President Truman and General Marshall had both preferred a Universal

Table 9-1. Active-Duty Military Personnel, 1950–1970

	Army	Air Force	Navy	Marine Corps	Total
1950	593,000	411,000	382,000	74,000	1,460,000
1953	1,500,000	974,000	808,000	246,000	3,528,000
1955	1,110,000	960,000	661,000	205,000	2,936,000
1960	873,000	815,000	617,000	171,000	2,476,000
1965	963,000	825,000	670,000	190,000	2,648,000
1970	1,300,000	791,000	691,000	260,000	3,042,000

Source: dmdc.osd.mil

Military Training (UMT) program: all eligible males would undergo several months of military training followed by a six-year stint in the reserves, producing a reserve ready in times of emergency to augment a relatively small standing force. Strong congressional and public opposition to UMT, however, ultimately prevented its implementation. Instead, Congress passed a new Selective Service Act in 1948 requiring all men eighteen or older to register for the draft. In the first two years, only about 30,000 men were actually inducted into the military, a paltry number compared with the millions conscripted in World War II.

Once the Korean War started, personnel needs increased dramatically. Some of these needs were met by calling up part-time military members in the reserve and National Guard. In addition, the number of conscripts rose steeply, ultimately to over 1.5 million. Most conscripts served in the Army; volunteers, 1.3 million of them, joined the Navy and Air Force. After Korea, the draft continued during Eisenhower's presidency, but relatively few conscripts entered the military and none died in combat. When the United States decided to build up ground forces in Vietnam, the draft administratively remained in place but had been used sparsely since the Korean War.

To expand the U.S. military's presence in Vietnam, however, Johnson decided to rely on the draft rather than call up a large number of reserve or National Guard units. Those who wanted to avoid ground duty in Vietnam knew to join the reserves, volunteer for the Navy or Air Force, or seek draft deferments. Of the almost 1.9 million men conscripted during the war, the vast majority went into the Army, especially the infantry. As a result, draftees suffered a disproportionate percentage of battlefield casualties. By 1966–67 widespread public protests against the Vietnam War had made it clear that Johnson had exceeded any national consensus in support of a draft. Six years later, on January 27, 1973, the day the Nixon administration announced the Vietnam cease-fire, conscription formally ended, and the All-Volunteer-Force era commenced.

The Reserve Component

The reserve component fell into disarray during the first decades of the Cold War. The rapid exodus of personnel after World War II made it immensely difficult to fill reserve ranks, much less bring them to combat effectiveness. Activation of the Air Force's reserve components compounded these challenges. The newly independent Air Force saw no value in part-time reserve forces and had fought vigorously against their establishment. But political pressure compelled it to create both an Air Force Reserve to fulfill assigned federal roles and an Air National Guard (ANG) for dual federal and state responsibilities.

Not surprisingly, given all these limitations, the reserve components performed poorly at the start of the Korean War. They were understrength and poorly trained; the ANG was considered nothing more than a subsidized flying club. As the war progressed these components increased in combat effectiveness, but their contributions remained minimal. Volunteer reservists and National Guardsmen accounted for only 1.5 percent of all Army soldiers on active duty, and most of the Air Guardsmen simply augmented active-duty units.

After Korea, both the reserves and the Guard turned their attention to responding to domestic crises. When the buildup of ground forces started in Vietnam, the military leadership expected an activation of the reserve component, as had been done for Korea. Johnson's 1965 decision to rely on draftees instead delayed even partial mobilization of the one-million-member reserve component until 1968. In that year, he called up about 600 naval reservists, 9,300 Air Guardsmen, and 4,900 air reservists. Activations from the Army reserve component were conspicuously absent. Later in 1968 Johnson directed the callup of about 25,000 more reservists, this time including the Army's, of which 7,000 ultimately went to Vietnam. The insignificance of the reserves' presence in Vietnam predictably earned them a reputation, especially among Army and Air National Guard, as a refuge for people avoiding the draft and the war.

Integration

The proportion of Americans eligible to serve in the active and reserve ranks increased under President Truman, a reflection of larger changes in American society. In 1948 Truman signed two executive orders, the first eliminating racial segregation in the armed forces and the second allowing women to become full-time, permanent members. On one level, racial integration proceeded quite quickly, accelerated by the draft and the demands of the Korean War. By the war's end in 1953, the military could, on paper, claim to have integrated its enlisted ranks successfully, though the officer corps remained almost all white. Below the surface, however, tensions simmered throughout the 1950s; they boiled over in the 1960s, largely paralleling the trajectory of the broader civil rights movement. In the most acute cases, raw racial tensions exploded into riots onboard ships and various military bases, rendering some units combat-ineffective. Only with the end of the Vietnam War and the simultaneous termination of the draft did the military leadership address these profound racial issues. As will be discussed in the next chapter, the viability of the All-Volunteer Force depended on their resolution.

Women also saw an increased opportunity to serve during the early decades of the Cold War. Truman signed the Women's Armed Services Integration Act in 1948, which, while it did not dramatically increase the military's overall personnel pool, allowed women to serve as career, active-duty service members for the first time. Career women continued to serve almost exclusively in medical corps or in administrative positions, in part because the legislation excluded them from serving on any ship or flying any aircraft that might become involved in combat. They were also excluded from the general-officer and flag ranks until the late 1960s. But even with these limitations, the legislation allowed women to make gradual inroads.

Training

Despite changes on the technological and personnel fronts, the services' overall approaches to basic training remained mostly consistent with their World War II models. As mentioned earlier, the services adjusted advanced training to account for new battlefield technology, most notably nuclear weapons, as well as expanded missions, most notably counterinsurgency. As a newly independent service, the U.S. Air Force faced the biggest training challenge, having no codified scheme for basic and advanced training. For the most part, it proceeded by centralizing basic training at Lackland Air Force Base in Texas and maintaining its large number of pilot-training bases. Perhaps most symbolically, in 1955 Congress authorized the U.S. Air Force Academy, outside Colorado Springs, Colorado, as the Air Force's counterpart to West Point and Annapolis.

Military Professionalism versus "Occupationalism"

Less tangibly, the dramatic technological change driven by the nuclear revolution started to change how service members viewed themselves, even in some cases to erode the traditional military ethos. An uneasy malaise afflicted portions of the Army, Navy, and the Air Force in the 1950s as service members saw themselves more as managers of technology than masters of organized violence. This led some to argue that service in the military was just another civilian occupation, albeit one that required a uniform. The Marine Corps fought off this demoralization by keeping its boot camp tough, intensely physical, and unforgiving; and by constantly training to keep the Corps the nation's force-in-readiness. Despite the infamous 1956 Ribbon Creek incident at Parris Island, where six recruits died when a drill instructor marched his platoon into a swamp, the Marine Corps did not change its fundamental approach to training, and certainly not the violence-based ethos that underpinned it.

Organizational Integration

On paper, compared to World War II, organizational integration across the services improved during the first decades of the Cold War. The Joint Chiefs of Staff met regularly to provide military advice to the president and secretary of defense on defense issues of the day (after 1952 including the

Commandant on matters impacting his service).[3] Moreover, the postwar Outline Command Plan, soon renamed the Unified Command Plan (UCP), went through a series of revisions aimed at identifying the missions or geographic regions critical enough to require "unified" (joint) or "specified" commands.[4]

In reality, however, JCS members found it impossible to rise above their service interests or to delegate management of their services to their vice chiefs in order to focus on national problems. Only the chairman, by dint of his position, could free himself from parochial constraints. Eisenhower, in fact, did everything he could to strengthen the CJCS. But, despite some legislative changes, the chairman never received special sway over the rest of the JCS—his advisory authority was only equal to that of the service chiefs.

Commanders of the unified and specified commands, too, were closely tied to their services and exercised uneven authority over their subordinate commanders from the other services during this period. This shortcoming helps explain why the services took individual and poorly aligned approaches to the Korean and Vietnam conflicts. Even in nuclear planning, the Air Force and the Navy formulated separate targeting plans initially. Only in 1960, after being forcefully prodded by President Eisenhower and two successive secretaries of defense, did they agree to the establishment of a Joint Strategic Target Planning Staff (JSTPS), responsible for producing the nuclear Single Integrated Operational Plan (SIOP) and reporting directly to the SAC commander.

Thus, despite the best efforts of General Marshall, President Truman, President Eisenhower, and others to achieve better unity of command among the services, little discernible progress had been made in joint operations almost three decades after World War II. Several factors contributed to this state of affairs. Certainly, services had legitimate disagreements over strategy, policy, and proper balance within the military force structure—questions that nuclear weapons and the emergence of the independent Air Force only compounded. But other factors also came into play, such as strong service organizational cultures that eschewed change, especially if it came at the expense of institutional independence; powerful constituencies on Capitol Hill willing to protect service interests; and incentive structures that encouraged service leaders to respond to service needs. Whatever the explanation, when the military withdrew from Vietnam it left having fought a disjointed, service-focused war.

Civilian Control

During the early decades of the Cold War, each president in his own way exercised energetically his constitutional authority as commander in chief. In addition to defense reform, Truman directly involved himself in the formulation of the Korean War strategy, ultimately firing General MacArthur when he refused to accept Truman's limited-war parameters. Eisenhower, of course, brought deep military expertise to the presidency. Like Truman, he used his prerogatives to push defense reform, tying force structure to national policy even at the cost of budgetary imbalance among the services. He also attempted to limit the peacetime size and budget of the military, fearing that an informal alliance between the military and industry would give rise to a self-serving military-industrial complex. Kennedy quickly became exasperated with the parochial nature of the Joint Chiefs and, unlike Eisenhower, chose to work around them. Poor counsel he received from the JCS during the Bay of Pigs debacle, in particular, convinced him that he needed to look elsewhere for military advice. Kennedy turned most notably to Gen. Maxwell Taylor, now retired, using him as a special adviser before recalling him to active duty as Chairman of the Joint Chiefs of Staff. Johnson exercised his role as commander in chief both in his decision against mobilization and in his choice to involve himself in operational details. Finally, Nixon, among other things, elevated his national security adviser, Henry Kissinger, to the stature of an alternative authority on defense matters as well as foreign policy.

Congress, for its part, exerted control over the military through its traditional legislative, especially budgetary, initiatives, and additional defense reform legislation it passed through the 1950s. It also used its legislative authority for narrower ends. For example, it insisted on creating an Air National Guard as well as an air reserve to ensure that the states directly benefited from the creation of an Air Force, and its 1952 defense legislation specifically protected the Marine Corps. Also noteworthy from a civilian-control perspective is that the presidents did not seek, nor did Congress insist on, declarations of war for either Korea or Vietnam.

Perhaps the least heralded, yet most disruptive, exercise of civilian control of the military came with the expansion and empowerment of the Office of the Secretary of Defense (OSD). By leveraging the various defense reform acts, as early as 1950 OSD had begun to transform itself from a small, personal staff directly supporting the secretary of defense into an expanding executive staff overseeing departmental affairs. This expanded staff included a deputy secretary and assistant secretaries with line responsibilities for budget, policy, public affairs, and legislative matters. In a similar fashion, formal and informal boards established during World War II to address issues like health, logistics, and research and development were brought under OSD and assumed line functions as well. This transformation happened gradually through the 1950s as successive secretaries used their congressionally expanded authority to grapple with the vastness and complexity of their responsibilities.

When Robert McNamara became secretary of defense in 1961, however, he quickly and significantly increased OSD's authority further. He believed this action essential to helping the president exercise civilian control. Specifically, he wanted to increase the department's efficiency and effectiveness by centralizing key activities in OSD. Centralization under the secretary of defense, moreover, meant a proportionate reduction in the military services' power and autonomy. McNamara employed a host of civilian experts in OSD, the "Whiz Kids," to force the department to accept new business practices, perform systems analyses, and adopt an integrated Planning, Programming, and Budgeting System (PPBS). By the time McNamara left office in 1968, his management revolution had had such effect that, whoever served as secretary of defense, OSD would have the power to intervene forcefully in areas where the military services believed it had no business. Starting with McNamara's term, OSD encroached on the services' traditional prerogatives in ways unimaginable to its Department of War and Department of the Navy antecedents.

Impact on the Common Defense

For the first time in the twentieth century, the American military of the Cold War could not demonstrate a firm and stable ability to provide for the common defense. During the early decades of the Cold War, it created and operated a nuclear deterrent force sufficient to deter the Soviet Union and reassure America's friends and allies in NATO and Asia. Yet for a host of reasons, some beyond its control, it could not win nonnuclear conflicts in Korea and Vietnam. In both wars, military involvement produced unsatisfactory outcomes—a status quo in the first, a failure in the second. America's failure in Vietnam, in particular, rocked the military to its core, leading to profound crises within the services and between the military and the nation. Paradoxically, less than three decades after World War II, the nation had come to loathe the very military services it had heralded as victors and protectors of democracy in 1945.

Further Reading

Primary sources include: U.S. Department of Defense, *Selected Manpower Statistics, Fiscal Year 1997*. Secondary sources include: Andrew Bacevich, *The Pentomic Era*, 1986; Chambers, *Oxford Companion to American Military History*; Chambers, *To Raise an Army*; Mark Clodfelter, *The Limits of Air Power*, 1989; Cohen, *Demystifying the Citizen Soldier*; Francis Duncan, *Rickover and the Nuclear Navy*, 1990; Joint History Office, *Organizational Development of the Joint Chiefs of Staff, 1942–2013*, 2013; Lawrence Kaplan, Ronald Landa, and Edward Drea, *The McNamara Ascendancy, 1961–1965*, 2011; Stephen McFarland, *A Concise History of the U.S. Air Force*, 1997; Millett, *Semper Fidelis*; Millet, Maslowski, and Feis, *For the*

Common Defense; Charles Moskos, "Success Story: Blacks in the Military," *Atlantic* (May 1986); Bernard Nalty, ed., *Winged Shield, Winged Sword*, 1997; O'Connell, *Underdogs*; Parker, *Concise History of the Marine Corps*; John Prados, *The U.S. Special Forces*, 2015; Rearden, *Formative Years*; Neil Sheehan, *A Fiery Peace in a Cold War*, 2009; Stewart, *American Military History*, vol. 2; John Stuckey and Joseph Pistorius, "Mobilization for the Vietnam War," *Parameters* (1985); Symonds, *U.S. Navy*; U.S. Marine Corps History Office, *The Marines in Vietnam, 1954–1973*; Weigley, *American Way of War.*

10

The Military's Revitalization and Redemption

The Cold War, 1974–1991

After Vietnam, the nation's military embraced once again the more familiar Cold War threats to the common defense—the Soviet military in Western Europe and the Soviet nuclear force. The U.S. military initially relied on a materially depleted (or "hollowed out") force, unevenly prepared and afflicted in places with personnel and morale problems.

The Common Defense

Military leaders had to account for an additional complication as well—the end of the draft. President Nixon's decision to shift to the All-Volunteer Force (AVF) concept in 1973 meant the services needed to rethink their fundamental approaches to filling their ranks. Thus, in the aftermath of Vietnam, restoring the military's organizational health, modernizing its capabilities, and ensuring that it provided for the common defense through continued containment of the Soviet Union became inextricably intertwined.

Organizational Responses

In the aftermath of Vietnam, the NSC, secretary of defense, and OSD began to provide more frequent guidance to the services about threats to plan for and the forces to expect to be available. This institutionalization of the "force-planning process," as it came to be called, was another manifestation of the growing power of the offices and organizations established by the National Security Act of 1947 and its subsequent amendments. Post-Vietnam force-planning guidance laid down as broad objectives rough nuclear parity with the Soviet Union; defense of Western Europe, acknowledging the increased possibility of a confrontation with the Soviet Union outside of Europe; and control of the sea-lanes in the Atlantic and Pacific. Services chose to focus on whatever aspects of this guidance best facilitated their rebuilding after Vietnam.

The Army

None of the services had escaped Vietnam unscathed, but the war had impacted the Army more than the others because of its size, experiences in that war, and reliance on the draft. Army leaders first had to ask what the Army needed to be able to do for the nation. They were relieved to be free to look beyond counterinsurgency: the post-Vietnam force-planning guidance presented them a national mission they knew well—defending Western Europe against a technologically and numerically superior enemy, in this case the Soviet-led Warsaw Pact. While the Army retained some tactical nuclear weapons, Army leaders looked for conventional paths, scrutinizing in particular Soviet conventional military modernization efforts and the 1973 Arab-Israeli War for ideas. What they concluded about the conventional battlefield led them to adopt a new Army–Air Force doctrine they called AirLand Battle.

The Army needed deeper integration among its own ground and air components, however, before it could work more closely with the Air Force. AirLand Battle relied on the ability of the Army to fight the "deep" as well as the "close" battle: it envisioned an expanded battlefield, one that extended 40 to 100 miles deep into the rear, well away from the fighting but where enemy reinforcements assembled. Army artillery, aviation, and special-operations forces, especially, would operate together (known as combined arms) to stop reinforcements from ever engaging. A numerically and technologically superior enemy like the Soviets would have to be fought on such a large battlefield; that success would require great mobility and extensive equipment modernization.

Five major weapons systems promised the needed firepower and mobility: the M1 Abrams tank, the M2 Bradley infantry fighting vehicle (IFV), the AH-64 Apache attack helicopter, the UH-60 Black Hawk utility helicopter, and the MIM-104 Patriot air-defense missile. The Army concluded that these systems, if purchased in large numbers and integrated at the division level, offered a decisive edge in the AirLand Battle.

The Abrams tank was significantly faster, better protected, and more heavily armed than its predecessors. The Bradley IFV was as fast as the Abrams, could destroy enemy tanks, and was designed to transport and protect six fully equipped infantry soldiers anywhere on the battlefield. The AH-64, armed with a machine gun and antitank missiles, provided the Army considerable air support independently of the Air Force. The UH-60 helicopter carried soldiers and equipment anywhere on the battlefield. The Patriot, originally designed as an antiaircraft missile, morphed into a system with some effectiveness against ballistic weapons. These Cold War systems remain integral to today's Army.

To prepare for the large, mobile, and dynamic battlefield it foresaw, the Army revamped almost every aspect of its education and training program. Most noteworthy was its emphasis on realistic, combined-arms training at the battalion and brigade levels. To this end, a demanding National Training Center was activated in the California desert along with a separate counterpart in Germany. There soldiers trained as they expected to fight, in intense, large-scale maneuvers shooting live ammunition.

Finally, as the Army returned its attention to the Soviet threat, it fundamentally changed its approach to the reserve component, both the Army Reserve and National Guard, under a new OSD policy called the Total Force. This concept sought to integrate the active and reserve components more closely. To reduce cost and minimize redundancy, the Army moved a large portion of its support capabilities from active to reserve units. Here was a lesson learned from Vietnam: the next time the nation went to war, the president would have to call up the Army Reserve and the National Guard. Army leaders believed this action essential to a continued strong connection between the American people and the military.

Ironically, the Army never fought the militaries of the Warsaw Pact, but this modernized force saw action in lower-level conflicts in Panama and Grenada and demonstrated its worth in 1990–91 during Operation Desert Storm in the Persian Gulf. Overall, the Army performed well, but it was aware that its combat effectiveness always rested on one major assumption—that the Army, as well as the other services, could always find enough people willing to serve. As will be discussed later, manning the All-Volunteer Force became an all-consuming task in the years after Vietnam.

The Air Force

The Air Force left Vietnam in organizational turmoil. During the war, SAC reluctantly moved some of its bombers into the nonnuclear realm, but SAC itself remained devoted to its core mission, readiness to execute the nuclear SIOP. The Air Force's fighter, or tactical, forces, conversely, embraced the nonnuclear mission in Vietnam and flew the missions that were among the war's most demanding and dangerous. Not surprisingly, when the war ended, the leaders of these two parts of the Air Force had diametrically opposed ideas of how the service should fulfill the force-planning guidance and shape its future.

On every level—from national mission to leadership to equipment—SAC's bomber generals and the tactical fighter generals were at odds about the future of their force. SAC leadership argued that the Air Force needed to return to its core strategic-deterrence mission and that this meant updating the strategic bomber fleet. The once-revolutionary B-52 had started to show its age and needed to be replaced. To a lesser extent, SAC also began to explore replacements for its Minuteman III ICBMs. Fighter generals, on the other hand, believed the time had come for them to take control of the Air Force's future. Like their Army counterparts, they argued that nuclear war was unlikely and that the service should prioritize conventional war in Europe. Moreover, because of their Vietnam experiences, the fighter generals believed they were best suited to lead the Air Force in such a conflict. They judged that thanks to rapid technological advances in stealth and precision, fighters, not bombers, would form the core of any European air campaign.

A result of these differences was that the institution did not always speak with one voice. Evolving concepts of deterrence, new arms-control initiatives, and a new presidential administration impacted SAC's efforts to modernize the bomber and missile legs of the triad. President Jimmy Carter's administration's decision to cancel the new B-1 bomber followed by President Ronald Reagan's administration's decision to restore it became the most memorable symbol of this uneven approach, in this case to nuclear modernization. To a lesser extent, the multiyear debate over the development and deployment of the Peacekeeper, or MX, ICBM—especially in light of advances in sea-launched ballistic missiles—was another reflection as well as of changing policies and attitudes toward nuclear deterrence.

The fighter-based Air Force made its own argument for modernization, but it was not couched in the arcane language of nuclear deterrence. It simply advocated for an Air Force suited to fight in Europe that would take on the dangerous air-to-air and air-to-ground missions that would arise in fighting the Soviet Union. It would require new fighters, like the F-15s and F-16s, full of the latest technologies and capable of air refueling, as well the A-10 tank-killing aircraft, intended to support ground troops directly. Starting in earnest in the late 1970s, the fighter generals would also pursue the F-117, a revolutionary "stealth" aircraft (i.e., its various detectable and identifiable characteristics minimized) intended to counter the deadly Soviet SAM threat first encountered in Vietnam. These aircraft would be armed with missiles that could be guided precisely to their targets. Together, stealth and precision should allow the fighter forces, it was projected, to offset the numerical advantages of their Warsaw Pact adversaries.

Finally, the fighter generals, like the Army, emphasized realistic training, developing intense programs like Red Flag and reinvigorating the Fighter Weapons School. Leaders of the fighter community within the Air Force cast themselves as aggressive, innovative airmen preparing for a dangerous conventional fight. They believed they stood in stark contrast to SAC's airmen, who constantly stood nuclear alert, performed repetitive tasks, and executed rote checklists.

While the Air Force's bomber and fighter communities vied for organizational primacy, on the periphery the mobility and space communities continued to develop separately. Because of the distinctiveness of the mobility and space missions, those engaged in them developed increasingly independent identities within the larger Air Force. Thus, by the end of the Cold War, the Air Force looked to be evolving into a collection of air and space forces, each part of the larger service yet possessing a unique culture.

The Navy

After Vietnam and for the remainder of the 1970s, the U.S. Navy centered its operational attention on conventionally balancing the Soviet navy, providing a continual sea-based nuclear deterrent with its SSBNs, and sustaining its long-term presence in the Pacific. To succeed, the Navy needed, successive CNOs argued, extensive modernization of its aircraft and submarines and accelerated production of its planned *Nimitz*-class aircraft carriers and the ships required for their battle groups. After a wide-ranging review by the NSC staff and OSD, President Carter disagreed; he reduced the Navy's modernization plan significantly. This constraint persisted until late in his term, when the overthrow of the shah of Iran and the 1979 Soviet invasion of Afghanistan suggested that the U.S. Navy would have to play a new and vital role in the Persian Gulf.

The Reagan administration stepped up the expansion that followed. Reagan's election campaign had called for a "six-hundred-ship Navy," a phrase that came to symbolize America's continued commitment to global leadership. Building toward this goal in the 1980s, the Navy accelerated production of the *Nimitz* supercarriers to control the seas and the *Los Angeles*–class attack submarines to kill their Soviet counterparts; recommissioned four World War II–era battleships; fielded new guided-missile cruisers capable of launching long-range cruise missiles; and started an aggressive program to construct and deploy the next-generation *Ohio*-class SSBN, armed with D-5 nuclear missiles. Carrier aviation similarly experienced revitalization. The new F-14 and F/A-18 fighter aircraft replaced Vietnam-era aircraft that had been the heart of carrier air wings. In short, for the Navy, the 1980s were the most robust decade of naval modernization since World War II. Much of what was built then remains in the fleet now, over thirty years later.

This revitalization of the U.S. Navy helped to deter its Soviet counterpart and gave the president more options for responding to other national security problems. Throughout the 1980s, naval forces were employed repeatedly in the Middle East. For example, battleships bombarded Lebanon in an effort to shore up a crumbling Lebanese government; carrier-based aircraft participated in attacks on Libya to punish its leadership for terrorist acts; and U.S. Navy ships escorted oil tankers through the Persian Gulf when Iran threatened to close it to shipping and destroyed most of the Iranian navy after the frigate USS *Samuel B. Roberts* struck a mine. But the disabling of the *Roberts* was not the Navy's only setback. It experienced additional losses when Iraqi missiles struck the frigate USS *Stark,* killing thirty-one and forcing the ship to leave the theater for repair. Conversely, it inadvertently inflicted civilian casualties, when the USS *Vincennes,* a new missile cruiser, negligently and tragically shot down an Iranian airliner. Notwithstanding these setbacks, deterring the Soviet navy had driven the Navy's revitalization, and its inherent flexibility was now available for presidents to use around the globe. By the late 1980s, clearly the Middle East, not Europe, occupied the epicenter of its employment.

The Marine Corps

Somewhat deflated by its Vietnam experience, the Marine Corps leveraged the defense guidance to refine its postwar missions and modernization. To the Corps' satisfaction, the Carter administration required it to defend NATO's northern flank by protecting airfields and anchorages in northern

Norway. More importantly, it directed the Marine Corps to prepare for deployment and "forcible entry" anywhere in the world, with or without an amphibious landing. To prepare for the former requirement, the Marine Corps pre-positioned equipment and supplies in Norway. For the latter, it did a comprehensive assessment of its doctrine and associated needs for equipment modernization.

Every aspect of the MAGTF received scrutiny. Were individual Marines adequately armed? Did the MAGTF have sufficient firepower and mobility? What type of aviation support did it need? How would the MAGTF get quickly to where it was needed? Like the other services, the Marine Corps identified essential equipment. To move Marines on land, the Marine Corps purchased large numbers of the Army's light, highly mobile tactical trucks—HMMWVs, better known as Humvees. It also adopted the Army's M1 tank (the M1A1 version) and separately procured the Light Armored Vehicle (LAV) to bring firepower as well as mobility to its ground forces. From the air, F/A-18 Hornets and vertical-takeoff AV-8 Harriers provided close air support; they flew from aircraft carriers and from the Navy amphibious assault ships that moved Marines around the globe. The largest of these amphibious assault ships, those of the *Wasp* class, carried 2,200 Marines, as well as the AV-8s, helicopters, and air-cushioned landing craft (LCACs) needed to move them ashore.[1]

Like the other services, Marine Corps modernization benefited from the Reagan administration's military buildup. But the Corps' leaders further argued that it offered a cheaper military option because it relied on the prowess of young, first-term enlisted Marines—not expensive technology or more senior personnel. How the Marine Corps calculated such cost then (and now) was (and is) hotly debated, especially because the Navy had the expense of building and operating amphibious ships. Nonetheless, post-Vietnam, this idea of "more military bang for the American taxpayers' dollar" emerged as a favorite Marine argument on Capitol Hill, and it still resonates today.

The Marine Corps found itself in a variety of contingencies in the latter part of the Cold War. In the early 1980s, Marines came under siege when terrorists attacked their barracks in Beirut, and they went ashore in Grenada. In the late 1980s the Commandant, Gen. Al Gray, anticipating the fall of the Soviet Union, refined the Corps' focus to prepare for a post–Cold War world characterized by Third World contingencies. These could be quick, violent confrontations with terrorists and narco-guerrillas or conflicts with radical, autocratic regimes (e.g., Libya) with small, arbitrarily violent militaries. To prepare for such eventualities Gray insisted that Marines receive additional infantry training before heading off to specialized training; that MAGTFs emphasize their expeditionary, combined-arms qualities over their amphibious one; and that doctrine reflect Eastern military theorists like Sun Tzu, to emphasize operational creativity. By the end of the Cold War, the Marine Corps was better organized, trained, and equipped than it had been for decades, and its post-Vietnam malaise was long past.

Personnel: The All-Volunteer Force and Total Force

The Vietnam War provided the catalyst for shifting from a draft to an All-Volunteer Force in 1973. Striking the appropriate balance between the rights and obligations of American citizens to serve in the military had challenged the nation's leaders from the start. As the public made clear during Vietnam, it had lost patience with the U.S. government drafting citizens to fight in a remote, unpopular war. Returning to a volunteer force was the obvious response. Moreover, free-market economists like Milton Friedman were convinced it would be cheaper.

For the military services, the shift to the AVF presented immense difficulties. For the first time since World War II, the military needed to compete directly with the civilian sector for manpower, and the large size of the military made the competition more intense. Where once it could round out its ranks with draftees, now it required a host of incentives. Initially the military did not compete effectively and had difficulty finding the qualified people it needed. This recruiting problem was addressed in three ways.

First, services started to rely on Madison Avenue expertise to assemble advertising campaigns that balanced individual appeal with unique service cultures. For example, the Army urged potential recruits, "Take the Army's 16-Month Tour of Europe"; the Marine Corps, characteristically, declared that it "Never promised you a rose garden." Second, prodded by Congress, the services increased their emphasis on both race and gender integration, so as to increase the pool of candidates. They did this by explicitly addressing root causes of racial tensions and by opening up more opportunities to women, including attendance at the military academies starting in 1976. The military, however, continued to exclude women from combat roles, starting a decades-long, public debate over women in combat. Third, the military competed more directly with the civilian sector in pay and benefits. Starting with the Reagan-era pay increases in the 1980s, the military gradually saw its direct and indirect compensation improve. Incentives included a strong retirement system and educational benefits as well as better pay. These encouraged more volunteers to join but also raised fundamental questions about what savings might be expected with the AVF (table 10-1).

Table 10-1. Active-Duty Military Personnel,
All-Volunteer Force, 1975–1990

	Army	Air Force	Navy	Marine Corps	Total
1975 (Ford)	784,000	613,000	535,000	196,000	2,128,000
1980 (Carter)	777,000	558,000	527,000	188,000	2,050,000
1985 (Reagan)	781,000	602,000	571,000	198,000	2,152,000
1990 (Bush)	761,000	531,000	578,000	198,000	2,068,000

Source: dmdc.osd.mil

The Department of Defense implemented the AVF at the same time it shifted to a Total Force Policy. As mentioned, the Total Force shifted as much military capability as possible into the reserve component, under the assumption that it would be cheaper to maintain key capabilities in the reserve and National Guard and harder to go to war without public support. In the years after Vietnam, however, the active-duty military found itself again at odds with the reserve components. Personnel shortages forced the active component to compete directly with its part-time reserve and Guard counterparts. Moreover, many in the active component doubted the reserve component would have sufficient training and experience to contribute meaningfully in combat.

Thus, the AVF and the Total Force Policy caused major shifts in the recruiting of military personnel and how they might be used in a conflict. The ultimate impact of these policies on military effectiveness would remain theoretical until a conflict erupted, against the Soviet Union or elsewhere in the world, in which to test this post-Vietnam force.

Organizational Integration

The 1986 Goldwater-Nichols Act affected military organizational integration as decisively as the AVF did its personnel composition.[2] The Goldwater-Nichols Act reflected mounting frustration within Congress over poorly executed, lower-level, contingency operations. Marginally successful or outright failed missions in the years after Vietnam included the tragic 1980 Desert One special-operations mission to rescue the U.S. hostages in Iran; the poorly coordinated El Dorado Canyon strikes against Libya; the confused 1983 invasion of Grenada; and the terrorist attack on the Marine Beirut barracks that same year. When Congress looked for overarching explanations for the operational problems, lack of unity of command and absence of interservice cooperation and integration emerged as common themes, just as they had during World War II.

In 1982 Gen. David C. Jones of the Air Force, the outgoing CJCS, voiced his own frustration to Congress about the inadequacy of existing command arrangements as well as the difficulty of providing sound military advice to the president and secretary of defense. He then asserted that despite his best efforts, internal reforms had failed and that only external intervention, by Congress, could improve matters. Jones' comments, it turned out, represented the first salvo in a fierce, four-year-long bureaucratic fight involving the secretary of defense, the Joint Chiefs, the services, Congress, and the White House. They passionately debated, among other things, how best to ensure unity of command, improve interservice cooperation and integration (i.e., "being joint," or "jointness"), enhance civilian control, and provide better military advice to the president and secretary.

The Goldwater-Nichols Act, passed and signed into law in 1986, addressed many of these issues by strengthening the roles of the CJCS and the combatant commanders while diminishing the roles of the service chiefs.[3] The combatant commanders would now exercise command over subordinate commanders regardless of service.[4] The chain of command above the combatant commanders went directly and solely to the secretary of defense and the president; the services had no authority over or within the combatant commands. To drive this point home, service chiefs were deprived of their former direct access to the secretary of defense; they were now required to go through their civilian secretaries or the CJCS. The Goldwater-Nichols legislation, in short, established a new military hierarchy in which the CJCS and combatant commanders were clearly elevated over the service chiefs.

In parallel with the Goldwater-Nichols Act, Congress worked on specific legislation for special operations, to address its shortcomings and protect it from the conventional military. To accomplish this, Congress directed the establishment of a new unified command that would take in all special-operations forces from the services—as well as from Joint Special Operations Command (JSOC), created in 1980—under the command of a four-star general or admiral.[5] Special Operations Command, or SOCOM, was unique among the combatant commands. In addition to the command authority the other unified commanders possessed, the SOCOM commander had prerogatives in such key personnel matters as promotions, assignments, and retention bonuses, as well as in the acquisition and development of specialized special-operations equipment. Moreover, SOCOM's civilian counterpart in the DOD was a new assistant secretary for special operations and low-intensity conflict (SO/LIC), a position that lacked the stature of a department secretary.

In short, from the moment of its creation SOCOM was one of a kind, a hybrid organization that could shift, chameleon-like, from an elite military service in its own right (albeit one that recruited from the four recognized services) to a combatant command and back again. When the final version of this bill was attached as a rider to the Goldwater-Nichols Act and signed into law on October 1, 1986, the nation created both a new combatant command and, de facto, a new military service.

The Goldwater-Nichols legislation proved the most revolutionary reorganization of the military since the National Security Act of 1947. It decisively shifted advisory and command authorities and operational responsibilities from the services to the CJCS and combatant commanders. It made joint education and experience with other services, whether on the Joint Staff or a unified command staff, a prerequisite for promotion to senior rank. Also, as amended, it created a new, independent special-operations unified command, moving control of special-operations forces out of their respective services and into the hands of a combatant commander.

Service chiefs, conversely, saw the scope of their responsibilities narrowed and their relative prestige among the most senior four-stars reduced. They assumed responsibility for providing well-selected, organized, trained, and equipped forces to the various combatant commanders, but they had no legal authority over how the commanders used them. Moreover, the service chiefs had to meet the diverse and changing needs of combatant commanders while anticipating what their own services would need to meet future threats. The combatant commanders' competing, insatiable demands for the services' finite resources required judicious allocation. The secretary of defense, aided at each step by advice from the CJCS, ultimately adjudicated the COCOMs' competing demands.

Civilian Control

Goldwater-Nichols symbolized the sweeping power of Congress, when united as a legislative body, to exercise civilian control. It rebalanced authorities and responsibilities across the Department of Defense. In addition to all the reforms outlined above, it strengthened the role of the secretary of defense with respect to the uniformed military, making it absolutely clear the secretary was the sole DOD authority on any defense issue. Everyone else in the department—service secretaries, combatant commanders, and service chiefs—was legally subordinate to the secretary on any departmental matter.

The Goldwater-Nichols Act similarly enhanced civilian control by designating the CJCS as the principal military adviser to the president and the secretary of defense. This meant that the chairman's voice outweighed those of the other four Joint Chiefs on national military matters for the first time. Moreover, the chairman would be assisted by a new four-star Vice Chairman of the Joint Chiefs of Staff, and the Joint Staff would now, specifically, to support the chairman rather than the corporate Joint Chiefs of Staff. Finally, the CJCS was given broad authority to revise military strategy and advise the secretary and president on potential changes to the UCP.

Although the chairman was not officially in the chain of command, his role as the principal military adviser made him the critical point of intersection between the president and secretary of defense on one hand and the combatant commanders and service chiefs on the other. Thus, by passing the Goldwater-Nichols Act, Congress fundamentally reshuffled civilian and military authority and responsibility within the Department of Defense and across the executive branch. Arguably Congress, as the driving force behind these changes, reached the apogee, to date, of its exercise of civilian control with this legislation.

Impact on the Common Defense:
The End of the Cold War

The Goldwater-Nichols Act's focus on integrating land, sea, and air components reflected the new reality that geographic dimensions of war, once separate, now overlapped and intertwined (figure 10-1). From this perspective, the reforms made sense; however, they also caused significant disruption within the military and raised questions about how the new system would work the next time the nation went to war. America's 1989 invasion of Panama gave the first indications of their impact. During the invasion, the commander of U.S. Southern Command, Army Gen. Maxwell Thurman, reported directly to the secretary of defense through the CJCS and later assessed that the reforms worked as designed. As the combatant commander, he exercised authority over forces from all the services without having to deal with individual service chiefs. He expressed satisfaction with his command authority and the operational outcome.

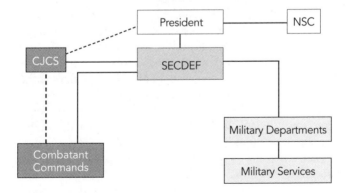

Figure 10-1. Goldwater-Nichols Act, 1986:
Department of Defense Relationships

The big test of all the post-Vietnam policy changes—the All-Volunteer Force, the Total Force, and Goldwater-Nichols—however, came several months after the Panama campaign, in, ironically, a conflict in the Middle East rather than against the Soviet Union. In 1990–91 the U.S. military waged Operations Desert Shield/Desert Storm to liberate Kuwait. The professionalism, competence, and esprit of the All-Volunteer Force revealed that the military had fundamentally changed since the end of the Vietnam War and had solved the core problems stemming from that conflict.

Moreover, the clear chain of command under Goldwater-Nichols allowed senior civilian leaders to hold their own vis-à-vis the military. Gen. Norman Schwarzkopf and Gen. Colin Powell, both Army officers, occupied joint positions recently strengthened by Goldwater-Nichols. General Schwarzkopf, commander of U.S. Central Command (CENTCOM), reported directly to Secretary of Defense Dick Cheney and the White House. But he worked very closely with the Chairman of the Joint Chiefs of Staff, General Powell. No other senior officers could challenge the authority of these three men. Indeed, Cheney quickly fired the Air Force Chief of Staff, Gen. Mike Dugan, when the latter spoke publicly about the upcoming Operation Desert Storm air campaign.

Thus, the 1990–91 Gulf War appeared to vindicate post–Vietnam War reforms, especially the AVF and the Goldwater-Nichols Act. From President George H. W. Bush down, many argued that the quick and relatively easy victory over Iraq showed the wisdom of radical changes within the Department of Defense and demonstrated that the nation had finally "kicked the Vietnam War syndrome"—in other words, the military had redeemed itself as a proud, capable, national institution.

The answers to other issues were less clear after Desert Storm: how to implement the Total Force Policy successfully and how to create systematically the general and flag officers who would lead an integrated, joint force. As to the former, of the three National Guard brigades called up to fill out active-component divisions, only one was ever certified as mission ready, and that came too late for the unit to deploy.

The Air Force Reserve and Air National Guard contributed more in terms of aircraft and crews, but they also fell short when it came to fully integrating with the active component.

The need to produce, in a deliberate way, qualified joint leaders was no less evident. Powell seemed uniquely prepared to serve as the nation's senior military officer, especially after demanding assignments at the White House. Schwarzkopf, however, had much less joint preparation. He served in two short, pre-Goldwater-Nichols, general-officer assignments, at Pacific and Southern Commands, but had spent most of his career in the infantry. His suitability for joint command was no more apparent than that of his general- and flag-officer contemporaries.

Goldwater-Nichols had attempted to rectify this problem by designating specific joint requirements for promotion to colonel or captain and to brigadier general or rear admiral (lower half). That was a far cry, however, from systematically developing senior leaders capable of moving with ease across the physical dimensions of war—much less of appreciating the value and dynamism of each dimension. Under the law, just serving in a joint assignment was what mattered, not what one learned there. Moreover, the services still largely controlled their own promotion systems, and outstanding performance in a specific service and loyalty to the same were still decisive in the most senior ranks.

The biggest challenge facing the military after the Gulf War, however, had nothing to do with the recent reforms. Instead it was a conundrum as old as the nation itself—how to draw down after threats to the common defense disappeared. A confluence of global events had ended the Gulf War and the Cold War within months of each other. Even as the nation reveled in these near-simultaneous victories, civilian and military defense leaders wrestled with what the post–Cold War, post–Gulf War military should look like. Members of the new All-Volunteer Force were about to discover that no matter how good and how professional they might be, they belonged to a military that was suddenly much larger than the nation needed—or at least wanted.

Further Reading

Primary sources include: U.S. Department of Defense, *Selected Manpower Statistics, Fiscal Year 1997*. Secondary sources include: Beth Bailey, *America's Army*, 2009; Carl Builder, *The Masks of War*, 1989; Chambers, *Oxford Companion to American Military History*; Cohen, *Demystifying the Citizen Soldier*; H. H. Gaffney et al., *U.S. Naval Responses to Situations, 1970–1999*, December 2000; Joint History Office, *Organizational Development of the JCS*; Kaplan, Landa, and Drea, *McNamara Ascendancy*; McFarland, *Concise History of the U.S. Air Force*; Millett, *Semper Fidelis*; Millett, Maslowski, and Feis, *For the Common Defense*; Moskos, "Success Story"; Nalty, ed., *Winged Shield, Winged Sword*; Walter Poole, *The Joint Chiefs of Staff and National Policy, 1973–1976*, 2015; Prados, *U.S. Special Forces*; N. A. M. Rodger, ed., *Naval Power in the Twentieth Century*, 1996; Bernard Rostker, *I Want You!*, 2006; Stewart, *American Military History*, vol. 2; Peter Swartz, *U.S. Navy in the World (1981–1990)*, 2011; Symonds, *U.S. Navy*; Weigley, *American Way of War*; Mike Worden, *Rise of the Fighter Generals, 1945–1982*, 1998.

11

Return to an Expeditionary Military, 1991–2001

The twin 1991 victories in the Persian Gulf and (at least in important senses) over the Soviet Union reinvigorated the military and the nation. Together these events restored the military's prestige with the American people while reducing threats to the homeland. However, with no looming crises on the horizon, America's leaders now began to consider significant reductions to this proven all-volunteer military. They sought a deliberate approach to force reductions, a way to avoid the chaos that had typically ensued after conflicts. With the end of the Cold War, they also wanted to reduce the military's personnel, force structure, and budget as much as possible and still meet defense needs.

The Common Defense: Downsizing amidst Uncertainty

As a result, a debate ensued in the 1990s between the civilian and military leadership over what it meant to provide for the common defense. The debate consumed considerable time and energy because its outcome would determine the military's size, equipment, and budget allocations. Inability to agree during the 1990s on the nation's specific security interests led civilian and military leadership to address them with three proxies—specific assumptions that would allow the nation to pursue whatever its future interests proved to be. First, the United States would continue to defend itself overseas; second, the end of the Cold War meant that the standing U.S. presence in Europe could be reduced dramatically;

and third, the drawdown in Europe should be matched by a significant reduction in the military's overall size.

At the same time, the convergence of the Goldwater-Nichols Act, the end of the Cold War, and victory in the Gulf War greatly strengthened the standing of the secretary of defense and the Chairman of the Joint Chiefs of Staff. Goldwater-Nichols directed the secretary of defense to provide written guidance on defense objectives, policies, mission priorities, and modernization programs; concurrently, it called on the chairman to "prepare strategic plans" and advise the secretary on "critical deficiencies and strengths in force capabilities." The secretary and chairman necessarily relied heavily on their respective staffs to draft these documents; there accordingly arose a new competitive-cooperative cycle between the Office of the Secretary of Defense and the Joint Staff in identifying potential national problems requiring military solutions.

The chairman, General Powell, was the first to use the Goldwater-Nichols legislation to shape the future military force. Anticipating the collapse of the Soviet Union, Powell used his expanded authorities to establish minimum military capabilities to meet future, as-yet vaguely defined, threats. Ultimately in this construct, known as the Base Force, the military provided for strategic deterrence, forward presence, crisis response, and additional "crisis response forces" based in the United States to reinforce the necessarily smaller, quick-reaction units that responded first. Powell estimated that these objectives, released in 1990, could be achieved with a military 25 percent smaller than the current one, especially with a concurrent drawdown in Europe.

OSD, similarly empowered by the Goldwater-Nichols legislation, not only coordinated with the Joint Staff on the Base Force but subsequently created several strategy and planning documents, tied to Goldwater-Nichols requirements, to help the secretary articulate his views. As the post–Cold War world began to reveal itself, OSD first issued the classified Defense Planning Guidance (DPG) to the services. This first DPG outlined for the services what their futures should look like: smaller, highly capable forces to underpin a "global hegemon" role for the United States. Because of a press leak, it also became the most publicized DPG. In April 1992 a hastily revised version of the planning guidance downplayed global hegemony and focused on a smaller force to counter future ill-defined threats while ensuring continued U.S. leadership.

When the William J. Clinton administration came into office less than a year later, it initiated its own broad strategic assessment known as the Bottom-Up Review (BUR). Like the Base Force and the first DPG, the 1993 BUR posited an uncertain world; it suggested as a force-sizing standard a requirement to fight two nearly simultaneous "major regional contingencies." However, the Clinton administration concluded, the BUR force could be smaller than the Base Force projections. Congress subsequently required each new administration to conduct a BUR every four years, and renamed it the Quadrennial Defense Review (QDR). The first QDR, delivered in 1997, envisioned a world of strategic opportunity for the United States. It endorsed the requirement to fight two major theater-scale wars while maintaining overseas presence, and it proposed that forces could be cut below the BUR and still meet this standard.

Successive CJCSs implicitly challenged some of the OSD projected force reductions based on these hypothesized future military challenges. They did so by offering their military advice in such congressionally required documents as the National Military Strategy, the Chairman's Risk Assessment, and future-oriented issuances like Joint Vision 2010 and 2020. These documents put on the record the chairmen's professional assessments on future force structure and force modernization, as well as their challenges to some of the vectors suggested by civilian leadership.

Goldwater-Nichols thus not only energized OSD and the Joint Staff but brought into being a sometimes onerous, bureaucratic burden, by creating an apparatus that posited national problems on a four-year cycle and then estimated the forces required to meet them. This set the service chiefs competing among themselves, with the Office of the Secretary of Defense, the Joint Staff, and even the combatant commanders at times over the mission, size, and composition of their respective services—a dynamic that persists today.

Organizational Responses

The rise of more complex defense debates meant that after 1991 the four services needed to work harder than ever to protect their organizational visions and cultures. Service chiefs well understood that they faced profound changes. They also believed that they best understood how to shepherd their services through those changes, and they worked aggressively to do so. The challenge to retain combat power while getting smaller and more expeditionary changed the shapes of all the services, but particularly the Army and the Air Force. Since the end of World War II, existing bases had allowed them to station forces in Europe rather than deploying from the United States. In the 1990s, accordingly, the Army and the Air Force were obliged to rediscover what it meant to be expeditionary, while the Navy and Marine Corps could capitalize on their inherently expeditionary qualities.

The Army

In the 1990s the Army embarked on a contentious decade of transformation. Mindful of the post-Vietnam "hollow force," its leaders committed themselves to a smaller, modernized, and expeditionary Army to respond to the needs articulated by OSD and the Joint Staff. What this force would ultimately look like remained an open question for much of the decade, but there was general agreement on three points.

First, the much smaller defense budgets meant the Army would need to deactivate several divisions and reduce active-duty personnel by about 275,000. The series of buyout incentives, early retirements, and involuntary separations that resulted, however, threatened the quality of the volunteer force the Army had so diligently built. Another consequence was a correspondingly, albeit reluctantly, increased dependence on the reserve and National Guard. In crises, reserve brigades would now necessarily be integrated into (or round out) active-duty divisions. The transformation of the

1990s made, for the first time, the reserve component integral to any Army operation.

Second, Army leaders began to rethink the division as the foundational organizational unit. They gradually concluded that given the need for mobility, the firepower of a modern brigade, and the potential of nascent information technology, the brigade should be the basic unit, not the division. Through a series of field experiments that started in the 1990s, the Army's active and reserve components began to conceptualize the "brigade combat team" as the fundamental, independent, deployable unit. Similarly, the Army's new expeditionary posture led to considerable interest in how to make the brigade more deployable without sacrificing firepower. A light armored vehicle, ultimately named the Stryker, offered one way to accomplish this; the Army decided in the late 1990s to design some brigades built around it.

Third, if it was once again to project large forces overseas to fight, the Army needed access to high-volume transport, both air and sea. The addition of C-17s to the Air Force's global cargo fleet allowed crisis-response units like the 82nd Airborne to "meet critical timelines" (military parlance for "arrive on time, in a hurry") anywhere in the world. But it was expanded sealift resources that made the Army into an expeditionary force. These capabilities included not only ships for moving heavy equipment but also large stockpiles of equipment prepositioned at sea. By 1996, for example, the Army had the use of thirty-six roll-on/roll-off (RO/RO) ships to move its heavy tanks even to theaters without improved ports. As the Army found itself involved in smaller operations like Somalia, the Balkans, and Haiti, one of the biggest challenges it faced, ironically, was that of differentiating itself from the Marine Corps, long recognized for its expeditionary, first-to-fight capabilities.

The Air Force

The decade after the Gulf War transformed the Air Force into, it argued, the nation's sole resource for global vigilance (air- and space-based intelligence, surveillance and reconnaissance), global reach (mobility aircraft), and global power (fighter and bomber aircraft, ICBMs). To prepare to meet the ill-defined, post–Cold War threats, Air Force leadership pursued three major initiatives. First, the Air Force significantly reduced its personnel and bases meant for the now-evaporated Cold War threat. The Air Force's active-duty strength fell from 531,000 in 1990 to approximately 370,000 in 1997. Also, it had closed several bases in the United States and overseas by the end of the decade.

Second, the Air Force focused on becoming expeditionary. In part, like the Army, it did so to compensate for diminished access to European bases; in addition, the Air Force had decided to place shorter-range fighters rather than long-range bombers at the core of its combat forces. This decision implied the need to be able to move fighters rapidly from domestic to overseas bases in conflict. To this end, the Air Force created ten air expeditionary forces (AEFs), built around fighters. As a corollary, LeMay's once legendary Air Force Strategic Air Command was disestablished in 1992; a new combatant command, U.S. Strategic Command, was simultaneously created to oversee the nuclear mission. As if to symbolize the demise of SAC, the Air Force leadership took another previously unthinkable action: it placed bombers under the command of a fighter general.

Third, as the Air Force's space mission matured in the 1990s, it significantly expanded, in conjunction with other government agencies, its capabilities in space-based intelligence, communication, weather, and navigation. Most notably, it launched and operated the Global Positioning System (GPS) satellites for precise navigation and timing anywhere on the globe. By the end of the decade, GPS was available to the American people, spurring dramatic change in numerous commercial technologies. This growing national role for space led some space leaders to begin a sustained campaign to create an independent space force. They argued an aviation-focused Air Force leadership "suboptimized" the use of space by the U.S. military, just as aviation pioneers had accused the Army leadership of suboptimizing the use of air in the early 1900s. Thus, the fighter pilots now leading the Air Force struggled to embrace a mission they thought was peripheral to the service's real purpose, and one it had only half-heartedly taken on.

Budget allocations provide some of the best evidence of the new Air Force priorities in the 1990s. During that decade the Air Force shifted its modernization emphasis from the expensive, revolutionary B-2 stealth bomber to the (also costly) stealth F-22 and F-35 fighters. To free up money, for the F-22 in particular, it reduced personnel and retired older aircraft. This action reflected the Air Force's long-standing top priority of maintaining a highly capable, modern fleet. It also symbolized the fighter's organizational ascendancy over the bomber, an ascendancy that defines the Air Force today.

These changes collectively made the Air Force well-suited to the operations it faced in the 1990s. Conflict in the Balkans and Operations Northern and Southern Watch in Southwest Asia kept the fighters busy. In the Balkans, the effects of precision air strikes led some to argue that airpower had single-handedly achieved U.S. political objectives there. In Southwest Asia, fighter units repeatedly deployed for years to bases in region to enforce "no-fly zones" over Saddam Hussein's Iraq. By their nature, these missions seemed to bear out the wisdom of moving to a fighter force, which, though limited by shorter endurance than bombers, was capable of conducting a variety of missions.

Because of the Air Force's operational successes, many of its leaders now argued it was time that more roles and missions were allocated to the Air Force. This view broke into the open in the mid-1990s before the congressionally mandated Commission on Roles and Missions (CORM) of the Armed Forces, when the Air Force squared off against the other services over which best provided expeditionary combat power to the nation. This renewed interservice competition over resources, doctrine, and strategy would persist throughout the decade—with the Air Force largely standing apart from the other services.

The Navy
With the end of the Cold War, the U.S. Navy dominated the oceans. But having no open-ocean, blue-water challenger,

the Navy, like the other services, prepared for significant drawdowns in personnel and ships and to recast what it offered the nation. By the end of the decade it had reduced its ranks by over 200,000 and decommissioned scores of ships. Addressing in documents like "From the Sea" and "Forward . . . from the Sea," the uncertain future highlighted by OSD and the Joint Staff, naval (and Marine) leaders argued for the continued relevance of a powerful navy. They observed that naval forces could, as no others could, operate forward, or well away from American waters, maintaining a routine, global presence while ensuring safe, unimpeded access to the world's sea-lanes. Naval leaders further contended that this forward presence could quickly be made a ready expeditionary force, unimpeded by land-access or overflight permissions—two issues that routinely confronted the Army and the Air Force. Finally, acknowledging that the great open-seas battles of World War II now belonged to history, the Navy shifted its emphasis to mastering the multiple dimensions of littoral (coastal, or brown-water) operations.

To reshape the Navy accordingly, its leadership did two things. First, the Navy altered how it thought about conventional global operations. The aircraft carrier remained the Navy's essential ship but as a platform for airpower against land targets. In Southwest Asia, where operations continued, the Navy in 1995 reactivated the Fifth Fleet, with headquarters in Bahrain, and cycled aircraft carriers and other warships in and out of the Persian Gulf.

Second, the Navy looked to exploit the much-touted revolution in military affairs of the 1990s to dominate any "battlespace" (i.e., in the air, at sea, under the sea, and projection from sea to shore). To this end, the Navy experimented with concepts like the "arsenal ship," sending massive salvos in support of land operations. Originally characterized as a "destroyer for the twenty-first century," or DD-21, this program ultimately produced the *Zumwalt*-class ship, although the first of three would not be built for two decades.[1]

For the Navy, then, the decade of the 1990s was not unlike the decade after World War II, if on a smaller scale. After tremendous success in blue-water operations during the

Cold War, when the threat from the Soviet navy disappeared, the U.S. Navy struggled to articulate a mission that would justify a large, oceangoing fleet. Moreover, as the military reshaped itself for ill-defined future threats, the Navy found itself enmeshed in another roles-and-missions debate with the Air Force. The two services once again wrangled over post–Cold War responsibilities and the associated forces to fulfill them. During the decade, however, the Navy carved out a forward-presence mission tied to America's long-standing desire to protect trade and sea-lanes, especially in the Pacific Ocean. In the process the aircraft carrier, with its battle group, became one of the most enduring symbols of American power.

The Marine Corps

Of all the services, the Marine Corps best weathered the shift to the post–Cold War world. Because it concentrated on being the nation's "first to fight," forcible-entry, expeditionary force, it adapted more easily to the radically altered security environment. The Marine Corps played a major role in articulating the ideas put forward in "From the Sea" and "Forward . . . from the Sea"—in fact, many naval officers thought the Marines' voice the dominant one in these maritime documents. Marine Corps leadership also issued its own planning concept, restating its core purpose to provide the nation an expeditionary force-in-readiness, using the MAGTF to provide that force. The Corps, in short, did not need to reinvent itself. It simply needed to emphasize what it had been doing for decades.

The value the nation placed on the Marine Corps' mission, as well as long-standing statutory requirements, kept its personnel reductions considerably smaller than the other services. The Marine Corps had to trim its ranks by approximately 13 percent, the other services by roughly 30 percent. Where once the Marine Corps could point to how much smaller in size it was than the other services, the gap was now reduced noticeably.

The shifting interservice personnel ratio, however, cut both ways: it meant that the Marines had to stress their uniqueness. The Commission on Roles and Missions was looking for redundancies across the services, and the Marine Corps needed to avoid renewed accusations that it was a second land army. It was in this context that the Commandant, Gen. Charles Krulak, held up the U.S. actions in Somalia of the mid-1990s as foreshadowing things to come. Krulak spoke of preparing junior Marines, "strategic corporals" (i.e., junior enlisted leaders whose decisions might have strategic significance), to fight and lead in the amorphous world of the "three-block war" in which Marines might confront a wide variety of threats in the space of three city blocks. Because most of the global population was concentrated on the coasts, he argued, the Marine Corps, unlike the Army, would operate in cities on the littorals—mostly, and unlike the Army, on those of the Pacific and Indian Oceans.

To conduct these expeditionary operations, the Marine Corps needed the Navy to maintain an amphibious fleet sufficient to keep a MEU-sized MAGTF of approximately 2,200 Marines at sea, ready to respond at a moment's notice. This rationale justified the building of eight *Wasp*-class amphibious assault ships. The Marines also lobbied for better aircraft, such as air transports to move personnel ashore. Most conspicuously, it pushed successfully for the controversial MV-22 to replace aging helicopters. The 1990s, in short, were hard on all the services, but the Marine Corps proved the most effective in mitigating the effects of the post–Cold War drawdown.

Personnel

Many members of the All-Volunteer Force watched anxiously as their services drew down. Where once conscripts eagerly awaited demobilization, members of the AVF equated the prospect to being fired with a severance package. The reserves absorbed some of those released from active duty, but only in small numbers, since the drawdown similarly impacted them and the National Guard (table 11-1).

At the same time, the expansion of defense agencies under the Office of the Secretary of Defense had the unintended effect of making more acute another personnel

Table 11-1. Active-Duty Military Personnel, 1990–2000

	Army	Air Force	Navy	Marine Corps	Total
1990 (Bush)	761,000	531,000	578,000	198,000	2,068,000
1995 (Clinton)	509,000	401,000	435,000	175,000	1,520,000
2000 (Clinton)	477,000	353,000	371,000	172,000	1,373,000

Source: dmdc.osd.mil

burden for the services. These agencies required hundreds, even thousands of military and civilian personnel, and OSD pressured the services to assign them. Indeed, the services saw themselves as sacrificing their own dwindling resources to keep these defense agencies manned.[2] Just as the military was experiencing one of the most precipitous manpower decreases since Vietnam, it had to supply more personnel to outside organizations than ever before.

Many former military personnel found work in a new and burgeoning privatized military-related industry. By the mid-1990s the military lacked the personnel to do all the U.S. government required of it. Sensing a profitable business opportunity, several firms—Blackwater, CACI, MPRI, Kellogg Brown and Root (KBR), DynCorp, and others—stepped forward to perform a wide variety of previously military-specific functions, such as personal and garrison security, host-nation training, supply and maintenance, and base support. As demand for military-outsourcing services grew, these businesses recruited aggressively and found a well-trained pool of candidates in people recently "downsized" from the military. Thus, ironically, all the uncertainty and change after the Cold War had shrunk the armed forces but stimulated a "shadow contractor force" of largely former military personnel.

Finally, the 1990s witnessed yet another reexamination of fundamental questions: Who is qualified to serve in the military? In what capacities? The former issue led to consideration of reversing a long-standing policy of prohibiting gays and lesbians from serving openly. Shortly after his swearing-in, President Clinton promised to open the military to both. However, the JCS warned him publicly that such a decision would threaten good order and discipline, and the president reluctantly agreed to a compromise, "Don't Ask, Don't Tell" (DADT). DADT allowed gays and lesbians to serve in the military as long as they kept silent about their sexual orientations. The latter question of capacities now centered on the service of women in combat and on board submarines. Women could serve in combat aviation and surface ships but remained excluded from ground-combat units and submarines. Despite numerous attempts to change this policy, these exclusions remained in place at the end of the twentieth century.

The military personnel picture, then, underwent dramatic changes in the 1990s—a downsized AVF military, a rapidly expanding contractor force, and new initiatives for changing the criteria of service. These changes made the decade a turbulent one for those associated with the military, and also, for individual service members, a difficult one in which to find deep purpose. Nothing had replaced the clear national problem faced during the Cold War, causing even many of those remaining in uniform to wonder why they served.

Organizational Integration

If the service chiefs thought their prestige diminished and their organizations under siege in the aftermath of the Cold War, the combatant commanders enjoyed a new ascendancy in the Goldwater-Nichols military. With the growing contingency requirements of the 1990s, they saw important reasons to exercise their new joint command responsibilities. By law, the combatant commanders relied on the military services to deal with the day-to-day matter of providing forces capable of any assigned mission. This freed the COCOM commanders to focus on planning for and, if necessary, executing joint missions. This distinctive structure and allocation of responsibilities allowed COCOM commanders to create a new, quasi-diplomatic role for themselves in the international travels their missions required.

Combatant commanders and their large staffs flew on dedicated (permanently assigned) military aircraft, arriving with fanfare in foreign capitals. These trips, in theory, reassured friends and allies and sent messages of overwhelming American military power to any nation that might need reminding. The commanders likewise hosted their counterparts at their headquarters to reinforce or build military-to-military relationships. Their efforts along these lines were so successful that the State Department raised concerns that the military was usurping the State Department's diplomatic role.

Indeed, for most of the decade the geographic combatant commanders were the predominant face of American power abroad. Analysts came to refer to them as "proconsuls," evoking a deliberate parallel between the provincial governors of the ancient Roman Empire and these senior military representatives of a new American one. Within the military, the breadth and power of the combatant commanders, as well as of the CJCS, made these senior joint positions more appealing to senior officers than the diminished, yet demanding, service-chief jobs. Ultimately, four-star joint assignments became an informal measure of the relative standing of services—the more officers a service had in important joint positions, the more, presumably, the nation valued that service.

Civilian Control

Preparation of required strategy and planning documents in many ways bureaucratized civilian-military relations within defense and Washington policy circles. Congress largely drove these debates by demanding a variety of studies and reports that military leadership, in turn, tried to leverage to protect people and equipment. The chairman and the Joint Chiefs engaged with civilian policy makers over potential challenges to the common defense. Ultimately, civilian-controlled documents like the BUR and the QDR represented an uneasy compromise between civilian policy makers and, in particular, the JCS.

The elevation of the combatant commanders, however, raised a new issue of civilian control. Who ensured that the COCOM commanders acted in ways consistent with presidential policy? Goldwater-Nichols gave the CJCS considerable latitude to comment on the performance and effectiveness of combatant commanders but not the legal authority to hire and fire them. Those prerogatives rested solely with the president and secretary of defense; meanwhile, the combatant commanders operated away from Washington with far fewer policy constraints than did officers in the capital. Sometimes disagreements reached the president, as during the Balkans campaign, but more often combatant commanders functioned with considerable autonomy and minimal civilian oversight. Thus, while Goldwater-Nichols strengthened some areas of civilian control, it introduced problems in others.

Impact on the Common Defense

Absent a shared understanding of the common defense in the 1990s, civilian defense officials and military leaders settled on yet another proxy challenge to ensure global supremacy: the nation needed a conventional military able to fight two major regional conflicts *almost* simultaneously. OSD, the services, CJCS, and the COCOM commanders throughout the 1990s hotly debated the size and composition of the military necessary to do this. Only two central assumptions were acceptable to all parties—the active and reserve components would be much reduced, and the military would be more expeditionary.

But in that decade, the military found itself involved not in the envisioned major regional contingencies but in a series of smaller operations around the globe. These contingencies, if smaller, nevertheless required considerable manpower, both for initial intervention and long-term peacekeeping. Campaigns in the Balkans, in particular, revealed that the U.S. military needed more personnel. Rather than seek to increase the active or reserve components, however, civilian leaders encouraged the expanded use of contractors. Arguably, this choice demonstrated in itself that the military was already too small, but the allure of the less politically charged contracting solution proved appealing. As the privatized military industry moved aggressively into this space, it added an entirely new dimension to the already vast military-industrial complex.

In the 1990s the maturing implementation of the Goldwater-Nichols Act deprived the service chiefs of operational responsibilities and relegated them to the less immediate and less prestigious Title 10 roles of recruiting, organizing, training, and equipping forces. The combatant commanders meanwhile emerged as esteemed warrior-diplomats who used these forces in joint operations around the globe. In short, at the organizational and policy levels, the military of the 1990s struggled to adapt to a changing world. Uncertainty drove reductions and attempted adaptations to amorphous threats. The military experienced substantial losses of personnel, equipment, and basing but also, at the same time, an increase in contingency response and military diplomacy. American leaders used, or attempted to use, this instrument of organized violence to shape an unsettled international environment to the nation's advantage. The military would not be able to assess the relative success of the changes it had made, however, until terrorists suddenly and violently attacked the nation on September 11, 2001.

Further Reading

Primary sources include: William Cohen, "Report of the Quadrennial Defense Review," May 1997; DoD Personnel, Workforce Reports and Publications, https://www.dmdc.osd.mil/appj/dwp. Secondary sources include: John Brown, *Kevlar Legions*, 2011; Chambers, ed., *Oxford Companion to American Military History*; Raphael Cohen, *Air Force Strategic Planning: Past, Present and Future*, 2017; Bradley Graham, "Air Force Chief on Attack," *Washington Post*, October 24, 1994; Lorna S. Jaffe, *The Development of the Base Force, 1989–1992*, 1993; Charles Krulak, "Operational Maneuver from the Sea," *Joint Force Quarterly*, Spring 1999; Charles Krulak, "The Strategic Corporal: Leadership in the Three Block War," *Marines*, January 1999; Benjamin

Lambeth, *The Transformation of American Air Power*, 2005; Eric Larson et al., *Defense Planning in a Decade of Change*, 2001; William Owens, *High Seas*, 1995; Stacie Pettyjohn, *Global Defense Posture, 1783–2011*, 2012; Prados, *U.S Special Forces*; Dana Priest, *The Mission*, 2004; P. W. Singer, *Corporate Warriors*, 2007; U.S. Navy, *Forward . . . from the Sea*, 1994; U.S. Navy, *From the Sea*, 1992; Cynthia Watson, *Combatant Commands*, 2010; John White et al., *Directions for Defense: Report of the Commission on Roles and Missions of the Armed Forces*, 1995.

12

"The Military the Nation Has,"
2001–2017

Speculation as to how best to provide for the common defense and to create the American military most suitable for that purpose ended abruptly on September 11, 2001. That day Al-Qaeda terrorists hijacked four airliners and crashed them into the twin World Trade Center towers in New York City, the Pentagon, and a field in rural Pennsylvania (reportedly when passengers thwarted a planned attack on the U.S. Capitol).

The Common Defense

Quickly responding to this terrorist act, Congress passed the "Authorization for the Use of Military Force" (AUMF) on September 14, granting broad powers to the president to prevent future acts of terrorism against the nation—specifically, to "use all necessary and appropriate force against those nations, organizations, or persons he determines planned, authorized, committed, or aided the terrorist attacks on September 11, 2001, or harbored such organizations or persons." In October 2001 President George W. Bush used this authority to direct the military to execute Operation Enduring Freedom (OEF) against Al-Qaeda and its Taliban supporters in Afghanistan.

Approximately a year later, Bush sought a related "Iraq Resolution" to address a specific terrorist threat he believed emanated from Iraq. After the resolution passed, Bush ordered the military to execute a second operation—Operation Iraqi Freedom (OIF)—against the regime of Iraqi leader Saddam

Hussein. Thus, after a decade of downsizing and reshaping the military to win two major conventional conflicts in two different regional theaters, the military instead found itself in two different operations in a single region falling within the CENTCOM combatant commander's area of responsibility.

Organizational Responses

The Army

Operations Enduring Freedom and Iraqi Freedom placed heavy demands on the land forces. To execute both operations, the Army grew to over 560,000 active-duty soldiers by 2010 and routinely relied on reserve personnel and National Guardsmen to send units for OEF and OIF. The Army especially relied on its reserve components to take on homeland security responsibilities in the immediate aftermath of the 9/11 attacks. National Guardsmen and Army reservists secured airports, key domestic facilities, and critical infrastructure around the nation. The decade after the terrorist attacks, in short, operationalized the reserve component, linking it more closely to its active-duty counterparts than at any time since World War II.

Meanwhile, the senior Army leadership struggled to understand the character of the conflicts in Afghanistan and Iraq. In the early days of both campaigns, land forces experienced fast, relatively easy victories. Special operations, combined with some conventional forces, captured many of the headlines in Afghanistan. In Iraq, the Army's armored "thunder run" into Baghdad won this nation's praise. Both conflicts, however, soon transformed into something more complex. The enemy fighters melted back into the civilian population, where they did everything they could to sow distrust of American forces. They also devised cheap but vicious weapons for deadly surprise attacks—most notably the roadside bombs, or improvised explosive devices (IEDs), and suicide bombers. By the end of 2005, American forces in both Afghanistan and Iraq found themselves fighting insurgencies.

The Army was ill-prepared for this challenge. To address it, the Army joined with the Marine Corps in writing the *Counterinsurgency* field manual (formally called FM 3-24 by the Army and MCWP 3-33.5 by the Marine Corps), which outlined a shared land-forces doctrine for COIN operations. It also completed the organizational shift away from the division to the approximately four-thousand-person brigade combat team as the fundamental, independent unit for battlefield operations. The BCT structure allowed the Army to handle forces more effectively. Geography and the type of conflict suggested that infantry BCTs were indicated for Afghanistan, and Stryker and armor BCTs for Iraq. But theater demands meant that BCTs sometimes deployed to wherever they were more needed, whenever they were available.

The BCT structure, combined with the COIN doctrine, empowered lower-ranking officers and enlisted soldiers to take more initiative, and they did so to great effect in places like Sadr City. But, as had happened in Vietnam, OEF and OIF operations bogged down, casualties increased, and lower-ranking soldiers began to question publicly the competence in and commitment of their seniors to fight a counterinsurgency. A widely known example was Lt. Col. Paul Yingling's "A Failure in Generalship" article. Army leadership, for its part, tried to respond to these criticisms, using them as sources of fresh ideas for improving operational effectiveness. Unlike in Vietnam, though, slow progress and mounting casualties did not stir up broad discontent with the war—a reflection of the nation's reliance on the AVF and of increasing distance between the military and civil society. Only volunteers deployed to OEF and OIF; no draft reached into American hometowns and families. As a result, citizens, telling themselves that soldiers (as well as airmen, sailors, and Marines) knew what they had signed up for, remained largely disconnected.

The Air Force

Institutionally, the Air Force's relative position among the services diminished in the post-9/11, COIN era. In the initial stage of OEF and OIF, the Air Force garnered considerable public attention, delivering impressive air strikes in support of special operations in Afghanistan and launching the famous "shock and awe" air campaign at the beginning of the Iraq invasion. For a while, the dominant role of airpower and of the Air Force seemed secure. But as both campaigns shifted from conventional to counterinsurgency operations, the Air Force's brash confidence in its ability to determine a conflict's outcome began to dissipate. Airpower alone could not stop the insurgencies, and the Air Force, to judge by the continued reduction in its overall personnel numbers, was a minor contributor in them.

Indeed, to its institutional dismay, supporting ground forces emerged as the Air Force's most important role during OEF and OIF. On the battlefield, the aging A-10 and its close-air-support missions garnered much more praise than the new, expensive F-22. Strategic bombers like the B-1 also supported land forces. Most mobility missions by the C-17s and C-130s were for moving forces to Afghanistan and Iraq and keeping them supplied. Space operators constantly fine-tuned their respective satellite "constellations" to ensure they provided the best possible navigation, timing, and communications support to the forces in theater.

But it was the maturation of unmanned aerial vehicles, commonly referred to as drones, that proved the greatest institutional challenge for the Air Force. Forced by Secretary of Defense Robert Gates to increase its drone capabilities, the service reluctantly built the world's largest drone fleet. For the first time, the operators were not themselves in the combat zone or even necessarily the theater. Drone operators flew their aircraft from locations hundreds, if not thousands, of miles away from the actual battlefields. These personnel fired missiles at insurgent targets and collected intelligence and surveillance for the land forces in Afghanistan and Iraq—all from the safety of a U.S. air base. Some airmen argued that these unmanned aircraft required a large number of personnel and detracted from airpower's decisive, independent role on the battlefield. Other airmen insisted that UAVs represented the Air Force's future and that its leaders needed to embrace this new reality.

Finally, there was increased reliance on using airmen on the ground, adding to organizational insecurity. When there was a shortage of soldiers or Marines, support airmen augmented them in a variety of ways, including escorting convoys and training host-nation forces in dangerous circumstances. They performed well, but their close alignment with ground operations undermined Air Force institutional interests. Many airmen in these roles started to identify more with their land-forces comrades than with their fellow airmen. Also, unlike in previous conflicts, these duties put support personnel at greater physical risk from day to day, driving the roads of Iraq or leading provincial reconstruction teams in Afghanistan, than their flying counterparts faced. Collectively, this emphasis on the Air Force's supporting capabilities in OEF, OIF, and subsequent operations led to an as-yet-unresolved Air Force leadership concern that appreciation for airpower's potential decisiveness in a conflict may be dwindling.

More substantively, general officers from the Air Force's manned-pilot community especially feared that their service could descend from the status of a decisive, technologically advanced force indispensable for countering states like China into one needed only to support the ground forces with fire, mobility, and personnel. Secretary Gates' 2009 cancellation of further production of F-22s fed this fear. In other words, these officers believed that the Air Force faced (and arguably it still faces) a threat to its institutional independence. Amidst this institutional uncertainty, highly charged debates about spending for current and future programs such as the F-35, "optionally manned" long-range bombers (i.e., that can operate either with or without human crews, as fits the mission), drones, advanced cyber capabilities, and future space systems became the de facto means for discussing the Air Force's future. Since the Air Force could not afford to buy all the forces it wanted, those programs that received the largest part of the budget, like the F-35, became the "winners" in these intra–Air Force debates.

Ironically, this sense of institutional "winners and losers" reinforced belief among some space-force advocates, in particular, that the nation needed an independent space service. They continued to argue the U.S. Air Force simply lacked the institutional wherewithal to recruit, organize, train, and equip both air and space forces with equal effectiveness. As of this writing, President Donald Trump has become the most prominent advocate for the creation of an independent space force, insisting the nation would be best served by creating a separate space service. Separately, in October 2018, Secretary of Defense Mattis asked President Trump to establish an eleventh combatant command, U.S. Space Command, to conduct space warfare.

What space operations might fall under the purview of an independent space force remain to be seen. The most easily established space force would have the Air Force's space operations at its core, supplemented by those of the other military services. However, that combination represents only a portion of the nation's space capabilities. Arguably, a fully integrated, capable space service would also include the satellite operations of the National Reconnaissance Office, National Aeronautics and Space Administration, and the National Oceanic and Atmospheric Administration. Creating such an organization would be more difficult, could (like the U.S. Coast Guard) reside under a cabinet-level department other than DOD, and ultimately might be more effective. In either case, for the Air Force, the potential loss of its space mission is a fundamental challenge to its institutional identity.

The Navy

To a certain extent, the Navy's role during OEF and OIF paralleled that of the Air Force. The Navy too saw its overall personnel decrease, and its role limited to strike missions in support of land forces, logistics, and augmenting troops on the ground. Nevertheless, the conspicuous presence of two carrier strike groups in the Persian Gulf area and the Navy's close ties to its maritime partner, the Marine Corps, muted comments about subservience to the land forces. Other responsibilities, out of the combat theater, further set the Navy apart from the Air Force: its counterpiracy mission off the Horn of Africa, its growing prominence in strategic deterrence, and its enduring presence in the Indo–Asia Pacific region.

The piracy problems stretching from the Horn of Africa into the Indian Ocean assumed added urgency in the post-9/11 world. Any unlawful activities that enabled insurgency and terrorism drew the attention of the United States and its partners—and piracy did both. To stop the related illegal flow of materials and individuals, the U.S. Navy and several of its partners formed Combined Task Force 150, specifically devoted to antipiracy operations in the waters off the Horn of Africa and stretching into the Indian Ocean. The Navy routinely sent destroyers and cruisers to participate in this multinational effort. Although it involved only a relatively small commitment, CTF-150 offered the Navy a role tied to counterterrorism and counterinsurgency that only it could fill.

Throughout the OEF and OIF years, the Navy also continued to provide the nation's most survivable nuclear deterrent. Where the Air Force had let the nuclear mission languish until a series of embarrassing problems refocused its attention, the Navy had demonstrated steady competence, continuously rotating fourteen SSBNs on deterrence patrols. In addition, the Navy converted four of the original SSBNs into special-operations-capable, conventionally armed cruise-missile-carrying submarines, finding yet another way to demonstrate the ability of naval power to influence actions ashore as well as at sea.

It was the Navy's sustained presence in another part of the world, however, that set it most dramatically apart from the other services during OEF and OIF. Throughout the Indo-Pacific region, U.S. Navy ships continued to patrol sea-lanes, provide relief after natural disasters, and operate with the navies of partner nations. The Navy's presence in the Indo-Pacific, even as operations in Afghanistan and Iraq were going on, embodied America's commitment to friends and partners there. This commitment became increasingly important as China grew economically and militarily, challenging the post–World War II status quo throughout the Indo-Pacific. While the U.S. military as a whole bogged down in Southwest Asia, the Chinese made advances in antiship ballistic missiles, making them able to threaten aircraft carriers hundreds of miles offshore.

Emerging threats like these prompted heated debates within the Navy over the long-term viability of the aircraft carrier in such dangerous environments. While the debate went on and continues today, Navy leadership remains committed to updating the carrier fleet—replacing the *Nimitz* class with the next-generation *Gerald R. Ford* class—and modernizing air wings with F-35 aircraft. Despite its post–Cold War, coastal-water focus, the Navy reduced its planned purchase of the fairly small littoral combat ship (LCS) because of cost, operational performance, and structural problems. It made a similar decision to cancel the stealthy, offensive DD-21 experimental program that had produced the first of three futuristic *Zumwalt*-class destroyers. In short, absent significant intervention, the mid-twenty-first-century Navy will look much like that of the late twentieth century.

The Marine Corps

The Marine Corps' size and prestige skyrocketed during OEF and OIF. At one point it grew to over 200,000, while the Navy remained steady at just over 320,000 personnel. The Navy had outnumbered the Marine Corps by almost 400,000 in 1990; this shifted balance between the two sea services represented how the nation's priorities changed after 9/11. Moreover, the Marine Corps found it easier to recruit than the Army. Its reputation for toughness and immediate readiness to fight made it the option of choice for many who wanted to join the land forces.

USS *Zumwalt* (DDG 1000). *U.S. Navy*

The small-war, counterinsurgency nature of both conflicts lent itself to the Marine Corps' combined-arms approach. At the height of the fighting, Marines deployed MEF-sized MAGTFs to Iraq and MEU-sized MAGTFs to Afghanistan. In Iraq, the Marines added to their combat lore in the first and second battles of Fallujah and, to a lesser extent, in the battle of Marja in Afghanistan. Some critics, especially in the Army, argued that the Corps had needlessly placed Marines in harm's way during these operations, but even critics acknowledged the courage of the Marines involved.

Preserving the uniqueness of the Marine Corps presented its leadership with a delicate balancing act during OEF and OIF. The Marine Corps needed first to retain its expeditionary and amphibious character even though it was now operating in one land-locked country and another largely so; second, to reinforce its status as an elite, quick-strike land force even though it had now rotated units through Afghanistan and Iraq for years; and finally, to emphasize the Marines' operational uniqueness even while its mission areas overlapped increasingly with those of high-profile and elite special-operations forces. The Marine Corps now worried about a blurring of its identity with that of the special-operations community, where it had once worried only about absorption into the Army. Today, these three imperatives continue to shape the Marine Corps as the United States shifts from COIN back to preparation for great-power conflict.

Special Operations

OEF and OIF transformed Special Operations Command, its forces, and its personnel. As outlined in chapter 10, the Goldwater-Nichols Act created SOCOM as a hybrid, on one hand, having most of the characteristics of a military service (funded to ensure new Special Operations Forces, or SOF, equipment reached the field quickly but relieved of major operating and personnel costs), on the other hand, clearly designated as a combatant command. In short, combatant command and service authorities for strategic, operational, personnel, and budgetary decisions rested solely with SOCOM's four-star commander.

Table 12-1. SOCOM Military Personnel
(Approximate Numbers)

	Army	Air Force	Navy	Marine Corps	Total
2002	25,000	10,500	6,000	1,000	42,500
2014	32,600	15,700	9,000	3,200	60,500

Source: U.S. Government Accountability Office

Until 9/11, the personnel strength of the command hovered around 42,000, over half of which came from the Army. Except for Somalia, in the years between Goldwater-Nichols and 9/11, special operators spent much of their time on missions, for which the Green Berets were famous—that is, training and advising other nations' military forces.[1] The September 11 terrorist attacks changed that. Shortly after 9/11, Secretary of Defense Donald Rumsfeld directed SOCOM to take the lead in the new Global War on Terrorism. This order changed SOCOM's focus to finding and destroying terrorist cells around the world.

These special operators conducting this new mission largely came from JSOC, the select, secretive, independent command within SOCOM. Among other things, JSOC went on to capture Saddam Hussein, hunt down Abu Musab al-Zarqawi, and kill Osama bin Laden. These successes helped to make the special operations community America's most celebrated military force and reinforced its separateness from the other military services. Furthermore, they reinforced presidential preference for special operations precisely because, under the AUMF, such missions could be executed without congressional or public scrutiny.

In the years after 9/11, Congress regularly authorized expansions of SOCOM to handle its ever-increasing mission load. By 2014 SOCOM included more than 60,000 military personnel, including the reestablished Marine Raiders (table 12-1). While this expansion increased military options available to the president, it also meant, from the service chiefs' perspectives, that SOCOM could skim off even more of their services' best talent than it had before 9/11. Today, with operations in Syria, Iraq, and North Africa, SOCOM remains one of the nation's preeminent forces.

Personnel

Even at the height of combat operations, from 2006 to 2010, the active-duty military increased by only about 100,000 members—the vast majority of whom joined the Army (table 12-2). To provide enough personnel for the OEF and OIF as well as other global obligations, the DOD took a series of actions. First, and most immediately, the services implemented a "stop loss" policy that involuntarily retained service members past their scheduled discharge or separation dates, in some cases for several months. Second, as mentioned above, the services routinely called their reserve partners to active duty. They relied on the National Guard and the reserves to help execute operations in Afghanistan and Iraq, as well as to handle missions at home and abroad for which active-duty units no longer had the time or personnel. Third, the Department of Defense expanded its cadre of government civilians to assume duties formerly performed by the military. Fourth, the services, especially the Army, lowered recruiting standards to enlarge the pool of possible volunteers. Finally, the military offered a wide array of incentive packages to enlist, and then retain, personnel. These incentives included the most generous GI Bill for veterans since World War II, and large retention bonuses, some well in excess of $100,000, to keep experienced individuals on active duty. Indeed, some

Table 12-2. Active-Duty Strength, 2001–2015

	Army	Air Force	Navy	Marine Corps	Total
2001	477,000	349,000	374,000	173,000	1,373,000
2005	489,000	349,000	359,000	180,000	1,377,000
2010	561,000	329,000	323,000	202,000	1,415,000
2015	487,000	307,000	323,000	183,000	1,300,000

Source: dmdc.osd.mil

policy advisers questioned the generosity of these initiatives, wondering if perhaps the nation had subtly replaced the all-volunteer force with a mercenary one.

Yet, despite all these efforts, the Department of Defense fell short of the personnel it needed in Afghanistan and Iraq. As we saw in chapter 11, the military accordingly turned to contractors. In some functions, like interrogations and drone operations, they became integral to mission execution. Security, however, became the highest-profile task assumed by contractors. Private security contractors (PSCs) like Blackwater provided security details for a variety of activities and senior officials. These contractors carried weapons, were not bound by the military's rules of engagement, and sometimes initiated violent exchanges outside of ongoing military operations. In both conflicts, total DOD contractor personnel (including American, host-nation, and third-country nationals) frequently represented more than 50 percent of the department's total presence (table 12-3). In 2016 contractors represented over 75 percent of the DOD's Afghanistan presence.

The larger contractor role offset the shortfalls in military manpower but raised a host of unresolved questions: Who is responsible for contractor conduct in a theater of war, since contractors report to company executives and not military commanders? What is the impact on personnel retention, especially since contractors constantly tried to lure away military personnel with large salaries and signing bonuses? What responsibilities does the military have to protect and provide medical services for contractors in-theater? Who keeps track of contractor casualties—not only Americans but those from other countries as well? The list of issues goes on, but the widespread use of contractors clearly revealed that, absent a draft or a much-expanded AVF, the nation could not meet its wartime personnel requirements otherwise. How comfortable the military and the nation are with this practice remains an important, persistent, and poorly explored issue.

The Afghanistan and Iraq conflicts also reignited debates over restrictions on service, specifically, allowing gays and lesbians to serve openly in the military and women to serve

Table 12-3. U.S. Military and Contractor Personnel
in Afghanistan and Iraq

	Afghanistan		Iraq	
	U.S. Military	Total Contractors*	U.S. Military	Total Contractors*
2007	24,056	29,473	165, 607	154, 825
2008 (OIF max contractors)	N/A	N/A	161,783	163,591
2010	96,600	70,599	48,410	74,106
2012 (OEF max contractors)	88,200	117,227	N/A	N/A

* Contractor data not reported prior to 2007.

Source: Congressional Research Service

in combat. American society's attitudes were changing; civilian leadership revisited and subsequently repealed DADT, removing any prohibition on gays and lesbians in uniform. Separately, civilian leadership also began to look at opportunities for transgender Americans. The Barack Obama administration removed all restrictions on service or medical support, but recent actions by the Trump administration put the future of this policy change in doubt.

In many ways, the boundary-less nature of the insurgencies removed lingering uncertainty about women in combat. Support forces frequently found themselves under fire; this fact and the constant demand for additional personnel led to calls to open all remaining combat roles to women. The Marine Corps opposed this proposal but to no avail. By 2016 the Department of Defense had removed all restrictions on women's service. They could now serve in any military capacity for which they met the requisite physical qualifications.

Thus the nation's understanding of who serves and why changed dramatically in the years after 9/11. These changes came from a potent mix of multiple conflicts being fought at once, selectively lowered standards, substantial reliance on contractors, and powerful social movements to integrate female, gay, lesbian, and transgender volunteers fully. Informally, some in the military argued this pattern of outsourcing and accommodation of social change in wartime raised serious questions about the focus and priorities of senior leaders. The most vociferous have accused civilian leadership of sacrificing military effectiveness to business interests and social agendas. However that may be, the personnel decisions taken over fifteen years of war fundamentally shifted the nation's conversation about who can serve and what it means to serve in the U.S. military.

Organizational Integration

The years after 9/11 tested Goldwater-Nichols in several respects. In many ways, the legislation worked as advertised. The role of the CJCS as the principal military adviser to the president and secretary of defense was firmly established. The CENTCOM commander, as the combatant commander responsible for Afghanistan and Iraq, exercised overall direction of coalition and joint military operations in both countries. The CENTCOM commander, in turn, oversaw two subordinate commanders, one for each theater, who handled the day-to-day demands of Operations Enduring Freedom and Iraqi Freedom. But their subordination to CENTCOM proved to be more theoretical; in reality, these theater commanders enjoyed considerable autonomy, frequently dealing directly with the president and secretary of defense.

As for the CENTCOM commander, he approved operational plans but spent most of his time addressing political-military matters with authorities in Washington, D.C.; exercising his quasi-diplomatic role throughout the region in order to keep complex coalitions together; and (in the military phrase) "working issues" that crossed geographic boundaries into areas of responsibility of other combatant commanders (i.e., "seams" between them). Such issues involved NATO (the province of European Command [EUCOM]), India (under what has recently become INDOPACOM), and the Horn of Africa (AFRICOM as of 2007), as well as certain matters that lacked seams altogether (SOCOM).

Goldwater-Nichols did not foresee the combatant commanders' "proconsular" duties or their amorphous lines of authority with subordinate joint commanders. It also did not anticipate DOD's persistent call for even broader, or "whole of government," organizational integration after 9/11. The secretary of defense, the Joint Chiefs, and the combatant commanders came to believe that all U.S. government departments needed to work together if the counterinsurgencies in Afghanistan and Iraq were to succeed. To institutionalize this view, the DOD leadership called for a new National Security Act of 1947 (or alternatively, a second Goldwater-Nichols Act) to improve interagency cooperation. Other departments, like State and Treasury, however, lacked similar enthusiasm. They feared such an initiative would cede too much of their institutional independence and that an already too-powerful DOD would end up militarizing other aspects of government.

Goldwater-Nichols also failed to anticipate new, hard-to-categorize, cross-cutting mission areas like cyber operations. Cyber emerged as a military mission after the 9/11 attacks but did not fit neatly into any one service or combatant command. Much of the nation's cyber capabilities resided outside of either realm, in DOD's secretive, largely civilian National Security Agency (NSA). No single organization existed to oversee specifically *military* cyber operations. To rectify this, the secretary of defense established U.S. Cyber Command in 2009 as a subordinate command under U.S. Strategic Command. Its commander, however, was the NSA director "wearing two hats."

This complicated relationship even confused people in DOD. Which organization actually commanded cyber operations, NSA or Cyber Command? Moreover, the dual responsibility gave the NSA director remarkable power under U.S. law, since his authorities now came from both military (Title 10) and intelligence (Title 50) legislation. What might be illegal under one might be permissible under the other. To make matters worse, the same people could well execute cyber missions under both Title 10 and Title 50. In 2017 President Trump decided to establish Cyber Command

(CYBERCOM) as an independent COCOM to address some of these issues and improve organizational integration. In May 2018 CYBERCOM became the nation's tenth combatant command, although its commander remains dual-hatted as the NSA director as well. It would seem that CYBERCOM is also the first unified command both remote from organized violence and reliant on civilian expertise. This development could further blur traditional distinctions between military and civilian roles, a process already well under way in Afghanistan and Iraq.

Civilian Control

Congress's passage of the AUMF shortly after 9/11 gave the president wide authority in his role as commander in chief. President George W. Bush and President Barack Obama took that role extremely seriously, sometimes challenging the military. President Bush, most notably, overruled the recommendations of the CENTCOM commander and JCS to order the 2007 "surge" of U.S. forces into Iraq. President Obama similarly took a hands-on approach as commander in chief, announcing new troop levels and withdrawals and firing commanders who publicly expressed doubts about his decisions.

Two powerful secretaries of defense helped their respective presidents exercise civilian control. Donald Rumsfeld, the irascible secretary of defense at the start of the Bush administration, took charge of joint promotions for all four- and three-star general and flag officers. This drew an outcry from many serving and retired admirals and generals, who argued that Rumsfeld had politicized the promotion process. Rumsfeld's simple rejoinder was that he needed to find the best senior officers, not just passively accept the nominations the services had agreed on. Robert Gates, who replaced Rumsfeld, became known for firing generals and admirals. For example, he fired the Chief of Staff of the Air Force for allowing standards to slip in the stewardship of nuclear weapons, and he fired the commander in Afghanistan for taking a conventional-war approach to an unconventional war. Gates also forcefully challenged the services to rethink their futures and their roles to keep themselves relevant.

Moreover, Goldwater-Nichols created unanticipated civilian-control problems. As seen in earlier chapters, service chiefs felt they were micromanaged by their civilian secretaries, while combatant commanders, especially those outside of the limelight, operated largely autonomously, subject only to the secretary of defense's direction. When allegations of abuse of authority (e.g., combining of official and personal travel, poor treatment of staff) emerged in AFRICOM and EUCOM, the extent of this autonomy raised civilian-oversight questions. Were the combatant commanders too powerful? Had the secretary of defense been burdened with too many oversight responsibilities? Goldwater-Nichols advanced joint operations considerably but arguably has empowered combatant commanders at the expense of civilian control.

Impact on the Common Defense

In the early years of the Iraq War, an Army NCO asked Secretary Rumsfeld why he (the NCO) and other soldiers had to scrounge around for parts to reinforce, or "up-armor," their vehicles. Rumsfeld famously responded, "You go to war with the army you have, not the army you might want or wish to have at a later time"—an unpalatable but accurate answer. Afghanistan and Iraq reshaped the U.S. military into the force America needed for counterinsurgency operations.

As they had in Vietnam, the Air Force and the Navy adjusted to, largely, supporting the Army and Marine land forces. For the Air Force in particular, a burgeoning inventory of drone aircraft added to its institutional unease. Senior civilian leaders' preference for classified, special operations put a tremendous burden on the highly skilled "niche" part of the military that conducted them. The existence of a secretive world of cyber operations created the impression that even when the nation returned to "peace" it would be waging cyber war. Also, paradoxically, even as the all-volunteer military grew increasingly remote from the civilian population, it relied more on civilians to provide expertise and offset shortages of uniformed personnel. During both Operations

Enduring Freedom and Iraqi Freedom, the military stumbled somewhat in its provision for the common defense, impeded by the confounding nature of the violent extremists in Afghanistan and Iraq and by the larger problems underpinning these insurgencies.

As the military moves beyond counterinsurgency and counterterrorism and thinks again about national challenges posed by an assertive and powerful China, a resurgent Russia, a bellicose North Korea, or an increasingly powerful Iran, it must reexamine the adequacy of its forces to meet them. All these problems are important, but none has yet emerged as the dominant threat to the common defense. Until then, the four services will, in particular, have to struggle with how to recruit, organize, train, and equip forces best suited to the nation's needs. Hopefully, the next time the nation goes to war, the force it has will look more like the force it needs.

Further Reading

Primary sources include: Authorization for Use of Military Force (AUMF), Pub. L. 107–40, September 18, 2001; DoD Personnel, Workforce Reports and Publications, https://www.dmdc.osd.mil/appj/dwp. Secondary sources include: Andrew Feickert, *U.S. Special Operations Forces (SOF)*, February 3, 2013; Robert Gates, *Duty*, 2014; Government Accountability Office, *Special Operations Forces*, July 2015; Jim Mattis and Kori Schake, *Warriors and Citizens*, 2016; Mark Moyar, *Oppose Any Foe*, 2017; Heidi Peters et al., *Department of Defense Contractor and Troop Levels in Iraq and Afghanistan: 2007–2016*, 2016; Prados, *U.S. Special Forces*; Stewart, *American Military History*, vol. 2; Peter Swartz, *American Naval Policy, Strategy, Plans and Operations in the Second Decade of the Twenty-First Century*, 2017; Symonds, *U.S. Navy*; Paula Thornhill, *Over Not Through*, 2012; U.S. Army/Marine Corps, *Counterinsurgency*, FM 3-24 / MCWP 3-33.5, 2006; U.S. Navy, *A Cooperative Strategy for 21st Century Seapower*, March 2015; U.S. Special Operations Command, *2017 Fact Book*, 2017; Andru Wall, "Demystifying the Title 10–Title 50 Debate,"

Harvard National Security Journal 3, no. 1 (2011); Paul Yingling, "A Failure in Generalship," *Armed Forces Journal*, May 1, 2007.

Conclusion

The American Military and the
Evolving Common Defense

Understanding the American military starts with realizing it has belonged to the nation since the nation's founding and exists to provide for an ever-evolving concept of the common defense. Individuals who join the military do so by becoming members of one of the four military services that trace their roots, directly or indirectly, to the U.S. Constitution. In all cases, America's military institutions have remained focused on mastering and managing organized violence on behalf of the nation.

Whither the Common Defense?

As the end of the second decade of the twenty-first century approaches, China, Russia, North Korea, Iran, and violent nonstate extremists all challenge the common defense. The AUMF remains in effect, allowing the executive branch to use the military to pursue violent extremists around the globe. No single looming challenge, however, is threatening enough to unite the nation and demand its full attention. Absent an urgent, immediate threat to American interests, as in the 1990s, the military services and combatant commands will continue to imagine threats and then propose solutions that capitalize on their respective responsibilities, capabilities, and approaches to problem solving. But, they will insist, their solutions promise success only given sufficient people, equipment, and training.

Organizational Responses

The four services, and the service members who bring them to life, remain at the core of any military solution for now. The services have evolved dramatically over time in response to national problems and available technology. The Army has mechanized most aspects of its operations, focused on sustained overseas operations, and gradually found ways to provide much of the airpower it needs on the battlefield on its own. The Navy has learned to operate above and below, as well as on, the water and to become a major player in land operations by projecting airpower from the sea. The Marine Corps has transformed itself from a naval auxiliary force into a large, expeditionary force capable of responding rapidly anywhere in the world with uniquely tailored ground and air task forces. When the Air Force—a service the Framers could not have imagined when they wrote the Constitution—emerged in the twentieth century, the bomber and nuclear weapons especially vaulted it to early prominence. But even this youngest service has changed dramatically. On one hand, it has developed advanced aircraft and weaponry that are the envy of other air forces around the world. On the other hand, as the other military services have generated airpower for their own purposes, the Air Force has arguably felt increasingly insecure about the uniqueness of its role. Moreover, it added space and cyber technologies, in particular, without fully integrating them into its organization, prompting periodic efforts to create separate space and cyber forces. As of this writing, the creation of an independent space force is under serious consideration.

All the services possessed unique organizational cultures through the end of the twentieth century. These cultures derived from the physical environments in which the respective services operated and from the specific ways in which they accordingly understood the nation's interests and the kinds of options they offered the civilian leadership. Now, as the services wrestle with new technologies that undercut their preferred ways of fighting, demanding deployments, and more diffuse threats, they are struggling to keep their organizational cultures intact while remaining relevant to the nation. Arguably, the Marine Corps is struggling a bit less than the other services, because of how it understands its core missions. But all of the services are seeking ways to provide for the common defense in a shifting threat environment.

In some ways, a hybrid organization like Special Operations Command is better suited than the individual services to strategic ambiguity. The command's mission provides its special operators with clarity of purpose, while its mix of service and combatant command attributes gives it organizational agility. As a result, SOCOM possesses a strong organizational culture, remains popular with the public, and continues to be the lead military organization in the fight against violent extremists. If sustainable, hybrid approaches could indicate a future evolutionary course for joint military organizations.

For the foreseeable future, however, the armed-service structure will remain fundamental to the military. The services are still the only federal military entities that volunteers can join directly. Volunteers seeking demanding physical experiences will, in general, join the land forces; those looking for technical challenges will be more inclined to serve in the Navy or Air Force; and those looking to join elite special operations units will seek out the services whose SOF structure best matches their goals. Combatant commands, for all the power of their four-star commanders, are not organizations that members volunteer for when entering the military. With the exception of SOCOM, these commands reflect more the personalities of their current commanders than any enduring, unifying culture. In short, combatant commands are largely the sum of the military services' contributions.

Personnel

In addition to the traditional need to recruit and train volunteers to keep the ranks filled, the military services are confronting a host of personnel questions associated with increasingly diverse operations. What types of individuals does the military need to conduct space, drone, and cyber operations? What are the personnel implications of machine learning and artificial intelligence for autonomous

machine-on-man and machine-on-machine operations? If a
job consists mostly of working at a console or with a com-
puter in the United States, do military volunteers need to
meet traditional physical demands, or should they meet a
different set of standards? Similarly, if cyber operations are
central to future success, should the military turn to reservists
and National Guardsmen having similar skills in the civilian
world to fill these roles, or should it bring people directly into
the field-grade officer ranks (i.e., lateral entry) to provide that
expertise? Fundamentally, are space, drone, and cyber operations in fact *military* operations at all, or are they important
national functions best performed by civilians? If they are
military, do they require separate, service-like organizations?

For the military, these are uncomfortable and, as yet
unanswered, questions that linger in the background of dis-
cussions about how to recruit, organize, train, equip, and
employ a future military force. They also foreshadow the
emergence of more difficult and ambiguous issues such as
artificial intelligence and algorithmic warfare, innovations
that further disrupt traditional understandings of organized
violence. Identifying who may (or in extreme circumstances,
must) serve in uniform and in what capacity—active duty
or reserve, officer or enlisted, entry level or lateral entry—
becomes increasingly complicated as the technology itself
becomes more complex. Whether the military consists largely
of draftees or solely of volunteers, a shared understanding
about who serves, under what terms, where, and in what
capacity remains as important to the nation today as it did
when the Framers fiercely debated these same issues.

Organizational Integration

The future of combatant commands as the points of integration for military operations remains open as well.
Conceivably, the military services could evolve into something like apprentice-level sources of qualified personnel
for functionally based, hybrid organizations like SOCOM,
Cyber Command, or a space force. The consolidation or dis-
establishment of the geographic combatant commands could
diminish accusations of American imperialism and erase

some of the awkward seams encountered when employing U.S. military power around the globe. But, consolidating these commands would also deny the military important, quasi-diplomatic voices in interactions with other nations' governments and especially their militaries. Any such change, of course, would require a shift in how America believes it can best organize and use its military. In any case, as occurred most recently with the Goldwater-Nichols Act, these changes usually happen when failure or unanticipated challenges shock the military into new ways of accomplishing its mission and Congress into new legislation that codifies them.

Civilian Control

The ability to take decisions about the combatant commands or anything else related to the military's future resides in authorities articulated in Articles 1 and 2 of the U.S. Constitution. Just as they did at the nation's founding, such questions—who serves in America's military, in what organizations, under whose command, and for what purpose—rest squarely with the Congress, the President as commander in chief, and, ultimately, the American people. How best to exercise effective civilian oversight of this vast institution in the twenty-first century raises important questions as well: Is OSD an important reflection of the president's defense policies or a powerful self-sustaining bureaucracy? Is OSD too small or too big? Are the service secretaries civilian positions that are legacies of a bygone era or essential elements of civilian control? Is it realistic to expect the secretary of defense to exercise effective civilian control over ten or more combatant commands? Did Congress cede too much authority by approving the AUMF? Should Congress restructure its defense committees to match the contemporary military? In short, the nation's leaders need to identify which areas require civilian control from the executive and legislative perspectives, and then either affirm existing mechanisms or create new ones to exert this control. Absent this analysis, ironically, military and civilian members could well disagree even on what *constitutes* civilian control, let alone how to exercise it effectively.

———

Ultimately, the U.S. military mirrors the nation it serves—
its government and citizens, its ideals and challenges, and,
fundamentally, its evolving understanding of the common
defense. The broader this conceptualization, the more likely
the military is to become overly and inappropriately involved
in national affairs. Conversely, the more narrowly the common defense is defined, the more the nation must spend to
sustain an institution it only infrequently uses.

When individual American citizens volunteer to join one
of the military services for a few years or a career, they are
making a unique and, in many cases, life-altering decision.
From their personal perspectives, and the organizational
ones of the services they join, nothing is more important than
clarity of purpose. Such clarity starts with clear articulation
by the nation's leaders of the interests vital to the common
defense and the general shape of the military needed to protect them. During national crises, such as World War II,
doing so is relatively easy. In transition periods after a conflict, however, the task can be daunting. Thus, an ongoing
national conversation about these interests as well as the
organizations, people, and equipment they employ is vital to
the health of this fascinating institution—and to the health of
the nation itself. In this conversation about the American military, we may hope, any lingering mystery will disappear, and
it will emerge for what it is—a direct reflection of America,
its history, and its people.

NOTES

Introduction

1. "Provide for the common defense" is the language used in the preamble to the U.S. Constitution. "Organized violence" is commonly employed in, for example, Hedley Bull, *Anarchical Society*, 178–93. For the importance of the murder/war distinction, see Dave Grossman, *On Killing*, and Karl Marlantes, *What It Is Like to Go to War*. Paula Thornhill, *Crisis Within*, also explores the concept of organized violence.

Chapter 1. Military Services, Organizational Integration, and Civilian Oversight

1. The U.S. Coast Guard is excluded because it reports to the Department of Homeland Security day to day and falls under the U.S. Navy in times of war. Services are discussed in chapters 1 and 2 based on the order in which they appear in U.S. Constitution and then in law.

2. Grossman and Marlantes both emphasize the importance those in uniform place on the distinction between organized violence and individual acts of violence.

3. "U.S. Code: Title 10—Armed Forces," *Cornell Law School Legal Information Institute*, https://www.law.cornell.edu/uscode/text /10.

4. The use of the expression "reserve component" is based on Title 10, U.S. Code (USC). These organizations are as follows: for the army, the Army National Guard of the United States (NG) and the U.S. Army Reserve (USAR); for the Navy, the U.S. Navy Reserve (USNR); for the Marine Corps, the U.S. Marine Corps Reserve (USMCR); and for the Air Force, the Air National Guard of the United States (ANG) and the U.S. Air Force Reserve (USAFR). These are discussed later in the chapter.

5. *Defense Manpower Report, FY 2017*, https://www.dmdc.osd .mil/appj/dwp/dwp_reports.jsp.

6. In certain armored cavalry units a brigade is called a "regiment" and a battalion a "squadron."

7. Since the nation's founding, the Army has used several of these terms to describe its organizations, the sizes of which vary.

8. Ship counting is surprisingly ambiguous, because the authorities vary as to what tonnage, type, construction status, and so on, constitutes a "ship."

9. Sometimes informally called "supercarriers," because of their large tonnage.

10. The new *Gerald Ford*–class aircraft carriers are over $13 billion per ship before adding the aircraft.

11. The name of a class of ships is usually that of the first to be commissioned. For example, the USS *Nimitz* was commissioned as the first of a series of carriers built to the same design, all of which are grouped as the *Nimitz* class.

12. *SS* (submersible ship) is the historical designation for submarine; *N* means it is nuclear powered; *B* means it carries sea-launched ballistic missiles (SLBMs); *G* means it carries cruise missiles.

13. The first generation of jet fighters goes back to World War II; the second generation to the Korean War era; the third generation, the Vietnam War era; the fourth generation, post-Vietnam, most notably the F-15 and F-16; and the fifth generation, F-22 and F-35, came on line post–Cold War. The sixth-generation fighter is now under design.

14. When discussing the four military services' reserve organizations in a general way, the term "reserve" will be used.

15. A former CJCS, Gen. Richard Myers, suggests in *Eyes on the Horizon* that the tank was named for the place where World War II service chiefs met—the basement of an office building, near its water tank (174).

16. The combatant commands and the Army, Navy, and Air Force service staffs use the same numerical system. The Army staff codes begin with *G-* for general staff, Navy with *N-*, and Air Force with *A-*. Only the Marine Corps staff does not adhere to this convention.

17. Technically, according to Joint Publication 1-02, "combatant command" is abbreviated CCMD (and its commander CCDR). However, COCOM will be used in this work, because it is much more widely recognized and used by journalists, scholars, and even military personnel.

18. Combatant command abbreviations are formally prefaced with US (e.g., USEUCOM for United States European Command). Informally, the US is usually dropped, making European Command, for example, EUCOM rather than USEUCOM.

STRATCOM has nuclear, missile defense, and space missions. It will lose the latter with the establishment of Space Command.

19. See in particular U.S. Constitution, Article 1, Section 8 (Congress), and Article 2, Section 2 (President).

Chapter 2. Those Who Serve and the Uniforms They Wear

1. Commitments usually range from four to ten years depending on the level of expertise and the extent of training required. In particular, highly skilled officers, such as pilots and nuclear submarine engineers assume longer commitments because of the time and expense involved in training them.

2. All generals and admirals, upon promotion, display flags (in prescribed circumstances) bearing the number of stars corresponding to their ranks; traditionally, however, only admirals are called "flag officers."

3. The Department of Defense has an excellent link showing officer ranks at https://dod.defense.gov/About/Insignias/Officers/.

4. This concept is based on Samuel Huntington's *The Soldier and the State*. Huntington discusses at length the unique responsibility officers have for developing specialized knowledge and skill in the management of violence.

5. Pictures, along with full descriptions of enlisted ranks, can be found at https://dod.defense.gov/About/Insignias/Enlisted.

6. Notable exceptions include wearing utility uniforms in the Pentagon since 9/11.

7. The saga of changing camouflage patterns provides fascinating insight into service cultures and identities. The Marine Corps initiated the latest competition with the introduction of a distinctive digital camouflage pattern in 2001; the other services followed with their own patterns and continued to change them. Recently, however, there has been a renewed effort to return, once again, to a standardized camouflage pattern.

8. The valor device is easily identified and can be found on lower-priority ribbons. A *V* can give to an otherwise less-consequential ribbon gravitas in the eyes of other service members. Conversely, a Bronze Star Medal with an *R* device for conducting remote actions contributing to a combat operation might be appreciated but would not elicit the same esteem as a *V* device does.

9. A full description of the ribbons, and in most cases their associated medals, can be found at https://www.marines.mil/portals/59/publications/NAVMC%202897.pdf.

Chapter 3. America's Military

1. See especially *Federalist Papers*, numbers 8, 11, 23, 24, 25, 29, 34, and 41, http://www.thefederalistpapers.org/federalist-papers.

2. *Anti-Federalist Papers*, numbers 8, 9, 23, 24, 25, 28, and 29, http://www.thefederalistpapers.org/anti-federalist-papers.

3. Richard Stewart's *American Military History*, vol. 1, ch. 6, is an excellent source on the size and relative effectiveness of the state militias and regular forces (roughly equal to modern-day active duty) during the War of 1812.

4. The USS *Constitution* remains in active service and is home-ported in Boston. It was one of the six original frigates in the U.S. Navy's fleet.

5. This organizational ambiguity caused considerable confusion until the Marine Corps was made a distinct service and placed solely under the Navy Department in 1834.

6. Henderson served as Commandant from 1820 to 1859. During this time, he was promoted from lieutenant colonel commandant to colonel, but he also held the mostly honorific rank of brevet brigadier general.

Chapter 4. Fighting to Preserve the Union

1. In practice, a brigade might comprise as few as two or as many as five regiments. Divisions had as few as two or as many as four brigades.

Chapter 5. The Military Services in Transition, 1880–1917

1. Most state militias had begun referring to themselves as "state national guards" by the end of the nineteenth century.

2. The Marine Corps was excluded, because it was a subordinate service in the Department of the Navy.

Chapter 6. The Common Defense Moves "Over There"

1. It was renamed the School of the Line in 1907. Today it is called the Command and General Staff College.

2. A July 1918 decision forbidding voluntary enlistments further ensured the draft's centrality in providing personnel to the services.

3. The school, later known as the Industrial College of the Armed Forces, is today the Dwight D. Eisenhower School for National Security and Resource Strategy, within the National Defense University.

Chapter 7. Global Expeditionary Conflict, 1941–1945

1. The Pentagon, begun in 1941 and soon to be the world's largest office building, symbolized the vast scope of this two-theater global war.
2. President Reagan immortalized the "boys" in a speech commemorating the fortieth anniversary of the Normandy invasion.
3. The Marine Corps shared the Army's nomenclature at lower levels of command—"aggregating up" in threes from platoon to company to battalion to regiment. A detailed pictorial explanation can be found at http://www.ibiblio.org/hyperwar/USMC/OOB/Regt-TOE-F/#1-.
4. These units were known as the Women's Army Corps (WAC), Women Accepted for Volunteer Emergency Service (WAVES), Women Marines (WM), and Women Airforce Service Pilots (WASP).
5. Hamilton, *Mantle of Command*, prologue.
6. As its role in advising the president became apparent, the JCS absorbed the advisory functions of earlier coordinating bodies like the Joint Board.

Chapter 8. The Services' Struggles for Relevance in the Atomic Age, 1945–1949

1. This legislation also created the Central Intelligence Agency (CIA).
2. Forrestal, tragically, committed suicide two months later.

Chapter 9. Containment and the Emergence of Two Militaries

1. Maxwell D. Taylor, *The Uncertain Trumpet* (New York: Harper and Row, 1960).
2. The book and movie *We Were Soldiers Once . . . and Young* tell the story of the 1st Cavalry Division in the battle of the Ia Drang Valley.
3. This relationship remained unchanged until the Commandant received coequal status in the JCS in 1978.
4. A specified command had a broad, continuing mission involving forces from a single military department. SAC was the best known specified command. When SAC was disestablished, DOD discontinued the use of the term.

Chapter 10. The Military's Revitalization and Redemption

1. See the photograph of the amphibious assault ship on page 19 of chapter 1.
2. The National Security Act of 1947, its subsequent amendments, and the Goldwater-Nichols Act of 1986 are now all integrated into Title 10, USC.
3. Although Title 10, Sec. 161, USC, gives specific definitions, the expressions "unified combatant commander," "unified commander," "combatant commander," and "COCOM commander" are used interchangeably in DOD. Combatant commanders were referred to as "commanders in chief," or CINCs, until 2002, when Secretary Rumsfeld changed them to "combatant commanders (or COCOMs)," arguing that only the president is commander in chief.
4. In theory, combatant commanders have had geographic or functional command responsibilities since the creation of the Outline Command Plan in 1946 and its successor, the Unified Command Plan (UCP). They lacked, however, command authority over the other services to match their responsibilities —hence the chronic lack of unity of command and jointness since World War II.
5. Marine Corps leaders agreed to join SOCOM only reluctantly, because they did not want to create an "elite" force when they believed the Corps was already an elite force. As a result, the Marines' special-operations Raiders were not fully integrated into SOCOM until 2005.

Chapter 11. Return to an Expeditionary Military, 1991–2001

1. See USS *Zumwalt* photograph, chapter 12, page 206.
2. There are over twenty defense agencies: the Defense Health Agency, Defense Logistics Agency, Missile Defense Agency, and National Reconnaissance Office are only a few of them.

Chapter 12. "The Military the Nation Has," 2001–2017

1. As mentioned in chapter 9, the Army's Green Berets are formally referred to as Special Forces. They are special operators of a specific type, specializing in training, advising, and assisting host-nations' forces.

BIBLIOGRAPHY

Primary Documents

Anti-Federalist Papers, 1787–89.

Authorization for Use of Military Force (AUMF). Pub. L. 107-40. September 18, 2001.

The Constitution of the United States of America, 1789.

The Declaration of Independence, 1776.

Hamilton, Alexander, James Madison, and John Jay. *The Federalist Papers.* 1787–88.

Lincoln, Abraham. *Emancipation Proclamation,* January 1, 1863.

———. *First Inaugural Address.* March 4, 1861

———. *Second Inaugural Address,* March 4, 1865.

The National Security Act of 1947.

The National Security Act of 1947 as Amended, 1949.

National Security Council Paper 68 (NSC-68), April 14, 1950.

Title 10, U.S. Code.

Truman, Harry. Executive Order 9877. June 6, 1947.

Books

Bacevich, Andrew. *The Pentomic Era.* Washington, DC: National Defense University Press, 1986.

Bailey, Beth. *America's Army.* Cambridge, MA: Belknap, 2009.

Boettcher, Thomas. *First Call: The Making of the Modern U.S. Military, 1945–1953.* Boston: Little, Brown, 1992.

Brown, John. *Kevlar Legions.* Washington, DC: Center of Military History, 2011.

Builder, Carl. *The Masks of War.* Baltimore, MD: Johns Hopkins University Press, 1989.

Bull, Hedley. *The Anarchical Society.* New York: Columbia University Press, 1995.

Center for Military History. *U.S. Army in World War II* ["the Green Books"]. Washington, DC: Center of Military History, 1946–92.

Chambers, John, ed. *The Oxford Companion to American Military History.* New York: Oxford University Press, 1999.

Chambers, John. *To Raise an Army.* New York: Free Press, 1987.

Clodfelter, Mark. *The Limits of Air Power.* New York: Free Press, 1989.

Coffman, Edward. *The Old Army: A Portrait of the American Army in Peacetime, 1784–1898*. New York: Oxford University Press, 1988.

———. *The Regulars: The American Army, 1898–1941*. New York: Oxford University Press, 2004.

Cohen, Eliot. *Supreme Command*. New York: Anchor, 2003.

Cohen, Raphael. *Air Force Strategic Planning: Past, Present and Future*. Santa Monica, CA: RAND, 2017.

———. *Demystifying the Citizen Soldier*. Santa Monica, CA: RAND, 2015.

Craven, W. F, and J. L. Cate, eds. *The Army Air Forces in World War II*. 7 vols. Washington, DC: Office of Air Force History, 1948–58.

Duncan, Francis. *Rickover and the Nuclear Navy*. Annapolis, MD: Naval Institute Press, 1990.

Gates, Robert. *Duty*. New York: Alfred Knopf, 2014.

Glatthaar, Joseph. *The American Military: A Concise History*. New York: Oxford University Press, 2018.

Goodwin, Doris. *Team of Rivals*. New York: Simon and Schuster, 2006.

Grossman, Dave. *On Killing*. New York: Back Bay Books, 2009.

Hamilton, Nigel. *The Mantle of Command: FDR at War, 1941–1942*. Boston: Mariner Books, 2014.

Hewes, James. *From Root to McNamara: Army Organization and Administration, 1900–1963*. Washington, DC: Center of Military History, 2005.

Huntington, Samuel. *The Soldier and the State*. Cambridge, MA: Harvard University Press, 1981.

Jablonsky, David. *War by Land, Sea and Air*. New Haven, CT: Yale University Press, 2010.

Jaffe, Lorna S. *The Development of the Base Force, 1989–1992*. Washington, DC: Joint History Office, 1993.

Joint History Office. *Organizational Development of the Joint Chiefs of Staff, 1942–2013*. Washington, DC: Joint History Office, 2013.

Kaplan, Lawrence, Ronald Landa, and Edward Drea. *The McNamara Ascendancy, 1961–1965*. Washington, DC: Office of the Secretary of Defense History Office, 2011.

Karsten, Peter. *The Naval Aristocracy*. Annapolis, MD: Naval Institute Press, 2008.

Kohn, Richard. *Eagle and Sword*. New York: Free Press, 1975.

Lambeth, Benjamin. *The Transformation of American Air Power*. Ithaca, NY: Cornell University Press, 2005.

Larson, Eric, et al. *Defense Planning in a Decade of Change.* Santa Monica, CA: RAND, 2001.

Lengel, Edward. *General George Washington.* New York: Random House, 2005.

Marlantes, Karl. *What It Is Like to Go to War.* New York: Atlantic Monthly, 2011.

Mattis, Jim, and Kori Schake. *Warriors and Citizens.* Stanford, CA: Hoover Institution, 2016.

McFarland, Stephen. *A Concise History of the U.S. Air Force.* Washington, DC: Office of Air Force History, 1997.

McPherson, James. *Battle Cry of Freedom.* New York: Oxford University Press, 2003.

Miller, Edward. *War Plan Orange.* Annapolis, MD: Naval Institute Press, 2007.

Millett, Allan. *Semper Fidelis.* New York: Free Press, 1991.

Millett, Allan, Peter Maslowski, and William Feis. *For the Common Defense.* New York: Free Press, 2012.

Morison, Samuel. *The Two-Ocean War.* New York: Little, Brown, 1963.

Moyar, Mark. *Oppose Any Foe.* New York: Basic Books, 2017.

Myers, Richard. *Eyes on the Horizon.* New York: Simon and Schuster, 2009.

Nalty, Bernard, ed. *Winged Shield, Winged Sword.* Washington, DC: Office of Air Force History, 1997.

O'Connell, Aaron. *Underdogs: The Making of the Modern Marine Corps, 1775–1969.* Cambridge, MA: Harvard University Press, 2012.

Owens, William. *High Seas.* Annapolis, MD: Naval Institute Press, 1995.

Parker, Capt. William. *A Concise History of the Marine Corps, 1775–1969.* Washington, DC: Headquarters, U.S. Marine Corps, Historical Division, 1970.

Pettyjohn, Stacie. *Global Defense Posture, 1783–2011.* Santa Monica, CA: RAND, 2012.

Poole, Walter. *The Joint Chiefs of Staff and National Policy, 1973–1976.* Washington, DC: Office of Joint History, 2015.

Prados, John. *The U.S. Special Forces.* New York: Oxford University Press, 2015.

Priest, Dana. *The Mission.* New York: W. W. Norton, 2004.

Rearden, Steven. *The Council of War.* Washington, DC: National Defense University Press, 2012.

———. *The Formative Years.* Washington, DC: Office of the Secretary of Defense History Office, 1984.

Rodger, N. A. M., ed. *Naval Power in the Twentieth Century*. Annapolis, MD: Naval Institute Press, 1996.

Rostker, Bernard. *I Want You!* Santa Monica, CA: RAND, 2006.

Sapolsky, Harvey, Eugene Gholz, and Caitlin Talmadge. *US Defense Politics*. New York: Routledge, 2009.

Schading, Barbara. *A Civilian's Guide to the U.S. Military*. Cincinnati, OH: Writer's Digest Books, 2007.

Sheehan, Neil. *A Fiery Peace in a Cold War*. New York: Vintage Books, 2009.

Sims, William. *The Victory at Sea*. London: Hasell, Watson, and Viney, 1920.

Singer, P. W. *Corporate Warriors*. Ithaca, NY: Cornell University Press, 2007.

Spires, David. *Beyond Horizons*. Maxwell Air Force Base, AL: Air University Press, 1998.

Stewart, Richard, ed. *American Military History*. Vol. 1. Washington, DC: Center of Military History, 2009.

———. *American Military History*. Vol. 2. Washington, DC: Center of Military History, 2010.

Stiehm, Judith. *The U.S. Military: A Basic Introduction*. New York: Routledge, 2012.

Stuart, Douglas. *Creating the National Security State*. Princeton, NJ: Princeton University Press, 2008.

Swartz, Peter. *American Naval Policy, Strategy, Plans and Operations in the Second Decade of the Twenty-First Century*. Arlington, VA: Center for Naval Analyses, 2017.

Symonds, Craig. *The U.S. Navy: A Concise History*. New York: Oxford University Press, 2016.

Thornhill, Paula. *The Crisis Within*. Santa Monica, CA: RAND, 2016.

———. *Over Not Through*. Santa Monica, CA: RAND, 2012.

Toll, Ian. *The Conquering Tide*. New York: W. W. Norton, 2015.

———. *Six Frigates*. New York: W. W. Norton, 2006.

U.S. Army/Marine Corps. *Counterinsurgency*. FM 3-24 / MCWP 3-33.5. Washington, DC, 2006.

U.S. Department of Defense. *The Armed Forces Officer*. Washington, DC: National Defense University Press, 2007.

U.S. Marine Corps History Office. *The Marines in Vietnam, 1954–1973*. Washington, DC: Marine Corps History and Museums Division, 1983.

Watson, Cynthia. *Combatant Commands*. Santa Barbara, CA: Praeger, 2010.

Weigley, Russell. *The American Way of War*. Bloomington: Indiana University Press, 1978.

Worden, Mike. *Rise of the Fighter Generals, 1945–1982*. Maxwell Air Force Base, AL: Air University Press, 1998.

Zegart, Amy. *Flawed by Design*. Stanford, CA: Stanford University Press, 2000.

Articles

Graham, Bradley. "Air Force Chief on Attack." *Washington Post,* October 24, 1994.

Krulak, Charles. "Operational Maneuver from the Sea." *Joint Force Quarterly* (Spring 1999).

———. "The Strategic Corporal: Leadership in the Three Block War." *Marines* (January 1999).

Moskos, Charles. "Success Story: Blacks in the Military." *Atlantic,* May 1986.

Stuckey, John, and Joseph Pistorius. "Mobilization for the Vietnam War." *Parameters* 15, no. 1 (1985).

Vandiver, Frank E. "Commander-in-Chief–Commander Relationships: Wilson and Pershing." *Rice University Studies* 57, no. 1 (1971).

Wall, Andru. "Demystifying the Title 10–Title 50 Debate." *Harvard National Security Journal* 3, no. 1 (2011).

Yingling, Paul. "A Failure in Generalship." *Armed Forces Journal,* May 1, 2007.

Reports and Websites

Cohen, William. "Report of the Quadrennial Defense Review." May 1997.

Congressional Budget Office. *U.S. Military Force Structure: A Primer.* 2016.

DMDC. *DoD Personnel, Workforce Reports and Publications,* https://www.dmdc.osd.mil/appj/dwp/dwp_reports.jsp.

Feickert, Andrew. *U.S. Special Operations Forces (SOF).* Congressional Research Service, February 6, 2013.

Gaffney, H. H., et al. *U.S. Naval Responses to Situations, 1970–1999.* Center for Naval Analyses, December 2000.

Peters, Heidi, et al. *Department of Defense Contractor and Troop Levels in Iraq and Afghanistan: 2007–2016.* Congressional Research Service, August 15, 2016.

Swartz, Peter. *U.S. Navy in the World (1981–1990).* Center for Naval Analyses, December 2011.

U.S. Department of Defense. *Selected Manpower Statistics, Fiscal Year 1997*. Washington, DC: Headquarters Services, n.d.

U.S. Department of Defense. https://www.defense.gov.

U.S. Government Accountability Office. *Special Operations Forces*. July 2015.

U.S. Marine Corps. https://www.marines.mil.

U.S. Marine Corps 101 Briefing (USMC_101 Brief [version 2].pptx). https://www.hqmc.marines.mil/Portals/138/USMC_101%20v2.ppt.

U.S. Navy. *A Cooperative Strategy for 21st Century Seapower*. March 2015.

———. *Forward . . . from the Sea*. 1994.

———. *From the Sea*. 1992.

U.S. Special Operations Command. *2017 Fact Book*. 2017.

White, John, et al. *Directions for Defense: Report of the Commission on Roles and Missions of the Armed Forces*. Defense Technical Information Center, 1995. https://apps.dtic.mil/dtic/tr/fulltext/u2/a295228.pdf.

INDEX

Italicized *page numbers* indicate photographs. Page numbers followed by *f* or *t* indicate figures or tables, respectively.

ABOUT THE AUTHOR

Paula G. Thornhill is a retired U.S. Air Force brigadier general, a RAND Corporation senior researcher, and an adjunct professor at Johns Hopkins University School of Advanced International Studies (SAIS). She has a D.Phil. in history from Oxford University.

The Naval Institute Press is the book-publishing arm of the U.S. Naval Institute, a private, nonprofit, membership society for sea service professionals and others who share an interest in naval and maritime affairs. Established in 1873 at the U.S. Naval Academy in Annapolis, Maryland, where its offices remain today, the Naval Institute has members worldwide.

Members of the Naval Institute support the education programs of the society and receive the influential monthly magazine *Proceedings* or the colorful bimonthly magazine *Naval History* and discounts on fine nautical prints and on ship and aircraft photos. They also have access to the transcripts of the Institute's Oral History Program and get discounted admission to any of the Institute-sponsored seminars offered around the country.

The Naval Institute's book-publishing program, begun in 1898 with basic guides to naval practices, has broadened its scope to include books of more general interest. Now the Naval Institute Press publishes about seventy titles each year, ranging from how-to books on boating and navigation to battle histories, biographies, ship and aircraft guides, and novels. Institute members receive significant discounts on the Press' more than eight hundred books in print.

Full-time students are eligible for special half-price membership rates. Life memberships are also available.

For a free catalog describing Naval Institute Press books currently available, and for further information about joining the U.S. Naval Institute, please write to:

Member Services
U.S. Naval Institute
291 Wood Road
Annapolis, MD 21402-5034
Telephone: (800) 233-8764
Fax: (410) 571-1703
Web address: www.usni.org